World Mythology: A Comprehensive Approach

World Mythology: A Comprehensive Approach

Selena Ellison

STATES
ACADEMIC PRESS
www.statesacademicpress.com

Published by States Academic Press,
109 South 5th Street,
Brooklyn, NY 11249, USA

ISBN: 978-1-63989-572-4

Cataloging-in-Publication Data

World mythology : a comprehensive approach / Selena Ellison.
    p. cm.
Includes bibliographical references and index.
ISBN 978-1-63989-572-4
1. Mythology. 2. Myth. 3. Gods. 4. Folklore. 5. Religions. I. Ellison, Selena.
BL312 .W67 2022
398.2--dc23

For information on all States Academic Press publications
visit our website at www.statesacademicpress.com

Table of Contents

Preface

This book is a culmination of my many years of practice in this field. I attribute the success of this book to my support group. I would like to thank my parents who have showered me with unconditional love and support and my peers and professors for their constant guidance.

Myths are the folklore which includes stories and narratives that play an important role in the society. It is referred to as the collection of sacred narratives and stories. The study of myths in general or a body of myths relating to a particular subject is known as mythology. Hindu mythology, lusitanian mythology, roman mythology, greek mythology and christian mythology are some of the important mythologies around the world. It refers to the stories that tell us how the world and humanity evolved into their present form. It also explains the fundamental worldview of a culture by delineating social and psychological practices of a society. Gods, supernatural humans or demigods are the central characters of this body of study. This field can be divided based upon time period and religion. This book unfolds the innovative aspects of this field which will be crucial for the holistic understanding of the subject matter. It presents the complex subject of mythology in the most comprehensible and easy to understand language. This book, with its detailed analyzes and data, will prove immensely beneficial to professionals and students involved in this area at various levels.

The details of chapters are provided below for a progressive learning:

Chapter – What is Mythology?

Myth can be defined as a folklore genre that consists of narratives, stories and tales which plays a significant role in the society. Mythology refers to a collection of myths about a specific person, culture, religion, etc. with shared beliefs. The topics elaborated in this chapter will help in gaining a better perspective of mythology.

Chapter – Concepts in Mythology

There are various concepts that are studied under mythology such as structuralist theory, mythological dances and religion, geomythology, myths and rituals, theology etc. This chapter closely examines the concepts related to mythology to provide an extensive understanding of the subject.

Chapter – European Mythology

European mythology is the collection of stories and myths associated with Christian mythologies, proto-Indo-European mythologies, Lithuanian mythologies, English mythologies, etc. This chapter sheds light on the subject of European mythology for an in-depth understanding of it.

Chapter – Greek and Roman Mythology

Greek mythology refers to the study of myths of ancient Greeks and legendary Greek genres. Roman mythology refers to the study of myths and culture of ancient Romans and legendary Roman genres. This chapter includes the origin, lives, deities, mythological creatures, ritual practices and the significance of ancient Greeks and Romans for a thorough understanding of the subject.

Chapter – Asian Mythology

Asian mythology includes Korean mythology, Hindu mythology, Japanese mythology, Vietnamese mythology, Philippine mythology, etc. This chapter delves into origin, ritual practices, gods and literature of the different Asian mythologies to provide an easy understanding of the subject.

Selena Ellison

1
What is Mythology?

Myth can be defined as a folklore genre that consists of narratives, stories and tales which plays a significant role in the society. Mythology refers to a collection of myths about a specific person, culture, religion, etc. with shared beliefs. The topics elaborated in this chapter will help in gaining a better perspective of mythology.

Myth

Myth is a symbolic narrative usually of unknown origin and at least partly traditional, that ostensibly relates actual events and that is especially associated with religious belief. It is distinguished from symbolic behaviour (cult, ritual) and symbolic places or objects (temples, icons). Myths are specific accounts of gods or superhuman beings involved in extraordinary events or circumstances in a time that is unspecified but which is understood as existing apart from ordinary human experience. The term mythology denotes both the study of myth and the body of myths belonging to a particular religious tradition.

Mythological figure, possibly Dionysus, riding a panther, a Hellenistic opus tessellatum emblema from the House of Masks in Delos, Greece, 2nd century BCE.

As with all religious symbolism, there is no attempt to justify mythic narratives or even to render them plausible. Every myth presents itself as an authoritative, factual account, no matter how much the narrated events are at variance with natural law or ordinary experience. By extension from this primary religious meaning, the word myth may also be used more loosely to refer to an ideological belief when that belief is the object of a quasi-religious faith; an example would be the Marxist eschatological myth of the withering away of the state.

While the outline of myths from a past period or from a society other than one's own can usually be seen quite clearly, to recognize the myths that are dominant in one's own time and society is always difficult. This is hardly surprising, because a myth has its authority not by proving itself but by presenting itself. In this sense the authority of a myth indeed "goes without saying," and the myth can be outlined in detail only when its authority is no longer unquestioned but has been rejected or overcome in some manner by another, more comprehensive myth.

Because myths narrate fantastic events with no attempt at proof, it is sometimes assumed that they are simply stories with no factual basis, and the word has become a synonym for falsehood or, at best, misconception. In the study of religion, however, it is important to distinguish between myths and stories that are merely untrue.

The Nature, Functions and Types of Myth

Myth has existed in every society. Indeed, it would seem to be a basic constituent of human culture. Because the variety is so great, it is difficult to generalize about the nature of myths. But it is clear that in their general characteristics and in their details a people's myths reflect, express, and explore the people's self-image. The study of myth is thus of central importance in the study both of individual societies and of human culture as a whole.

Relation of Myths to other Narrative Forms

In Western culture there are a number of literary or narrative genres that scholars have related in different ways to myths. Examples are fables, fairy tales, folktales, sagas, epics, legends, and etiologic tales (which refer to causes or explain why a thing is the way it is). Another form of tale, the parable, differs from myth in its purpose and character. Even in the West, however, there is no agreed definition of any of these genres, and some scholars question whether multiplying categories of narrative is helpful at all, as opposed to working with a very general concept such as the traditional tale. Non-Western cultures apply classifications that are different both from the Western categories and from one another. Most, however, make a basic distinction between "true" and "fictitious" narratives, with "true" ones corresponding to what in the West would be called myths.

If it is accepted that the category of traditional tale should be subdivided, one way of doing so is to regard the various subdivisions as comparable to bands of colour in a spectrum. Within this figurative spectrum, there will be similarities and analogies between myth and folktale or between myth and legend or between fairy tale and folktale.

Fables

Like mythos, it came to mean a fictitious or untrue story. Myths, in contrast, are not presented as fictitious or untrue.

Fables, like some myths, feature personified animals or natural objects as characters. Unlike myths, however, fables almost always end with an explicit moral message, and this highlights the characteristic feature of fables—namely, that they are instructive tales that teach morals about human social behaviour. Myths, by contrast, tend to lack this directly didactic aspect, and the sacred narratives that they embody are often hard to translate into direct prescriptions for action in everyday human terms. Another difference between fables and myths relates to a feature of the narratives that they present. The context of a typical fable will be unspecific as to time and space—e.g., "A fox and a goose met at a pool." A typical myth, on the other hand, will be likely to identify by name the god or hero concerned in a given exploit and to specify details of geography and genealogy—e.g., "Oedipus was the son of Laius, the king of Thebes."

Fairy Tales

The term fairy tale, if taken literally, should refer only to stories about fairies, a class of supernatural and sometimes malevolent beings—often believed to be of diminutive size—who were thought by people in medieval and postmedieval Europe to inhabit a kingdom of their own; a literary expression of this belief can be found in Shakespeare's A Midsummer Night's Dream. The term fairy tale, however, is normally used to refer to a much wider class of narrative, namely stories (directed above all at an audience of children) about an individual, almost always young, who confronts strange or magical events; examples are "Jack and the Beanstalk," "Cinderella," and "Snow White and the Seven Dwarfs." The modern concept of the fairy tale seems not to be found earlier than the 18th century in Europe, but the narratives themselves have earlier analogues much farther afield, notably in the Indian Katha-saritsagara (The Ocean of Story) and in The Thousand and One Nights.

Like myths, fairy tales present extraordinary beings and events. Unlike myths—but like fables—fairy tales tend to be placed in a setting that is geographically and temporally vague and might begin with the words "Once upon a time there was a handsome prince." A myth about a prince, by contrast, would be likely to name him and to specify his lineage, since such details might be of collective importance (for example, with reference to issues of property inheritance or the relative status of different families) to the social group among which the myth was told.

Folktales

There is much disagreement among scholars as to how to define the folktale; consequently, there is disagreement about the relation between folktale and myth. One view of the problem is that of the American folklorist Stith Thompson, who regarded myths as one type of folktale; according to this approach, the particular characteristic of myth is that its narratives deal with sacred events that happened "in the beginning." Other scholars either consider folktale a subdivision of myth or regard the two categories as distinct but overlapping. The latter view is taken by the British Classicist Geoffrey S. Kirk, who in Myth: Its Meaning and Functions in Ancient and Other Cultures uses the term myth to denote stories with an underlying purpose beyond that of simple story-telling and the term folktale to denote stories that reflect simple social situations and play on ordinary fears and desires. Examples of folktale motifs are encounters between ordinary, often humble, human beings and supernatural adversaries such as witches, giants, or ogres; contests to win a bride; and attempts to overcome a wicked stepmother or jealous sisters. But these typical folktale themes occur also in stories normally classified as myths, and there must always be a strong element of arbitrariness in assigning a motif to a particular category.

A different and important aspect of the problem of defining a folktale relates to the historical origin of the concept. As with the notion of folklore, the notion of folktale has its roots in the late 18th century. From that period until the middle of the 19th century, many European thinkers of a nationalist persuasion argued that stories told by ordinary people constituted a continuous tradition reaching back into the nation's past. Thus, stories such as the Märchen ("tales") collected by the Grimm brothers in Germany are folktales because they were told by the people rather than by an aristocratic elite. This definition of folktale introduces a new criterion for distinguishing between myth and folktale—namely, what class of person tells the story—but it by no means removes all the problems of classification. Just as the distinction between folk and aristocracy cannot be transferred from medieval Europe to tribal Africa or Classical Greece without risk of distortion, so the importing of a distinction between myth and folktale on the later European model is extremely problematic.

Sagas and Epics

The word saga is often used in a generalized and loose way to refer to any extended narrative re-creation of historical events. A distinction is thus sometimes drawn between myths (set in a semidivine world) and sagas (more realistic and more firmly grounded in a specific historical setting). This rather vague use of saga is best avoided, however, since the word can more usefully retain the precise connotation of its original context. The word saga is Old Norse and means "what is said." The sagas are a group of medieval Icelandic prose narratives; the principal sagas date from the 13th century and relate the deeds of Icelandic heroes who lived during the 10th and 11th centuries. If the word saga is restricted to this Icelandic context, at least one of the possible terminological confusions over words for traditional tales is avoided.

While saga in its original sense is a narrative type confined to a particular time and place, epics are found worldwide. Examples can be found in the ancient world (the Iliad and Odyssey of Homer), in medieval Europe (the Nibelungenlied), and in modern times (the Serbo-Croatian epic poetry recorded in the 1930s). Among the many non-European examples are the Indian Mahabharata and the Tibetan Gesar epic. Epic is similar to saga in that both narrative forms look back to an age of heroic endeavour, but it differs from saga in that epics are almost always composed in poetry (with a few exceptions such as Kazak epic and the Turkish Book of Dede Korkut). The relation between epic and myth is not easy to pin down, but it is in general true that epics characteristically incorporate mythical events and persons. An example is the ancient Mesopotamian epic of Gilgamesh, which includes, among many mythical episodes, an account of the meeting between the hero Gilgamesh and Utnapishtim, the only human being to have attained immortality and sole survivor (with his wife) of the flood sent by the gods. Myth is thus a prime source of the material on which epic draws.

Legends

In common usage the word legend usually characterizes a traditional tale thought to have a historical basis, as in the legends of King Arthur or Robin Hood. In this view, a distinction may be drawn between myth (which refers to the supernatural and the sacred) and legend (which is grounded in historical fact). Thus, some writers on the Iliad would distinguish between the legendary aspects (e.g., heroes performing actions possible for ordinary humans) and the mythical aspects (e.g., episodes involving the gods). But the distinction between myth and legend must be used with care. In particular, because of the assumed link between legend and historical fact, there may be a tendency to refer to narratives that correspond to one's own beliefs as legends, while exactly comparable stories from other traditions may be classified as myths; hence a Christian might refer to stories about the miraculous deeds of a saint as legends, while similar stories about a pagan healer might be called myths. As in other cases, it must be remembered that the boundaries between terms for traditional narratives are fluid, and that different writers employ them in quite different ways.

Parables

The term myth is not normally applied to narratives that have as their explicit purpose the illustration of a doctrine or standard of conduct. Instead, the term parable, or illustrative tale, is used. Familiar examples of such narratives are the parables of the New Testament. Parables have a considerable role also in Sufism (Islamic mysticism), rabbinic (Jewish biblical interpretive) literature, Hasidism (Jewish pietism), and Zen Buddhism. That parables are essentially non-mythological is clear because the point made by the parable is known or supposed to be known from another source. Parables have a more subservient function than myths. They may clarify something to an individual or a group but do not take on the revelatory character of myth.

Etiologic Tales

Etiologic tales are very close to myth, and some scholars regard them as a particular type of myth rather than as a separate category. In modern usage the term etiology is used to refer to the description or assignment of causes. Accordingly, an etiologic tale explains the origin of a custom, state of affairs, or natural feature in the human or divine world. Many tales explain the origin of a particular rock or mountain. Others explain iconographic features, such as the Hindu narrative ascribing the blue neck of the god Shiva to a poison he drank in primordial times. The etiologic theme often seems to be added to a mythical narrative as an afterthought. In other words, the etiology is not the distinctive characteristic of myth.

Approaches to the Study of Myth and Mythology

The importance of studying myth to provide a key to a human society is a matter of historical record. In the middle of the 19th century, for instance, a newly appointed British governor of New Zealand, Sir George Grey, was confronted by the problem of how to come to terms with the Maori, who were hostile to the British. He learned their language, but that proved insufficient for an understanding of the way in which they reasoned and argued. In order to be able to conduct negotiations satisfactorily, he found it necessary to study the Maori's mythology, to which they made frequent reference. Other government officials and Christian missionaries of the 19th and 20th centuries made similar efforts to understand the mythologies of nations or tribes so as to facilitate communication. Such studies were more than a means to an end, whether efficient administration or conversion. They amounted to the discovery that myths present a model or charter for human behaviour and that the world of myth provides guidance for crucial elements in human existence—war and peace, life and death, truth and falsehood, good and evil. In addition to such practically motivated attempts to understand myth, theorists and scholars from many disciplines have interested themselves in the study of the subject. A close study of myth has developed in the West, especially since the 18th century. Much of its material has come from the study of the Greek and Roman classics, from which it has also derived some of its methods of interpretation.

The growth of philosophy in ancient Greece furthered allegorical interpretations of myth—i.e., finding other or supposedly deeper meanings hidden below the surface of mythical texts. Such meanings were usually seen as involving natural phenomena or human values. Related to this was a tendency toward rationalism, especially when those who studied myths employed false etymologies. Rationalism in this context connotes the scrutiny of myths in such a way as to make sense of the statements contained in them without taking literally their references to gods, monsters, or the supernatural. Thus, the ancient writer Palaiphatos interpreted the story of Europa (carried off to

Crete on the back of a handsome bull, which was actually Zeus in disguise) as that of a woman abducted by a Cretan called Tauros, the Greek word for bull; and Skylla, the bestial and cannibalistic creature who attacked Odysseus's ship according to Homer's Odyssey, was by the same process of rationalizing interpreted as simply the name of a pirate ship. Of special and long-lasting influence in the history of the interpretation of myth was Euhemerism (named after Euhemerus, a Greek writer who flourished about 300 BCE), according to which certain gods were originally great people venerated because of their benefactions to humankind.

The early Church Fathers adopted an attitude of modified Euhemerism, according to which Classical mythology was to be explained in terms of mere men who had been raised to superhuman, demonic status because of their deeds. By this means, Christians were able to incorporate myths from the culturally authoritative pagan past into a Christian framework while defusing their religious significance—the gods became ordinary humans. The Middle Ages did not develop new theoretical perspectives on myth, nor, despite some elaborate works of historical and etymological erudition, did the Renaissance. In both periods, interpretations in terms of allegory and Euhemerism tended to predominate.

In early 18th-century Italy, Giambattista Vico, a thinker now considered the forerunner of all writers on ethnology, or the study of culture in human societies, built on traditional scholarship—especially in law and philosophy—to make the first clear case for the role of the creative imagination of human beings in the formation of distinct myths at successive cultural stages. His work, which was most notably expressed in his Scienza nuova had no influence in his own century. Instead, the notion that pagan myths were distortions of the biblical revelation (first expressed in the Renaissance) continued to find favour. Nevertheless, Enlightenment philosophy, reports from voyages of discovery, and missionary reports (especially the Jesuits' accounts of North American Indians) contributed to scholarship and fostered greater objectivity. Bernhard Le Bovier de Fontenelle, a French scholar, compared Greek and American Indian myths and suggested that there was a universal human predisposition toward mythology. In De l'origine des fables, he attributed the absurdities (as he saw them) of myths to the fact that the stories grew up among an earlier, more primitive human society. About 1800 the Romantics' growing fascination with language, the postulation of an Indo-European language family, the study of Sanskrit, and the growth of comparative studies, especially in history and philology, were all part of a trend that included the study of myth.

The relevance of Indo-European studies to an understanding of Greek and Roman mythology was carried to an extreme in the work of Friedrich Max Müller, a German Orientalist who moved to Britain and undertook important research on comparative linguistics. In his view, expressed in such works as Comparative Mythology, the mythology of the original Indo-European peoples had consisted of allegorical stories about the workings of nature, in particular such features as the sky, the sun, and the dawn. In the course of time, though, these original meanings had been lost (through, in Müller's notorious phrasing, a "disease of language"), so that the myths no longer told in a "rationally intelligible" way of phenomena in the natural world but instead appeared to describe the "irrational" activities of gods, heroes, nymphs, and others. For instance, one Greek myth related the pursuit of the nymph Daphne by the god Phoebus Apollo. Since—in Müller's interpretation of the evidence of comparative linguistics—"Daphne" originally meant "dawn", and "Phoibos" meant "morning sun", the original story was rationally intelligible as "the dawn is put to flight by the morning sun." One of the problems with this view is, of course, that it fails to account for the fact that the Greeks continued to tell this and similar stories long after their supposed meanings had been forgotten; and they did so, moreover, in the manifest belief that the stories referred, not to nature, but precisely to gods, heroes, and other mythical beings.

Interest in myth was greatly stimulated in Germany by Friedrich von Schelling's philosophy of mythology, which argued that myth was a form of expression, characteristic of a particular stage in human development, through which men imagine the Absolute (for Schelling an all-embracing unity in which all differences are reconciled). Scholarly interest in myth has continued into the 20th century. Many scholars have adopted a psychological approach because of interest aroused by the theories of Sigmund Freud. Subsequently, new approaches in sociology and anthropology have continued to encourage the study of myth.

Allegorical

An example of an allegorical interpretation would be that given by an ancient commentator for the Iliad, book 20, verse 67. Referring to an episode in which the gods fight each other, the commentator cites critics who have explained the hostilities between the gods allegorically as an opposition between elements—dry against wet, hot against cold, light against heavy. Thus, the gods Apollo, Helios, and Hephaestus represent fire, and the god Poseidon and the river Scamander represent water. Similarly, the goddess Athena is interpreted as wisdom/sense, the god Ares as the absence of that quality, the goddess Aphrodite as desire, and the god Hermes as reason. An allegorical interpretation of a myth could be said to posit a one-to-one correspondence between mythical "clothing" and the ideas being so clothed. This approach tends to limit the meaning of a myth, whereas that meaning may in reality be multiple, operating on several levels.

Romantic

In the late 18th century artists and intellectuals came increasingly to emphasize the role of the emotions in human life and, correspondingly, to play down the importance of reason (which had been regarded as supremely important by thinkers of the Enlightenment). Those involved in the new movement were known as Romantics. The Romantic movement had profound implications for the study of myth. Myths—both the stories from Greek and Roman antiquity and contemporary folktales—were regarded by the Romantics as repositories of experience far more vital and powerful than those obtainable from what was felt to be the artificial art and poetry of the aristocratic civilization of contemporary Europe.

This new attitude is illustrated in a work of the German critic and philosopher Johann Gottfried von Herder entitled "Auszug aus einem Briefwechsel über Ossian und die Lieder alter Völker". Ossian is the name of an Irish warrior-poet whose Gaelic songs were supposedly translated and presented to the world by James Macpherson in the 1760s. Although largely the work of Macpherson himself, these songs made a colossal impact when they were published. Herder believed that the more "savage," that is, the more "alive" and "freedom-loving" a people (ein Volk) was, the more alive and free its songs would be. In opposition to the culture of the educated, Herder exalted the Kultur des Volkes ("culture of the people"). In 1769 Herder abandoned his job as a schoolteacher and took a boat from Riga, on the Baltic, to Nantes, on the Atlantic coast of France. In Journal meiner Reise im Jahre 1769, a description of the experience, he wrote:

> "In everything (on board ship) there is experience to illuminate the original era of the myths. Then (i.e., in antiquity) every man, ignorant of nature, listened for signs and had to listen for them. Then, Jupiter's lightning was terrifying—as indeed it is (i.e., now) on the Ocean. There are a thousand new and more natural explanations of mythology if one reads, say, Orpheus, Homer, Pindar on board ship".

In other words, for Herder ancient myths were the natural expressions of the concerns that would have confronted the ancients; and those concerns were the very ones that, according to Herder, still confronted the Volk—e.g., ordinary sailors—in Herder's own day.

Comparative

Since the Romantic movement, all study of myth has been comparative, although comparative attempts were made earlier. The prevalence of the comparative approach has meant that since the 19th century even the most specialized studies have made generalizations about more than one tradition or at the very least have had to take comparative works by others into account. Indeed, for there to be any philosophical inquiry into the nature and function of myth at all, there must exist a body of data about myths across a range of societies. Such data would not exist without a comparative approach.

Folkloric

The classic folklore approach is that of Wilhelm Mannhardt, a German scholar, who attempted to collect data on the "lower mythology," which he considered to be more or less homogeneous in ancient and popular peasant traditions and basic to all formation of myth. Mannhardt saw sufficient analogies and similarities between the ancient and modern data to permit use of the latter in interpreting the former. Like Herder, he saw the source of mythology in the traditions passed on among the Volk. He collected information not only about popular stories but also about popular customs. He interpreted ancient Greek rituals by relating them to customs of the agricultural peoples of northern Europe, proposing this link in his book Antike Wald- und Feldkulte. Other people who examined myth from the folklore standpoint included Sir James Frazer, the British anthropologist, the brothers Grimm (Jacob, who influenced Mannhardt, and Wilhelm), who are well-known for their collections of folklore, and Stith Thompson, who is notable for his classification of folk literature, particularly his massive Motif-Index of Folk-Literature. The Grimms shared Herder's passion for the poetry and stories of the Volk. Their importance stems in part from the academic diligence and meticulousness that they brought to the recording and study of popular tradition. In addition to their collection of Märchen ("tales"), they published volumes of Deutsche Sagen ("German Legends"). These were tales that purported to record actual events and that were ostensibly set in a specific place and period, as opposed to the "once-upon-a-time-in-the-forest" setting characteristic of the Märchen. Collecting and classifying mythological themes have remained the principal activities of the folklore approach.

Functionalist

One of the leading exponents of the functionalist approach to myth was the French sociologist Marcel Mauss, who used the phrase "total social facts" in reference to religious symbols and myths and their irreducibility in terms of other functions. In his Essai sur le don, Mauss referred to a system of gift giving to be found in traditional, preindustrial societies. Observing that there was a mass of complex data on the subject, Mauss continued- in these "early" societies, social phenomena:

> "Are not discrete; each phenomenon contains all the threads of which the social fabric is composed. In these total social phenomena, as we propose to call them, all kinds of institutions find simultaneous expression: religious, legal, moral, and economic."

In his introduction to the English edition Edward Evans-Pritchard commented on that passage:

> "Total is the key word of the Essay. The exchanges of archaic societies which he examines are total social movements or activities. They are at the same time economic, juridical, moral, aesthetic, religious, mythological phenomena. Their meaning can therefore only be grasped if they are viewed as a complex concrete reality."

Functionalism is primarily associated with the anthropologists Bronisław Malinowski and A.R. Radcliffe-Brown, however. Both ask not what the origin of any given social behaviour may be but how it contributes to maintaining the system of which it is a part.

In this view, in all types of society, every aspect of life—every custom, belief, or idea—makes its own special contribution to the continued effective working of the whole society. Functionalism has had a wide appeal to anthropologists in Britain and the United States, especially as an interpretation of myth as integrated with other aspects of society and as supporting existing social relationships.

Structuralist

Structuralist approaches to myth are based on the analogy of myth to language. Just as a language is composed of significant oppositions (e.g., between phonemes, the constituent sounds of the language), so myths are formed out of significant oppositions between certain terms and categories. Structuralist analysis aims at uncovering what it sees as the logic of myth. It is argued that supposedly primitive thought is logically consistent but that the terms of this logic are not those with which modern Western culture is familiar. Instead they are terms related to items of the everyday world in which the "primitive" culture exists. This logic is usually based on empirical categories (e.g., raw/cooked, upstream/downstream, bush/village) or empirical objects (e.g., buffalo, river, gold, eagle). Some structuralists, such as the French anthropologist Claude Lévi-Strauss, have emphasized the presence of the same logical patterns in myths throughout the world.

In earlier anthropology, "primitive mentality" was characterized by the inability to make distinctions, by a sense of "mystic participation" or identity between human beings, the cosmos, and all other beings. Beginning with complex kinship systems and later exploring other taxonomies, structuralists argue to the opposite conclusion: the supposedly primitive human beings are, if anything, obsessed with the making of distinctions; their taxonomies reveal a complexity and sophistication that rival those of modern humanity.

Formalist

In contrast to the structuralists' search for the underlying structure of myths, the 20th-century Russian folklorist Vladimir Propp investigated folktales by dividing the surface of their narratives into a number of basic elements. These elements correspond to different types of action that, in Propp's analysis, always occur in the same sequence. Examples of the types of action isolated by Propp are "An interdiction is addressed to the hero"; "The interdiction is violated"; "The false hero or villain is exposed"; and "The hero is married and ascends the throne."

An important development of Propp's approach was made in the late 20th century by the German historian of religion Walter Burkert. Burkert detected certain recurrent patterns in the actions described in Greek myths, and he related these patterns (and their counterparts in Greek ritual) to basic biologic or cultural "programs of action." An example of this relation is given in Burkert's Structure and History in Greek Mythology and Ritual. Burkert shows how certain Greek myths have a recurring pattern that he calls "the girl's tragedy." According to this pattern, a girl first leaves home; after a period of seclusion, she is raped by a god; there follows a time of tribulation, during which she is threatened by parents or relatives; eventually, having given birth to a baby boy, the girl is rescued, and the boy's glorious future is assured. The reason for the frequency and persistence of this pattern is, in Burkert's view, the fact that it reflects a basic biologic sequence or "program of action"; puberty, defloration, pregnancy, delivery. Another pattern Burkert explains in a similar way is found in myths about the driving out of the scapegoat. This pattern, Burkert argues, stems from a real situation that must often have occurred in early human or primate history; a group of humans, or a group of apes, when pursued by carnivores, were able to save themselves through the sacrifice of one member of the group. The persistence of these patterns through time is explained, according to Burkert, by the fact that they are grounded in basic human needs—above all, the need to survive.

Functions of Myth and Mythology

Explanation

The most obvious function of myths is the explanation of facts, whether natural or cultural. One North American Indian (Abenaki) myth, for example, explains the origin of corn (maize): a lonely man meets a beautiful woman with long, fair hair; she promises to remain with him if he follows her instructions; she tells him in detail how to make a fire and, after he has done so, she orders him to drag her over the burned ground; as a result of these actions, he will see her silken hair (viz., the cornstalk) reappear, and thereafter he will have corn seeds for his use. Henceforth, whenever Abenaki Indians see corn (the woman's hair), they know that she remembers them. Obviously, a myth such as this one functions as an explanation, but the narrative form distinguishes it from a straightforward answer to an intellectual question about causes. The function of explanation and the narrative form go together, since the imaginative power of the myth lends credibility to the explanation and crystallizes it into a memorable and enduring form. Hence myths play an important part in many traditional systems of education.

Justification or Validation

Many myths explain ritual and cultic customs. According to myths from the island of Ceram (in Indonesia), in the beginning life was not complete, or not yet "human": vegetation and animals did not exist, and there was neither death nor sexuality. In a mysterious manner Hainuwele, a girl with extraordinary gift-bestowing powers, appeared. The people killed her at the end of their great annual celebration, and her dismembered body was planted in the earth. Among the species that sprang up after this act of planting were tubers—the staple diet of the people telling the myth. With a certain circularity frequent in mythology, the myth validates the very cultic celebration mentioned in the myth. The cult can be understood as a commemoration of those first events. Hence, the myth can be said to validate life itself together with the cultic celebration. Comparable myths are told in a number of societies where the main means of food production is the cultivation of root crops; the myths reflect the fact that tubers must be cut up and buried in the earth for propagation to take place.

Ritual sacrifices are typical of traditional peasant cultures. In most cases such customs are related to mythical events. Among important themes are the necessity of death (e.g., the grain "dies" and is buried, only to yield a subsequent harvest), a society's cyclic renewal of itself (e.g., New Year's celebrations), and the significance of women and sexuality. New Year's celebrations, often accompanied by a temporary abandonment of all rules, may be related to or justified by mythical themes concerning a return to chaos and a return of the dead.

In every mythological tradition one myth or cluster of myths tends to be central. The subject of the central mythology is often cosmogony (origin of the cosmos). In many of those ceremonies that each society has developed as a symbol of what is necessary to its well-being, references are made to the beginning of the world. Examples include the enthronements of kings, which in some traditions (as in Fiji or ancient India) are associated with a creation or re-creation of the world. Analogously, in ancient Mesopotamia the creation epic Enuma elish, which was read each New Year at Babylon, celebrated the progress of the cosmos from initial anarchy to government by the kingship of Marduk; hence the authority of earthly rulers, and of earthly monarchy in general, was implicitly supported and justified.

Ruling families in ancient civilizations frequently justified their position by invoking myths—for example, that they had divine origins. Examples are known from imperial China, pharaonic Egypt, the Hittite empire, Polynesia, the Inca empire, and India. Elites have also based their claims to privilege on myths. The French historian of ancient religion Georges Dumézil was the pioneer in suggesting that the priestly, warrior, and producing classes in ancient Indo-European societies regarded themselves as having been ordained to particular tasks by virtue of their mythological origins. And in every known cultural tradition there exists some mythological foundation that is referred to when defending marriage and funerary customs.

Inasmuch as myths deal with the origin of the world, the end of the world, or a paradisiacal state, they are capable of describing what people can never "see for themselves" however rational and observant they are. It may be that the educational value of myths is even more bound up with the descriptions they provide than with the explanations. In traditional, preindustrial societies myths form perhaps the most important available model of instruction, since no separate philosophical system of inquiry exists.

Healing, Renewal and Inspiration

Creation myths play a significant role in healing the sick; they are recited (e.g., among the Navajo Indians of North America) when an individual's world—that is to say, his life—is in jeopardy. Thus, healing through recitation of a cosmogony is one example of the use of myth as a magical incantation. Another example is the case of Icelandic poets, who, in singing of the episode in Old Norse mythology in which the god Odin wins for gods and men the "mead of song" (a drink containing the power of poetic inspiration), can be said to be celebrating the origins of their own art and hence renewing it.

The poetic aspect of myths in archaic and primitive traditions is considerable. Societies in which artistic endeavour is not yet specialized tend to rely on mythical themes and images as a source of all self-expression. Mythology has also exerted an aesthetic influence in more modern societies. An example is the prevalence of themes from Greek and Roman Classical mythology in Western painting, sculpture, and literature.

Myth in Culture

Myth and Psychology

One of the most celebrated writers about myth from a psychological standpoint was Sigmund Freud. In his Die Traumdeutung; he posited a phenomenon called the Oedipus complex, that is, the male child's repressed desire for his mother and a corresponding wish to supplant his father. (The equivalent for girls was the Electra complex.) According to Freud, this phenomenon was detectable in dreams and myths, fairy tales, folktales—even jokes. Later, in Totem und Tabu, Freud suggested that myth was the distorted wish-dreams of entire peoples. More than that, however, he saw the Oedipus complex as a memory of a real episode that had occurred in what he termed the "primal horde," when sons oppressed by their father had revolted, had driven out or killed him, and had taken his wives for themselves. That subsequent generations refrained from doing so was, Freud suggested, due to a collective bad conscience. The relevance of Freud's investigations to the study of myth lies in his view that the formation of mythic concepts does not depend on cultural history. Instead, Freud's analysis of the psyche posited an independent, trans-historical mechanism, based on a highly personal biologic conception of human beings. His anthropological theories have since been refuted (e.g., totemic (symbolic animal) sacrifice as the earliest ritual custom, which he related to the first parricide), but his analysis is still regarded with interest by some reputable social scientists. Criticism, however, has been leveled against the explanation of myths in terms of only one theme and in terms of the "repression" of conscious ideas.

Another theorist preoccupied with psychological aspects of myth was the Swiss psychoanalyst Carl Jung, who, like Freud, was stimulated by a theory that no longer has much support—i.e., the theory of Lucien Lévy-Bruhl, a French philosopher, associating myth with prelogical mentality. This, according to Lévy-Bruhl, was a type of thought that had been common to archaic human beings, that was still common to primitives, and in which people supposedly experienced some form of "mystical participation" with the objects of their thought, rather than a separation of subject and object. Jung's theory of the "collective unconscious," which bears a certain resemblance to Lévy-Bruhl's theory, enabled him to regard the foundation of mythical images as positive and creative, in contrast with Freud's more negative view of mythology. Jung evolved a theory of archetypes. Broadly similar images and symbols occur in myths, fairy tales, and dreams because the human psyche has an inbuilt tendency to dwell on certain inherited motifs (archetypes), the basic pattern of which persists, however much details may vary. But critics of Jung have hesitated to accept his theory of archetypes as an account of mythology. Among objections raised, two may be mentioned. First, the archetypal symbols identified by Jung are static, representing personal types that conflate aspects of the personality: they do not help to illuminate—in the way that the analyses of Propp and Burkert do—the patterns of action that myths narrate. Second, Jungian analysis is essentially aimed at relating myth to the individual psyche, whereas myth is above all a social phenomenon, embedded in society and requiring explanation with reference to social structures and social functions.

Myth and Science

Attention has sometimes focused on changes occurring in the way the real world is apprehended by different peoples and how these changes in "reality" are reflected in myths. This reality changes continually throughout history, and these changes have especially occupied philosophers and historians of science, for a sense of reality in a culture is basic to any scientific pursuit by that culture, beginning with the earliest philosophical inquiries into the nature of the world. Though it would perhaps be going too far to identify the images and concepts that make up a culture's scientific sense of reality with myth, parallels between science and myth, as well as the presence of a mythological dimension to science, are generally reckoned to exist.

The function of models in physics, biology, medicine, and other sciences resembles that of myths as paradigms, or patterns, of the human world. In medicine, for instance, the human body is sometimes likened to a machine or the human brain to a computer, and such models are easily understood. Once a model has gained acceptance, it is difficult to replace, and in this respect it resembles myth, while at the same time, just as in myth, there may be a great variety of interpretations. In the 17th century it was assumed that the universe could be explained entirely in terms of minute corpuscles, their motion and interaction, and that no entities of any other sort existed. To the extent that many models in the history of science have partaken of this somewhat absolutist character, science can be said to resemble myth. There are, however, important differences. Despite the relative infrequency with which models in science have been replaced, replacement does occur, and a strong awareness of the limitations of models has developed in modern science. In contrast, a myth is not as a rule regarded by the community in which it functions as open to replacement, although an outside observer might record changes and even the substitution of a new myth for an old one. Moreover, in spite of the broad cultural impact of theories and models such as those of Newton and Einstein, it is in general true to say that models in science have their principal value for the scientists concerned. Hence, they function most strongly for a relatively small segment of society, even though, for instance, a medical theory held in academic circles in one century can filter down into folk medicine in the next. As a rule, myth has a much wider impact.

Modern science did not evolve in its entirety as a rebellion against myth, nor at its birth did it suddenly throw off the shackles of myth. In ancient Greece the naturalists of Ionia (western Asia Minor), long regarded as the originators of science, developed views of the universe that were in fact very close to the creation myths of their time. Those who laid the foundations of modern science, such as Nicholas of Cusa, Johannes Kepler, Sir Isaac Newton, and Gottfried Leibniz, were absorbed by metaphysical problems of which the traditional, indeed mythological, character is evident. Among these problems were the nature of infinity and the question of the omnipotence of God. The influence of mythological views is seen in the English physician William Harvey's association of the circulation of the blood with the planetary movements and Darwin's explanation of woman's menstrual cycles by the tides of the ocean.

Several thinkers (e.g., the theologian Paul Tillich and the philosopher Karl Jaspers) have argued convincingly for a mythological dimension to all science. Myth, in this view, is that which is taken for granted when thought begins. It is at the same time the limit reached in the course of scientific analysis, when it is found that no further progress in definition can be made after certain fundamental principles have been reached. In recent scientific researches, especially in astronomy and biology, questions of teleology (final ends) have gained in importance, as distinct from earlier concerns with questions of origin. These recent concerns stimulate discussion about the limits of what can be scientifically explained, and they reveal anew a mythological dimension to human knowledge.

Myth and Religion

The place of myth in various religious traditions differs.

Ritual and other Practices

The idea that the principal function of a myth is to provide a justification for a ritual was adopted without any great attempt to make a case for it. At the beginning of the 20th century many scholars thought of myths in their earliest forms as accounts of social customs and values. According to Sir James Frazer, myths and rituals together provided evidence for humanity's earliest preoccupation—namely, fertility. Human society developed in stages—from the magical through the religious to the scientific—and myths and rituals (which survived even into the scientific stage) bore witness to archaic modes of thought that were otherwise difficult to reconstruct. As for the relationship between myth and ritual, Frazer argued that myths were intended to explain otherwise unintelligible rituals. Thus, in Adonis, Attis, Osiris he stated that the mythical story of Attis's self-castration was designed to explain the fact that the priests of Attis's cult castrated themselves at his festival.

In a much more articulate way, biblical scholars stressed the necessity to look for the situation in life and custom (the "Sitz im Leben") that mythical texts originally possessed. A number of scholars, mainly in Britain and the Scandinavian countries and usually referred to as the Myth and Ritual school (of which the best-known member is the British biblical scholar S.H. Hooke), have concentrated on the ritual purposes of myths. Their work has centred on the philological study of the ancient Middle East both before and since the rise of Islam and has focused almost exclusively on rituals connected with sacred kingship and New Year's celebrations. Of particular importance was the discovery that the creation epic Enuma elish was recited at the Babylonian New Year's festival: the myth was, it was argued, expressing in language that which the ritual was enacting through action. Classical scholars have subsequently investigated the relations between myth and ritual in ancient Greece. Particularly influential has been the study of sacrifice by Walter Burkert titled Homo Necans: The Anthropology of Ancient Greek Sacrificial Ritual and Myth.

Connections between myths and cult behaviour certainly exist, but there is no solid ground for the suggestion, following Frazer, that, in general, ritual came first and myth was then formulated as a subsequent explanation. If it is only the subsequent myth that has made the sense of the earlier ritual explicit, the meaning of the ritual may remain a riddle. There is in fact no unanimous opinion about which originated first. Modern scholars are inclined to turn away from the question of temporal priority and to concentrate instead on the diversity of the relationship between myth and ritual. While it is clear that some myths are linked to rituals, so that it makes sense to say that the myth is expressing in the language of narrative that which the ritual expresses through the symbolism of action, in the case of other myths no such ritual exists.

The content of important myths concerning the origin of the world usually reflects the dominant cultural form of a tradition. The myths of hunter-gatherer societies tell of the origin of game animals and hunting customs; agricultural civilizations tend to give weight to agricultural practices in their myths; pastoral cultures to pastoral practices; and so on. Thus, many myths present models of acts and organizations central to the society's way of life and relate these to primordial times. Myths in specific traditions deal with matters such as harvest customs, initiation ceremonies, and the customs of secret societies.

Religious Symbolism and Iconography

Sacred objects are found in all religious traditions, and sacred images in most. They are the material counterparts of myth inasmuch as they represent sacred realities of figures, as myths do in narrative form. Representing does not entail faithful copying of natural or human forms, and in this respect religious symbolism is again like myth in that both depict the extraordinary rather than the ordinary. Many symbolic representations have their sources in myths. Representations in human form, especially "natural" human form, are rare. The sculptures of divine figures in Classical Greece (by sculptors such as Phidias and Praxiteles) are the exception. Usually the degree of representation occurring in cult practices and the depiction of mythical themes has been considerably less humanistic. An example is the way geometric and animal figures abound in the history of religions. Another example is the use of sacred masks, as in the mysteries of Dionysus, an ecstatic cult in the Aegean world of Classical antiquity, and the indigenous traditions of Australia, America, prehistoric Europe, and elsewhere.

Sacred Texts

The Hebrew Bible is usually regarded as embodying much material that anthropologists would regard as containing mythical themes in just the same way as the practices of the ancient Greeks, Chinese, or Abenaki Indians are bound up with myths. Yet the religion of Israel was in many respects critical of myths (in the sense of noncanonical, approved narratives). Similarly, it rejected any representation of God in natural forms. Anti-mythological tendencies exist in the religions that have their roots in Israel. The New Testament of Christianity in some instances derogates myths by describing them as "godless" and "silly." Islam's emphasis on the transcendence of God, as attested in the Qur'ān, similarly allows little room for mythological stories. The activities of the supernatural beings known as jinn, however, are acknowledged even by official Islam, besides being prominent in popular belief (as in The Thousand and One Nights); and other mythological themes, for example motifs relating to the end of time (eschatology), also figure in Islamic religion, above all in its Shī'ite form. Orthodox Shī'ite Muslims believe in the existence of 12 imams, semidivine descendants of the Prophet Muhammad through his son-in-law 'Alī. Toward the end of time, according to the beliefs of Shī'ism, the 12th imam will return to bring truth and justice to humankind.

Other traditions with sacred scriptures are more tolerant of myth, for example Hinduism and Buddhism. Running through certain central texts of the Hindu sacred tradition is the theme of the contrast between the One and the Many. Thus, the philosophical poem known as the Bhagavadgita contrasts the person who sees Infinity within the ordinary finite world with the person who merely sees the diversity of appearances. Yet this ascetic and abstract view by no means excludes a rich and extraordinarily diverse mythology, which is reflected in the tremendous variety of Indian religious statuary and which mirrors the religious complexity of Indian society. A justification for the coexistence of an ideal of unity with a pluralistic reality is found in the Rigveda, where it is written that although God is One the sages give him many names. Buddhism also finds room for exuberant mythology as well as for the plainer truths of sacred doctrine. Buddhism embraces not only the teachings of the Buddha about the pursuit of the path to enlightenment and nirvana but also the exotic mythical figures of Yamantaka, who wears a necklace of skulls, and the grossly fat god of wealth Jambhala.

Myth and the Arts

Oral Traditions and Written Literature

Myths in ancient civilizations are known only by virtue of the fact that they became part of a written tradition. In the case of Greece, virtually all myths are "literature" in the form in which they have survived, the oldest source being the works ascribed to the Greek poets Homer and Hesiod (usually dated, in written form, to the 8th century BCE). Literary forms such as the epic have frequently served as vehicles for transmitting myths inasmuch as they present an authoritative account. The Homeric epics were both an example and an exploration of heroic values, and the poems became the basis of education in Classical Greece. The great epics of India (Mahabharata and Ramayana) came to function as encyclopaedias of knowledge and provided models for all human existence.

Visual Arts

In principle, the sort of relationship that exists between myth and literature exists also with respect to the other arts. In the case of architecture and sculpture, archaeological discoveries confirm the primacy of mythical representations. Among the earliest known three-dimensional objects built by human beings are prehistoric megalithic and sepulchral structures. Mythological details cannot actually be discerned, but it is generally believed that such structures express mythological concerns and that mythical images dictated the shape. An especially intriguing example is the stone circle at Stonehenge in southern England. Axes of this construction are aligned with significant risings and settings of the sun and moon, but the idea that the circle was built for a religious purpose must remain likely rather than certain.

Grave monuments of rulers are among the most important remains of ancient civilizations (e.g., the Egyptian pyramids; and the sepulchral structures of Chinese rulers since the Zhou dynasty. There is worldwide evidence that in archaic cultures human beings considered the points of the compass to have mythological affiliations (e.g., the west and death or the east and a new beginning). Mythological views even influenced building activity. One architectural feature that can have mythological significance is the column. In a number of popular traditions the sky is believed to be supported by one or more columns. The relatively strict separation between religious and civil architecture that modern people are perhaps inclined to take for granted has not existed in most cultures and periods and perhaps is not universal even in modern times.

Even when art ceases to represent mythological matters outright, it is still usually far from representational. That art has ceased to represent mythology is challenged by some theorists, who argue that what seems to be abandonment of mythological forms is really only a change in mythology. The opposing arguments are analogous to the favourable or unfavourable attitudes toward myth that religions have developed.

Performing Arts

Myth is one of the principal roots of drama. This is particularly obvious in the earliest Western drama, the tragedies of Classical Greece, not only because of the many mythological subjects treated and the plays' performance at the festival of Dionysus but also because of the playwrights' myth like presentation of events and facts. An example of such presentation is the story pattern, notably the way retribution follows transgression. Another feature of Greek drama that is relevant to the subject of myth is the fact that the role of the chorus was taken by a group of ordinary citizens. In Greek tragedy the heroic past was presented and explored by a chorus of nonheroic individuals; hence the meaning of the inherited myths was examined by a collectivity that can be seen as standing for the wider collectivity (more than 10,000 in number) that constituted the audience at the plays. In its songs the chorus frequently had recourse to expressions of a proverbial kind, using the distilled wisdom of the community to account for the strange and often disturbing events represented in the plays. The origins of drama are obscure, but Theodor Gaster, an American historian of religion, has suggested that in the ancient eastern Mediterranean world the interrelationship of myth and ritual created drama. Elsewhere, dramatic presentations (as in Japanese nō plays and the Javanese wayang) are similarly rooted in myth.

Dance has been a medium for the expression of mythological themes throughout the world and in all periods for which there is evidence. Especially common are dances aimed at ensuring the continuity of fertility or the success of hunting, at curing the sick, or at achieving shamanistic trance states. An aspect of the decay of ritual in the modern West is the tendency for dance to lose its close and direct connection with the life of the community. A further consequence is that the role of dance in embodying and exploring a community's myths has often been overlooked, and dance may have become further removed from myth than any other form of art in the Western world. There are important and significant exceptions, however. One of the most notable is the work of the American choreographer Martha Graham, who frequently used mythical themes—often drawn from Greek antiquity—as the inspiration for her ballets.

Music

Myth and music are linked in many cultures and in various ways. For example, numerous stories ascribe the origins of music to a figure, usually divine, who lived in the mythical past. Thus, in ancient Greece the lyre was said to have been invented by the god Hermes, who handed it on to his brother Apollo as part of a bargain. From then on Apollo played the lyre at the banquets of the gods, while the Muses sang to his accompaniment. An ancient Chinese myth tells of the discovery of the "foundation tone," which, in addition to being a musical note of specific pitch, also had political implications, since each dynasty was thought to have its own "proper pitch." The foundation tone was produced when Ling Lun, a scholar, went to the western mountain area of China and cut a bamboo pipe in such a way that it produced the correct sound.

Throughout the world music is played at religious ceremonies to increase the efficacy and appeal of prayers, hymns, and invocations to divinities. The power of music to charm the gods is movingly expressed in the Greek story of Orpheus. This mythical figure goes to the underworld to try to have his dead wife, Eurydice, restored to life. By means of his lyre playing and singing he is able to win over even the god of death, so that Eurydice is allowed to leave the underworld. The continuing potency of the myth (including its tragic conclusion—Orpheus is forbidden to look back at his wife but does so and thus loses her again) is shown by the fact that it has been retold in Europe by numerous composers of opera since the early 17th century.

That a particularly close connection exists between myth and music has been argued by Claude Lévi-Strauss. In an analysis of the myths of certain South American Indians he explains that his procedure is "to treat the sequences of each myth, and the myths themselves in respect of their reciprocal interrelations, like the instrumental parts of a musical work and to study them as one studies a symphony." His treatment is divided into such subsections as "The 'Good Manners' Sonata", "Fugue of the Five Senses", and "The Opossum's Cantata". In Myth and Meaning Lévi-Strauss returned to the link between myth and music, which had proved difficult for his readers to understand. To make his point clearer Lévi-Strauss took the example of a theme from an opera by Richard Wagner. Each time the theme is repeated its overall meaning grows clearer, as each instance is superimposed on the others in the series, so that it becomes possible to see what the different occurrences of the theme have in common. Analogously, the meaning of a myth is found not simply by reading its narrative in sequence, but by superimposing upon one another similar mythical events from one narrative and boiling down each resulting "bundle" to a common denominator. It is the relationship between these bundles that constitutes the logic of the myth.

The use of music for religious ends has declined in modern Western societies, but mythical themes (e.g., in opera and oratorio) are still used with genuine artistic effect. The repertoires of late 20th-century opera companies may include, for example, Giacomo Puccini's Turandot, about a princess who asks her suitors three riddles and beheads them if they fail to answer correctly and a prince who will die if his name is discovered; Richard Strauss's Die Frau ohne Schatten ("The Woman Without a Shadow"), about a princess who must gain a shadow or her husband will be turned to stone; and Wagner's Tannhäuser, Lohengrin, Der Ring des Nibelungen, and Parsifal, all loosely based on tales from medieval Germanic mythology.

Myth and History

Myth and history represent alternative ways of looking at the past. Defining history is hardly easier than defining myth, but a historical approach necessarily involves both establishing a chronological framework for events and comparing and contrasting rival traditions in order to produce a coherent account. The latter process, in particular, requires the presence of writing in order that conflicting versions of the past may be recorded and evaluated. Where writing is absent, or where literacy is restricted, traditions embedded in myths through oral transmission may constitute the principal sources of authority for the past. Hence, myths may be cited when a situation in the present is materially affected by what version of the past is accepted. For instance, if a dispute arises among the Iatmul of Papua New Guinea over the rights of different clans to possess land, the contending parties take part in oral contests involving the recitation of long lists of mythological names and other details from the myths. Since each clan's view of the mythic past has implications for the ownership of estates by persons living in the present, victory in these contests is a matter of direct practical importance to the participants.

Even in societies where literacy is widespread and where a considerable body of professional historians is at work, it may still be the case that a majority of the population form their views of the past on the basis of inherited mythlike traditions. Examples from the 20th century in Europe would be the polarized communities (Protestant and Roman Catholic) of Northern Ireland, or pro- and anti-Communist sympathizers in Greece. In the former case, the two communities have different and irreconcilable pictures of the events related to the partition of Ireland. In the latter case, the course of the civil war (after the end of World War II) is viewed quite differently by the two groups. These rival traditions may be described as mythlike because they are narratives with a strong validating function—the function of justifying current enmities and current loyalties—and they are believed with a quasi-religious faith against which objective historical testing is all but powerless.

Finally, similarities to myths may be present even in the work of those who are justifiably described as historians. A clear instance of this is the ancient Greek writer Herodotus, the so-called "father of history." He had the radically original idea of writing an account of the struggle between the Greek world and its "barbarian" neighbours during the Persian Wars, an account that combined and evaluated a range of disparate and often conflicting pieces of information. On these grounds he should certainly be described as a historian. Yet, his work is full of themes and story patterns that also occur in Greek myths—for example, transgression against the gods leads to retribution; again, people who live at the margins of the Greek world are imagined as having customs that are the exact inverse of their Greek equivalents. In the work of Herodotus there is no incompatibility between myth and history; both historical events and the patterns into which such happenings are perceived as falling form part of his overall enterprise: namely, to conduct an inquiry (the meaning of the Greek word historia) into the past. As with the distinction between myth and science, then, that between myth and history is by no means a straightforward one.

Major Types of Myth

Myths of Origin

Cosmogony and creation myth are used as synonyms, yet properly speaking, cosmogony is a preferable term because it refers to the origin of the world in a neutral fashion, whereas creation myth implies a creator and something created, an implication unsuited to a number of myths that, for example, speak of the origin of the world as a growth or emanation, rather than an act. Even the term origin should be used with caution for cosmogonic events (as well as for other myths purporting to describe the beginning of things), because the origin of the world hardly ever seems the focal point of a mythological narrative—as a mythological narrative is not a matter of inquiry into the first cause of things. Instead, cosmogonic myths are concerned with origins in the sense of the foundation or validity of the world as it is. Creation stories in both primitive and advanced cultures frequently speak of the act of creation as a fashioning of the earth out of raw material that was already present. In African cosmogonies, especially, the earth is preexistent. A creation out of nothing occurs as a theme much less frequently, for all that such creation myths are more satisfying to the philosophical mind. Philosophical questions, however, are less important in the justificatory systems set up by myth.

Water, though important everywhere as a source of life and image of endless potentiality, has a special role in Asia and North America, where the creator (often an animal) is assisted by another figure, who dives for earth in the primordial ocean. The earth-diver helper sometimes develops into an opponent, or Satan-like character, in other areas—e.g., those touched by Zoroastrianism, an ancient Persian dualistic religion. Though hardly an explanation in the ordinary sense of the word, the theme accounts for the fact that evil is constitutive of the cosmos without holding the creator responsible for it. Other widely diffused motifs are: the cosmogonic egg, found in the Pacific world, parts of Europe and southern Asia (e.g., in Hinduism); the world parents (usually in the image of sky and earth); and creation through sacrifice or through a primordial battle. Creation through the word of the creator also occurs outside the biblical account (in Polynesia).

Cosmogony sets the pattern for everything else in most traditions; other myths are related to it or derived from it. Because human beings' inhabitable world, the cosmos, is the crucial issue, no matter how various the contents may be and how different from one period to another, cosmogony probably is the clearest expression of humanity's basic mythological propensity. All cosmogonic accounts have certain formal features in common. They speak of irreconcilable opposites (e.g., heaven and earth, darkness and light) and, at the same time, of events or things totally outside the common range of perception and reason (e.g., a "time" in which heaven and earth were not yet separated and darkness and light intermingled). In other words, the basic ingredients of the human world and its orientation are presupposed yet are realized, constituted, or brought about anew in the narration. The narrative can arrive at such a reconstitution only by transcending the limits of ordinary perception and reason.

The origin of human beings is usually linked immediately to the cosmogony. Humans, for instance, are placed on the earth by God, or in some other way their origin is from heaven. Nevertheless, it is only in mythologies influenced by philosophical reflections that the place of humans becomes the conspicuous centre of the cosmogony (e.g., Pythagoreanism, a Greek mystical philosophical system; Orphism, a Greek mystical religious movement; gnosticism, a Christian dualistic and esoteric movement; and Tantrism, a Hindu and Buddhist esoteric meditation system). Humans are sometimes said to have ascended from the depths of the earth (as with the Zuni, an American Indian people) or from a certain rock or tree of cultic significance. These images are often related to the idea of a realm of ancestors as the origin of newborn children. Humans are also said to be fashioned from the dust of the ground (as in Genesis) or from a mixture of clay and blood (as in the Babylonian creation myth). In all cases, however, humans have a particular place (because of their duties to the gods, because of their limitations, or even because of their gifts), even though—especially in many hunters' civilizations (e.g., the African San peoples and many North American Indian tribes)—the harmony of humanity and other forms of nature is emphasized.

In most cosmogonic traditions the final or culminating act is the creation of human beings. The condition of the cosmos prior to humanity's arrival is viewed as separate and distinct from the alterations that result from the beginning of the human cultural world. Creation is thus seen as a process of periods or stages, frequently in a three-stage model. The first stage consists of the world of gods or primordial beings, the second stage is the world of human ancestors, and the third stage is the world of humanity itself. The three stages are sometimes seen as interrelated; for example, the gods may be either the creators or the ancestors of human beings; there are also mythical accounts in which the ancestors of human beings undergo a transformation to become human.

Among innumerable tales of origin, one of the most common types is related to the origins of institutions. Certain initiation ceremonies or ritual acts are said to have originated in the beginning, in mythical times, this primeval moment of inception constituting their validity.

Myths of Eschatology and Destruction

Myths of eschatology deal with "the end." The end is conceived of as the opposite of the cosmogony; it means first and foremost the origin of death but also, in a wider sense, the end of the world. Special forms of eschatology are prevalent in messianism (belief in a future salvation figure) and millenarianism (belief in a 1,000-year reign of the elect).

Myths about the origin of death, for which an added explanation has to be found in the sense that death is not seen as automatically the end of life, are probably as widely diffused as creation stories. One of the most common types of such myths speaks of a primordial time in which death did not exist and explains that it arose as the result of an error, as a punishment, or simply because the creator decided the earth would get too crowded otherwise. One example of a myth about the origin of death may be regarded as characteristic; it occurs, with variations, in many parts of the world. Among the Zulus the story is told that the supreme being Unkulunkulu instructed the chameleon to take a message to humankind, saying that they would be immortal. But the chameleon moved slowly, since he stopped to have something to eat (or, according to a variant, basked in the sun and fell asleep). In due course the supreme being changed his mind and sent a lizard to human beings, telling them that they would die. The lizard arrived and delivered his message. When the chameleon eventually arrived, his message conflicted with what humankind had already been told by the lizard. The chameleon was not believed, and human beings were mortal from then on.

Expectations of a cataclysmic end of the world are also expressed by myths. A universal conflagration with a final battle and defeat of the gods is part of Germanic mythology and has parallels in other examples of Indo-European eschatological imagery. In many "primitive" religions specific expectations about the end of the world do occur, but until recently they have not received much scholarly attention. An example of such a belief about the end of the world is found among the Pawnee Indians. In their view, there will come a time when everything will disappear and the star of death will govern the world. The moon will turn red, the sun will be extinguished, and men will be turned into stars flying along the route to heaven now taken by the dead.

Messianic and Millenarian Myths

The hope of a new world surges up from time to time in many civilizations. Many such religious movements have flourished in the 20th century in Melanesia, Africa, South America, and Siberia. Christian elements are usually detectable, but the basic element in virtually all cases is indigenous. These cults and movements centre on prophetic leaders, often emphasize the return of the dead at the renewal to come, and are convinced of a catastrophic end of the present world. In many cases, the culture hero is expected to return and lead believers in battle against the evil forces. In the history of Judaism and Christianity, as in many primitive millenarian and messianic movements, there is an expectation of a new heaven and a new earth.

Myths of Culture Heroes and Soteriological Myths

A great many nonliterate traditions have myths about a culture hero (most notably, one who brings new techniques or technology to humankind—e.g., Prometheus, who supplies fire to humans in Greek mythology). A culture hero is generally not the person responsible for the creation but the one who completes the world and makes it fit for human life; in short, the culture hero creates culture. Another example of a culture hero is Maui in Polynesia, who brought islands to the surface from the bottom of the sea, captured and harnessed the sun, lifted the sky to allow human beings more room, and, like Prometheus, gave them fire.

The bringer of culture is often also the bringer of health. Thus, the culture hero of the Woodlands and Plains Indians in North America is at the same time related to the foundation of the medicine society. A comparable figure occurs in many traditions of Classical antiquity or the Mediterranean basin generally as the "good son"—e.g., Horus, the son of the god Osiris in Egypt, or the figure of the king in the Psalms. Health and (spiritual) salvation are synonymous, and this is implied in the Greek word sōtēr, which can mean both "saviour" and "preserver from ill health." Related to soteriological myths in many cases is the hope for a final and total salvation in which the "good" powers will triumph, such as through Saoshyant, the saviour in Zoroastrianism. In fact, Zoroastrianism shared with the Judeo-Christian tradition the notion of a Last Judgment followed by the ultimate salvation of the world. According to Zoroastrian belief, as the end approached heroes from the past would come to life and help in the struggle of good against evil. Saviours, the Saoshyants, would work toward the triumph of virtue and the spreading of heavenly light over all creation.

Myths of Time and Eternity

The apparent regularity of the heavenly bodies long impressed every society. The sky was seized as the very image of transcendence, and what seemed to be the orderly course of sun, moon, and stars suggested a time that transcended that of humanity—in short, eternity. Many myths and mythological images concern themselves with the relationship between eternity and time on earth. The number four for the number of world ages figures most frequently. The Zoroastrians of ancient Persia knew of a complete world age of 12,000 years, divided into four periods of 3,000 each, at the end of which Ormazd (Wise Lord) would conquer Ahriman (Destructive Spirit). Similarly, the Book of Daniel (in the Bible) mentions four kingdoms—of gold, silver, bronze, and a mixture of iron and clay, respectively—after which God will establish an everlasting kingdom. The notion of four world ages, sometimes associated with metals, occurs also in the works of Classical writers and in later speculative writings on human history. Judaism developed the view of a 1,000-year period between the four world ages and the everlasting kingdom (hence the words millennium and millenarian). Although other numbers occur (three, six, seven, 12, and 72), four is dominant. In ancient Mexico this world was held to be preceded by four other worlds. India, in both Hindu and Buddhist texts, has developed the most complex system of world ages and worlds that arise and come to an end. Here, too, the number four is important—e.g., the four ages (yugas) of decreasing length and increasing evil. Many writings, often with large numbers, reflect exact astronomical observations and calculations. Some mythologies—e.g., those of the Maya in Central America—have developed sophisticated views interrelating time and space. Mythological accounts of repetitions of worlds after their destruction occur not only in India but also elsewhere, such as in Orphism and in the Stoic philosophy that flourished in Classical antiquity.

Myths of Providence and Destiny

In attitudes to the idea of a link between human activity and the stars, the most familiar example of which is probably astrology, there is a broad range of mythical motifs between astrological calculations (in the sense of an attempt at an intellectualized account of what is happening) and devotional self-surrender. There are many occasions at which humans may be filled with doubt about their fate or the fate of their communities. In some myths divine supremacy is marked by a god's mastery over fate. Marduk, the patron god of Babylon, acquires the "tablets of fate" in his primordial battle preceding the creation. There is no doubt about Zeus's supremacy in the Greek poet Hesiod's genealogical account of the gods, yet in the works of Homer, Zeus is powerless to defy fate and save the life of his son Sarpedon. Mythological views of providence, destiny, or fate are given precise shades of meaning vis-à-vis dominant views in a tradition concerning justice and divine law, the philosophical problem of determinism, the theological problems of theodicy (justification of a good god with observable facts of evil), and predestination. An important difference in mythological accounts of providence exists between those traditions that speak of the creation of the world as a result of God's will (as in Judaism, Christianity, and Islam) and those that attribute worldly phenomena to causation by a lesser being (as Buddhism does).

Myths of Rebirth and Renewal

Myths of archaic traditions generally imply a conception of the world, nature, and humanity in terms of cyclic time. According to Australian Aboriginal myth, human beings are reincarnated into profane life at the moment of birth. At their initiation they reenter sacred time, and through their burial ceremonies they return to their original "spirit" state. Similar beliefs are held by many tribal peoples, and their myths are expressed in terms of cosmic cycles. Special myths are narrated in many places in preparation for initiation procedures. In agricultural societies, in addition to the themes of cosmic renewal, renewal through birth, and rebirth through initiation ceremonies at the attainment of manhood and womanhood, the theme of seasonal renewal is of great importance. The cyclic concept of time in all these traditions is present in many of the great religious and philosophical systems, such as Brahmanism (a Hindu system), Buddhism, and Platonism, and to some extent it is at variance with the idea of linear time typical of Judaism, Christianity, and Islam. But no culture, not even that of Jews, Christians, or Muslims, completely disregards the cyclic patterns of the seasons, work, festivities, or existence. Such patterns seem to be engraved on humanity's perception of the world.

Myths of Memory and Forgetting

Some of the North American medicine men claim to remember their prenatal existence. Such memory, according to their mythology, is lost in ordinary people. Similar myths of memory and forgetting are related to the hierarchy that exists in all archaic societies. The fundamental knowledge of the world, transcending ordinary consciousness, is not equally attainable by everyone. Myths of memory can take the form of collective nostalgia. In South America the Yaruros, whose material existence was so simple that they lacked the skills of the agricultural and pastoral life, were one of the many tribes that in the face of modern Western cultural expansion gave up the struggle for their own social and cultural identity, becoming assimilated into a more complex society. As the Yaruros ceased to struggle for the preservation of their tribal identity, they expressed a yearning to return to the Great Mother ruling the land of the dead and awaiting them in her paradise. Mythologies of memory and forgetting have a role in many traditions. They are of great significance in traditions where the idea of rebirth or reincarnation exists. Some people have claimed to remember previous existences, and a few (among them the Buddha) the very first. The veil of maya ("illusion") in many Indian stories prevents a man from remembering his true origin and goal. In gnosticism there is talk of a similar forgetfulness, which must be resisted. In ancient Greek myth, Mnemosyne (Memory), the mother of the Muses, is said to know everything, past, present, and future. She is the Memory that is the basis of all life and creativity. Forgetting the true order and origin of things is often tantamount to death (as in the case of Lethe, the river of death in Greek mythology, which destroys memory). Anamnesis, "commemoration" or "recollection," is one of the crucial parts of the Christian celebration of Holy Communion. Through the anamnesis, the Passion and death of the Lord is "applied" to the congregation. In philosophy, the imagery of forgetting and remembering occurs in the thought of Shankara, a medieval Indian philosopher, and of Plato in connection with the paramount calling of the thinker and the difficulty of living up to that calling.

Myths of High Beings and Celestial Gods

Supreme celestial deities occur in many mythologies, with various qualities and attributes, in many shapes, and with great diversity in cultic significance. A cardinal distinction exists between the supreme being in many archaic or polytheistic traditions and the God of the great monotheistic systems (Judaism, Christianity, and Islam). Even though certain qualities seem alike in many cases (e.g., transcendence, omniscience), the God of the latter arose historically in a reaction to polytheistic views and practices and demonstrates his supremacy accordingly, whereas the more archaic types of supreme beings nowhere show that aggressive aspect in their mythologies. The exalted status of archaic supreme beings and celestial gods does not necessarily involve exclusion of other supreme beings. Outstanding examples are Vishnu, Shiva, and the great goddess in Hindu literature, who are each described as supreme yet do not reduce the "reality" of the others. "Supremacy" is not as unambiguous and general a term as it seems, and in Hinduism it refers first and foremost to the perfection (i.e., the idea that a deity is supremely perfect) of a deity in himself.

The sky seen as a sacred entity is an all but universal belief. It is often related to or identical with the highest divinity. Nevertheless, supreme beings are always more than what can be explained from celestial phenomena alone, for they are often called creators of the world, founders of the order of the world, and protectors of law; and they are praised for their eternity and goodness. Often, the supreme being that created the world does not—or has ceased to—receive attention in the cult, although he may still be invoked in moments of great crisis. In a good many ancient agricultural societies, the idea of a great goddess prevailed instead of a male creator-god. The great goddess (as in the ancient Middle East and India) is venerated principally because of her omnipotence, especially her power over life. The sky god-creator sometimes cedes to a divinity who is also related to the sky but apparently is experienced more concretely because of his activity. Such a divinity (especially in pastoral cultures) can be a god of atmospheric phenomena (storm, rain, thunder, or lightning), whose power for the good of the people is extolled. In spite of his power, however, he is one of several gods, and in some cases (Yahweh in ancient Israel and Allah in Islam) one such God retains the full creative function of early creator gods, and in him all "true" divinity is concentrated. In addition, a divinity related to the sun rather than the heavens can assume preeminence; this has happened in some ancient imperial traditions (e.g., Egypt, Inca empire). Among sky gods who remained important in the mythologies of ancient civilizations are Zeus in Greece, Jupiter in Rome, and Tian in China.

Myths Concerning Founders of Religions and other Religious Figures

Although the founders of great religions (Confucius, Zoroaster, the Buddha, Moses, Jesus, Mani, Muhammad) are generally conceded to have had actual existence, information about them is couched in legendary terms that have many mythological features. The same is true of many other religious figures (prophets, saints, or gurus (Hindu spiritual teachers)). Those traditions that have preserved the memory of their founders have, as a rule, carefully emphasized the elements that function most mythologically, in the sense that they state categorically realities that could not be known in any ordinary fashion or that raise the founder above ordinary historical conditions. Examples are the account of Jesus' prayer in Gethsemane, which no one heard according to the text itself, his statement that he was before Abraham, and his prophecies. Buddhist texts state that the Buddha not merely surpassed all yogis in knowledge of previous existences but, in fact, had conquered time. Well known too are his predictions concerning the course and decline of Buddhism and (in Mahayana texts) his promises as to the future spiritual attainments of the bodhisattvas. Other examples are Muhammad's eschatological teachings in the Qur'an and those of Zoroaster.

Myths of Kings and Ascetics

Genuine myths concerning kings are found only in traditions that know a form of sacred kingship. Temple records from ancient Babylon mention offerings to kings who were considered divine. Hymns addressed to them make references to the king's union with a goddess—i.e., the mythological motif of the "sacred marriage." One of the epithets for the king in ancient Egypt was "endowed with life" or "imparting life." The twofold meaning of the epithet is significant and can serve to make the mythology of sacred kingship understandable in other places as well, because the function of the king is in fact double. He mediates between the divine world and the human world, representing each to the other. Hence, in Egypt a sacrifice by an individual was understood as offered to the king and at the same time by the king. The king's role of mediator and protector brings royal mythologies close to myths of culture heroes. Solemn procedures in which kings become divinities occur relatively late in history. An early and most conspicuous case of such an apotheosis (becoming divine) is that of Alexander the Great, who was called a god in his lifetime. Later, apotheosis took place for Roman emperors, although there are no cases of an emperor being accorded divine honours in his lifetime. A great many legends have accumulated around the figures of kings (e.g., around King Ashoka of India and King Arthur in Britain). Stories about the Holy Roman emperor Frederick I Barbarossa and Charlemagne have a somewhat eschatological mythical flavour, because they are said to dwell each in his mountain (in the Kyffhäuser and the Untersberg, respectively) until they appear again to act as saviours in a crisis.

Most narratives about great ascetics, as well as other saints, could be regarded as legends rather than myths. There are, however, instances of saints or ascetics who are presented as a more than worldly model, so that a case can be made for the mythological function of their legends (e.g., al-Hallāj in Islam and St. Francis in Christianity). In the case of traditions that have asceticism as an integral part, certain figures and the legends around them do indeed function as exemplars.

Myths of Transformation

Countless stories exist concerning the origin of peculiar rocks, properties of animals, plants, stars, or other features in the world. In addition to such etiologic tales there are several myths that speak of cosmic changes brought about at the end of primordial times. An altogether different and extensive mythology exists concerning initiation rites and other "rites of passage" that involve transformation of an individual's being.

Cosmic transformation may concern an original world, without proper human means of existence and without death, that was transformed through a certain event (e.g., the death of Hainuwele, a type of primal being known as a dema, or ancestral, deity) into the world known to human beings, a truly inhabitable world with vegetation, animals, and other features that had not existed before.

On a wider scale are myths that could be appendages to cosmogonic myths but that have not turned into mere etiologies. Many myths akin to the type of the dema deity (like Hainuwele) and to the culture-hero type (like Prometheus) account for events—such as the invention of agriculture, domestication of animals, and the use of fire—that have transformed the world for the benefit of humankind. Many others are just as closely related to cosmogonic accounts but tell of "setbacks" in primordial times. In agricultural societies, for example, myths have been collected that ascribe the unevenness of land or the formation of mountains to an ancient mishap or evil force.

In rites of passage (e.g., rites accompanying birth, attainment of maturity, marriage, death) the contents of myths are acted out. In each case the intention behind the rites is that an individual's mode of being be affected, indeed transformed. Through the birth ceremony the child "becomes" a person, and through initiation an adolescent "becomes" an adult, a member of a sodality, or a warrior. There is a great variety of customs in different communities and traditions, but everywhere these rites dramatize graphically the cosmic processes and realities expressed in language in myths. In many traditions the myths of the community are conveyed to the novice at the time of his initiation. Even in the major world religions rites of passage are still performed, as evidenced in such ceremonies as circumcision, Baptism, weddings, and mortuary rites. In all instances, the rites derive their meaning from the core of the tradition, and for that reason human existence is regarded as transformed. In some cases the transformation derived from the dominant myth is far-reaching. The initiated shaman is able to transcend the ordinary human condition and overcome dangers that would cause the death of a noninitiate. Through his initiation he is believed to have gone through death and thus conquered it. In certain Hermetic (an occult magical tradition) and gnostic texts the certainty of attaining divine being is clearly expressed.

Myth in Modern Society

Secularization of Myth and Mythology

Deciding the extent to which there has actually been any secularization of myth involves a problem of definition. If myth is seen as the product of a past era, it is difficult to determine at what actual moment that era ended. Thus, it is virtually impossible to state precisely when a certain mythical theme becomes a mere literary theme or to determine in general when myths are no longer being created. It is more fruitful to recognize that symbols, myths, and rituals are all subject to change over time. Nor is secularization an irreversible process. It is instead a process that takes place time and again. Secularization movements and movements toward "mythification" of a phenomenon, narrative, or idea are aspects of the same historical processes. There have also been many types of secularization; the one brought about in Western society since the Middle Ages is only a single example. Another instance was the development in Archaic and Classical Greece (sometimes referred to—with great oversimplification—as a movement "from myth to reason") whereby fundamental questions about the nature of the universe came increasingly to receive answers in terms of philosophical, as opposed to mythical, reasoning.

On the other hand, although the secularization of modern times is not a unique phenomenon, it is a new and complex type, to which many factors have contributed. Scientific, particularly astronomical, discoveries of the late medieval and Renaissance periods were accompanied by a new trust in cosmic laws and an increasingly abstract notion of God. More or less Euhemeristic historical accounts that were common in the Middle Ages and were a symptom of a certain secularization process themselves gave way to history writing, focusing on psychological, social, and economic facts. In philosophy, naturalism of various sorts opposed notions of transcendence that earlier systems had taken for granted. The most common tendency in modern society has been to regard the characters and events in mythical accounts as not real or as by-products of realities that are not transcendent but rather immanent.

This secularization in modern society, like earlier secularization processes, is accompanied by a process whereby new myths are formed.

Demythologization of Major Religious Traditions

Demythologization should be distinguished from secularization. Every living mythology must come to terms with the world in which it is transmitted and to that extent inevitably goes through processes of secularization. Demythologization, however, refers to the conscious efforts people make to purify a religious tradition of its mythological elements. The term demythologization (Entmytho-logisierung) was coined by Rudolf Bultmann, a German theologian and New Testament scholar. In the strict sense of the word, demythologizing efforts have been limited to theological discussions in 20th-century Christianity.

Even after secularization has taken place, a certain mythological residue may persist. Edward B. Tylor, one of the founders of anthropology as an academic discipline in the 19th century, coined the use of the word survival for customs and beliefs that continued to be adhered to long after the context in which they had had their meaning had ceased to exist. Because such customs and beliefs may be regarded as mere superstitions, the word survival usually has a slightly derogatory overtone. There are many survivals of myth in this sense. The myth of "the noble savage," well known from the 18th-century writer Jean-Jacques Rousseau, can be understood as a survival of a paradisiacal mythology: Western man expecting to find evidence of paradise on earth.

The secularization process in modern times has affected symbolic behaviour (cult, ritual, liturgy) and symbolic objects (sacred places) more than myth, however. Nevertheless, commonly accepted forms of mythology in modern society do not permeate all parts of society or fulfill all needs. (In all likelihood, no society has ever been perfectly homogeneous in its myths.) At the same time there exist profound mythological needs in modern society, and some are filled by myths borrowed from submerged or alien traditions. Modern society's neglect of cosmic symbolism (which in contrast was widespread in archaic tradition) has provoked certain reactions, such as the continuing interest in astrology, which may even be seen as an attempt to present a coherent account of the cosmos. And the huge scientific advances of the 20th century have given rise to a literature, science fiction, that resembles myth, even down to an eschatological element.

Political and Social uses of Myth

In the industrialized Western society of the 20th century, myths and related types of tales continue to be told. Urban folklorists collect stories that have much in common with the tales collected by the Grimm brothers, except that in the modern narratives the lone traveler is likely to be threatened, not by a werewolf, but by a phantom hitch-hiker, and the location of his danger may be a freeway rather than a forest. Computer games use sophisticated technology to represent quests involving dragons to be slain and princesses to be saved and married. The myth of Superman, the superhuman hero who saves the world and preserves "the American way," is a notable image embodying modern Americans' confidence in the moral values that their culture espouses. Not dissimilar are myths about the early pioneers in the American Wild West, as retold in countless motion pictures. Such stories often reinforce stereotypical attitudes about the moral superiority of the settlers to the native Indians, although sometimes such attitudes are called into question in other movies that attempt to demythologize the Wild West.

A particular illustration of the power that myths continue to exert was provided as late as the 1940s by the belief in the existence of an Aryan racial group, separate from and superior to the Semitic group. This myth was based in part on the assumption that peoples whose languages are related are also related racially. The fact that this assumption is spurious did not prevent the Aryan myth from gaining wide acceptance in Europe from the 18th century onward, and it was eventually to provide a supposed intellectual justification for the persecution of the Semitic Jews by their Aryan Germanic "superiors" during the period of Nazi domination. This episode suggests that, in politics, a myth will take hold if it serves the interests and focuses the aspirations of a particular group; the truth or falsity of the myth is irrelevant. In a sense, of course, this function is merely an extension of its more general role in religion, where a myth, as well as addressing questions such as a society's place in the cosmos, may serve to justify a particular kind of governmental organization.

Although politics is often regarded as having taken over the role once played by religion or myth in Western society, the situation is more complex than such a generalization would imply. Just as myth has always had a strong social and political element, so political movements and theories have mythical dimensions. For instance, a mythological component has always been important in keeping political units together, from villages to nations. Recently, however, this mythical dimension has gained prominence with the rise of competing mythlike ideologies such as capitalism and communism; the word ideology might indeed be replaced, in much contemporary discussion about politics, by the term mythology. Finally, crucial terms in modern sociopolitical discussion, such as freedom and equality, although they have a long and complex philosophical history, are often posited in a manner analogous to the function of myth presenting its own authority.

Animals and Plants in Myth

Animals and plants have played important roles in the oral traditions and the recorded myths of the peoples of the world, both ancient and modern.

Mṛga ("deer") Jātaka showing the bodhisattva (Buddha-to-be) as a deer, stone bas-relief from Bhārhut, 2nd century BC; in the Indian Museum, Calcutta.

Human beings have always been intrigued by the problem of boundaries: what distinguishes one individual from another; what marks off one culture from another; what the dividing lines are between humans and nonhumans, be they other forms of mortal life or divine beings. At times humans have maintained a rigid sense of separation and viewed the breaking of distinctions as transgression. At other times they have sought to cross the boundaries in order to gain power or knowledge. In some myths, they have glorified an age when distinct categories had not yet come into existence, and they have yearned for a return to this paradisiacal condition. In other traditions, they have viewed with horror the monsters that result when different spheres of being are mixed.

According to a view prevalent in many traditional societies, humans were formed by the gods. Human history is given in the myths of the primordial establishment of things, and the solemn responsibility of human individuals, along with every other living thing, is to fit themselves within this given world. This does not mean that people living in such traditional societies lack distinctions. Among the African Lele, for example, animals are distinguished from humans by their lack of manners, their immense fecundity, and by their sticking to their own sphere and avoiding contact with humans. Animals that violate this third characteristic are understood to be human-animals, the product of sorcery or metempsychosis (transmigration of souls).

The Great Chain of Being that dominated Western thought throughout the Middle Ages made human beings both the highest of the animals and the lowest of the gods. The human body was like that of the animals: corporeal, sensate, and mortal. But the human spirit or intellect resembled the gods: incorporeal, rational, and immortal. The great surge of ethnological and biologic data and theories from the 16th century on tended to undermine this point of view. New types of human beings were encountered (e.g., the "savage") who seemed to their first describers closely akin to the brute; new biologies were proposed that placed humans wholly within the animal kingdom, merely as one species among many, and postulated their descent from animals. More recently, psychology and ethology have emphasized the irrational (or brutish) elements of human beings and suggested close analogies between animal and human behaviour. Since the 18th century humanity has been defined in a new, nonbiological way: as a cultural being rather than as the inhabitant of a natural realm. There have been many forms of this dichotomy: a human is the only being who has a language, uses symbols, employs tools, freely plays, is self-conscious, or possesses a history. Humans, in short, create themselves as cultural beings in distinction to animals or plants, which are created by their environment or heredity. These questions of human identity and the way humans resemble or differ from other sentient beings may be found in every culture and during every age.

Human beings tend to draw boundaries, both conceptually and practically. Not only does their existence demand that they find a position in a complex system of relationships, but also their social life and biological survival depend on the making of distinctions. To speak with the gods, to have relations with another human, to take possession of another's territory, or to eat this or that plant or animal involves individuals in a host of decisions upon which their existence depends. One of the chief resources for answering such questions is that of the myths and legends mapping the world in which individuals dwell.

Myths and legends concerning animals and plants employ a wide variety of motifs but express a limited number of relationships. Humans, animals, and plants may stand in a relationship of (1) opposition or difference, (2) descent, (3) mixture, (4) transformation, (5) identity, or (6) similarity. These are determined by and expressive of the total worldview of a people. The hunter, for example, has a different understanding of the animal from that of the agriculturalist or pastoralist; the tuber planter has a different view of plants from that of the cultivator of grains. Even within these broad categories sharp differences occur. The Kalahari San of southern Africa, who, alone, naked, and crawling on the ground, blends in with his environment in order to kill an animal for food, reveals a way of looking at the human relation to nature different from that of the Masai tribesman of eastern Africa, who, costumed and walking upright as part of a line of chanting hunters in order to slay a lion as a symbol of his manhood, stands forth visibly as the ruler of the world through which he moves. The Cretan bull dancer of ancient Mediterranean culture, playing with the animal by somersaulting over his back, expresses a conception of the human relation to this powerful animal and the forces of fecundity and death that it symbolizes different from that of the Spanish bullfighter who slays the beast.

Relationships of Opposition or Difference

The fundamental religious boundary is that between the sacred and the profane, the sacred being conceived of as a sphere of power superior to or opposed to the mundane. That which is sacred may be either creatively or chaotically powerful. If the former, it is primarily expressed in creation myths; if the latter, in demonic traditions.

Cosmogonies

The notion of a creator deity in animal or plant form is comparatively rare. There are stories of animals, birds, or insects creating the world and of creators with animal attributes or animal companions, but these are isolated traditions. Even in the widespread motif of the birth of the world from a cosmic egg there is rarely the notion of a bird laying or incubating the egg (the most notable exception is the world egg laid by a beautiful bird in the beginning of the Kalevala, the national epic of Finland). There are, however, a number of cosmogonic (origin of the world) motifs that employ a fundamental animal or plant symbolism: the cosmic tree that supports and nourishes the world; the earth surrounded by a serpent or supported on a turtle or on some other animal's back; the features of the present world created by the actions of some primeval animal—e.g., lakes and rivers caused by the digging of an animal or hills raised by the flapping wings of a bird. Sacrificial motifs abound, such as the world being formed from the cut-up parts of an animal or restored by its primordial sacrifice.

A number of important traditions associated with animals occur in dualistic creation accounts in which animals oppose creation, acting as a foil to the creator, or creation is accomplished by combat between the creator and animal monsters representative of chaos who must be slain or bound before the world can be established. The widely distributed earth-diver myth is the most familiar example of dualistic creation.

Other oppositions occur with respect to the creation of the human species. Perhaps the most frequent myth of the origin of death is that of the "perverted message" or "two messengers." In one, an animal is sent with a message from the creator that humans are immortal, but the animal alters the message to state that humans must die. In the other, two animals are sent, one with the word that humans are immortal, one with the message that humans will die. A mishap occurs to the first, and only the fatal message arrives.

In some traditions, there is a union of disparate features or opposites in a given mythic being. This does not express a chaotic hybrid but rather a creative totality (the "coincidence of opposites"). Though most frequently expressed by androgyny (having both male and female characteristics), either in traditions of an androgynous creator or first human, the theme is present in some animal and plant traditions as well (e.g., the emergence of the human species from the androgynous rīvās plant in Iranian mythology). Although it occurs in cosmogonic settings (e.g., the tree that unites heaven and earth), motifs of the reconciliation of animal and plant opposites more usually occur in paradisiacal imagery that promises the harmonious mingling of realms.

Animal and Plant Deities

Belief in sacred plants or animals is widespread. Common to all of these is the notion that the plant or animal is a manifestation of the sacred and thus possesses the dual attributes of beneficence (in healing, hunting, or agricultural magic) or danger (as expressed in taboos against their destruction or consumption). More rarely, gods are believed to have animal (theriomorphic) or plant (phytomorphic) forms. Influenced by ancient Greek disparagement of contemporary Egyptian religion and Judeo-Christian antipathy to "idolatry," Western scholars have tended to speak of such traditions as "animal worship," although it is usually not the animal itself but rather the sacred power revealed by the animal that is being revered. Other deities possess animal or plant attributes or are incarnations associated with particular animals or plants. Here the animals or plants possess a symbolic function. Certain qualities are associated with certain species (e.g., wisdom with the owl, strength with the lion, immortality with the eagle, inspiration with the grape), and the god's possession of these qualities is indicated by his being identified with the appropriate animal or plant. In other traditions, natural phenomena are associated with the actions of certain species (e.g., wind as a bird, lightning as a snake), and the god who controls such phenomena is identified with the species. At times, the animal or plant achieves a divine identity of its own—e.g., the thunderbird or the earthquake monster.

Hunting and Agricultural Deities

In the traditions of archaic hunting peoples there is frequently a figure whom scholars term the master of the animals or the protector of game. He is the ruler of the forest, of all animal species, or of only one particular species (usually a large game animal—e.g., the northern master of the caribou). The master controls all game animals (frequently by penning them up). He dispenses a certain number to humans as food and can be invoked by a shaman when he withholds game. He guides the hunter and, in some traditions, avenges the spirits of slain animals, whose souls return to his enclosures when they die. He is sometimes pictured in human form, on occasion having animal attributes or riding an animal; in other traditions, he is a giant animal or can assume animal form.

In a related complex, a deity in animal form demonstrates to humans the art of hunting, serving as the first victim (a motif found in some of the American Indian bear mother or buffalo woman tales). Or the deity appears among humans as an animal who must be slain and eaten so that he may return to his heavenly home (e.g., the Ainu Iyomante feast in Japan).

A similar pattern is found among archaic agricultural peoples. An ancestral (dema) goddess, at times in plant form, produces food asexually from her body. She is slain by the tribe, and from the dismembered portions of her body crops appear.

The archaic pattern of the dema deity needs to be distinguished from the widespread tradition among technically more sophisticated agricultural peoples of the bountiful mother earth or the god or goddess of vegetation or special crops. In the latter case, the deity, frequently depicted or associated with the appropriate animal and vegetative characteristics, is the principle of inexhaustible vitality. The god frequently has a human consort who participates in a sacred marriage in order to gain fecundity for humans (this happens in ancient Mesopotamian religions, for instance).

Culture Heroes

The master of the animals or corn mother is frequently found in association with animal culture heroes. An animal or trickster who can assume animal form secures for humans the various attributes of culture (acting either in consort with or opposition to the gods). These traditions are found in etiologic stories about how humans first learned to hunt, discovered tobacco, and accomplished other things. The most frequent motif is that of the animal who stole fire from the gods for the benefit of humanity. Frequently, such traditions lie behind etiologies of specific animal or plant characteristics; e.g., the bat is black and blind because it stole fire and was singed by the flames and blinded by the smoke. In other tales, the animals oppose the acquisition of culture by humans and must be overcome by a human culture hero.

A closely related theme is the myth of a life-giving tree or other healing magical plant, growing in paradise or some other inaccessible place, to which the culture hero must travel in order to gain a boon for humankind. He is frequently assisted by or has to overcome supernatural animals. This is an especially widespread type of myth, with numerous instances found throughout the world.

Demonic Plants and Animals

Opposed to these positive conceptions of the creative powers of plants and animals is the notion that their sacred power is chaotic or demonic. Rather than aiding human beings, they are destructive. The most common examples are monstrous plants and animals, which figure especially in heroic quests as guardians of boons or threats to be overcome; mythical animals associated with destructive natural phenomena, such as the earthquake monster or the monster who according to some traditions causes eclipses by devouring the Sun or Moon; and personifications of evil powers such as death or disease (e.g., the hound of hell) or chaos beasts (such as dragons) whose release marks the end of the world or who will be slain in a final battle by a saviour deity. A universal phenomenon is the association of certain species of animals with sorcerers and witches. The most frequent form of this belief is that of the familiar—an animal whose soul is bound up with that of the sorcerer, whose form the sorcerer can assume, and who may be commanded to serve his evil master.

Some species (e.g., animals such as the serpent and various narcotic plants) exhibit the ambivalence of the sacred—they are conceived as being both beneficent and dangerous. This reflects a crucial aspect of the sacred—that it is a region of power. As was stated above this power is ambivalent—i.e., it can act for humanity's benefit or detriment—and is perceived therefore as the location either of creativity or of chaos.

Relationships of Descent

One of the major ways humans have of organizing their world is through genealogy or relations of descent. In theogonies, or tales of the origin of gods (e.g., that by Hesiod), or in legendary lists of human offspring (such as the genealogies in the Hebrew Bible), relations of descent and the association of characteristics, territories, and spheres of influence with descendants provide a means of mapping the cosmos and the human world. In traditions concerning animals and plants, relations of descent are most prominent in myths of human origin and in totemic (animal-clan relational) materials. Central to both is the figure of the plant or animal ancestor.

Creation of Human Beings from Plants or Animals

A widespread motif, especially among archaic peoples, concerns the supposed descent of the human species from plants or animals. These descent traditions usually name a particular species as humanity's ancestor, and the tribe frequently takes its name from the plant or animal.

In some myths, an asexual mode of creation is implied; a child, for example, appears from the bud of a tree or from a split fruit, or man is a featherless bird sent from the sky. Even the motif of the birth of man from an egg is predominantly an asexual motif inasmuch as no preliminary coition is mentioned. Other traditions, particularly agricultural ones, see man as the product of the mating of a plant or animal species. In some myths, fabrication rather than descent is emphasized. Man is fashioned from a plant or animal by the gods, or his parts are modeled after other species. In these descent traditions, the primal man who results is usually the progenitor of a particular people. Other peoples are created from different or less favourable species. These traditions persist in folkloric accounts of the birth of individuals from plants or animals. Such myths express a close relationship between man and the animal and plant world. Man does not represent a new type of being but rather a new manifestation or form.

The widely distributed notion of animal or plant ancestors places considerable emphasis on transformation. The ancestral myths describe a primeval time of creation (or successive creations) followed by a decisive alteration in the conditions of life in the shift from the ancestral to the present human mode of being. Compared with the "fixed" characteristics of the present period, the ancestral era is represented as having been one of flux, lacking definite boundaries. In it animals, plants, and humans are much the same: they can speak with each other, have sexual relations with each other, and engage in other relationships. The ancestors are polymorphic (many formed) and are frequently depicted as emerging from the ground. In such cases their movement toward the surface is represented as an increasing differentiation, away from compound hybrids and toward forms somewhat resembling present species. But even on the surface, the ancestors remain relatively fluid: some resemble plants, others animals or humans, and all have shared characteristics and the power to change their form at will.

The ancestors are depicted as primordially powerful beings, but due to a variety of causes their world becomes transformed, and the present order of things comes into existence. Human culture and the decisive features of the world as humans now know it are established during the transformation: a person's labour, sexuality, and death are due to some action of the ancestors; the topography of the land is the "tracks" left by the ancestors; humans, animals, and plants are depicted as having received their present form after the ancestral age.

Totemism

The relations to an animal or plant ancestor are frequently associated with the complex phenomenon of totemism. Totemism is primarily a social relationship. It expresses the belief that there is a connection between a group of persons, on the one hand, and a species of animal or plant, on the other. The relationship to the totem (animal or plant symbol) occurs in a variety of forms; associated phenomena (e.g., exogamy, or marriage outside the clan, and taboos against killing the totem species) may or may not be present. The myths associated with such traditions narrate the origin of a social group and the discovery of its totem. It was commonly believed in the 19th century that there was a stage in the development of human thought that could be called "totemic," a stage at which primitive peoples perceived a mystical connection between particular social groups and the animals or plants that were their totems. Totemism apparently covered a bewilderingly wide range of phenomena: the list of totems among the Nuer, for instance, includes lion, waterbuck, tortoise, papyrus, rafters, and certain diseases. Utilitarian explanations for the choices of totems—"good to eat," "useful," etc.—do not fit the ethnographic data, and to say that the totems are chosen because they have some special mystical significance is merely to rephrase the problem, without identifying why only certain items have mystical significance. In Le Totémisme aujourd'hui Lévi-Strauss advocated a different approach. He suggested that totemism, far from being a special stage in human development, was merely an instance of the use, within so-called primitive systems of classification, of objects and categories from the world of everyday experience to divide and order that experience.

A phenomenon that has, at times, been confused with the social relations of totemism is that of the individual guardian. It involves a relationship between a particular person and a particular species, usually revealed to the individual in a vision, such as in the vision quests among the North American Plains Indians. These guardians become a source of knowledge and good fortune for the individual. To these traditions, other folkloric motifs may be related, such as the birth of various individuals from intercourse between humans and animals or plants; the animal wife; animal nurses; or the ability of certain persons to understand or converse with animals or plants.

Hierarchy

The fluidity of boundaries characteristic of relations of descent raises important questions as to the status of human beings or of culture in relation to nature. Are animals and plants more like humans than not? Is the human world superior to or inferior to the natural sphere? Such questions lie behind a variety of motifs associated with descent traditions: that the first humans were undeveloped, amorphous, or resembled animals; that animals resisted the creation of humans; and that the primordial man is the ruler of the natural world. The characteristic fluidity of the descent traditions persists in traditions such as the wild man and in relations of transformation and identity.

Relationships of Mixture

For some societies boundaries and the maintenance of distinctions guarantee the continued existence of the cosmos as an integrated totality. There are rituals that periodically reenact the original process whereby the cosmos was divided up and established in its present form. In such cases a new beginning, for example New Year's celebrations as carried out in modern Western society, re-create the original beginnings of things as they are today. Other rituals foster remembrance of the decisive deeds of the ancestors in fixing the present state of things; ritualized social structures (such as the caste structure of India) maintain a complex system of distinctions; and religious ideologies (such as astrology) foster the notion of spheres of power that control all members of a class, be they gods, planets, animals, plants, minerals, or human beings. In such societies, to be real is to affirm and repeat the structures of the cosmos. Each being is called upon to dwell in a limited world in which everything has its given place and role to fulfill. To be sacred is to remain in place. To break out, to cross boundaries, is to open the world to the threat of chaos, to commit transgression. Associated with this worldview is the notion that the mixing of realms is the result of evil influence and leads to monsters, hybrids, and uncleanliness. An alternative view in the history of religions sees positive sacred power to be gained from the violation of the given boundaries of the world. Each being, in such a view, is called upon to challenge its limits; to break them and to create new possibilities for existence, to achieve freedom. Associated with this view is either the necessity for a periodic loosening of restraint or the celebration of gods or sacred persons who have achieved freedom. Religiously expressed, for the one view, the sacred is the ordinary, that which remains in place; for the other, the sacred is the extraordinary, that which is not restricted to its allotted place.

These two points of view—i.e., that power comes from conformity to class or freedom from class—may be illustrated by the widespread category of taboo. Research in the second half of the 20th century led to the conclusion that taboo is primarily a taxonomic (classificatory) system. Those things that are forbidden involve the crossing of boundaries or are beings that fall between classes. Thus, one may not with impunity enter other spheres (e.g., the realms of the gods) or touch sacred objects, transport an object from one realm to another, cross sexual or class lines, or have relations with a being not of one's class. Many food taboos have been shown to reflect taxonomic anomalies. An animal such as the bat is tabooed because it has fur like a mammal but flies like a bird; it has wings like a bird but has fur rather than feathers—and therefore is neither mammal nor bird and must be shunned. On the other hand, the consumption of forbidden foods or engaging in forbidden sexual practices (including homosexuality and bestiality) is part of the ritual of transcendence in many cultures. If an individual can survive the crossing of boundaries, he will obtain extraordinary sacred power (e.g., adherents of Tantrism, a system of esoteric practices performed in both Buddhism and Hinduism, who violate both eating and sexual taboos; the Jewish magicians mentioned in the biblical Book of Isaiah, chapter 65, who eat the forbidden swine and say "do not come near me, for I am holy").

From the earliest times, human beings have shown a readiness to be fascinated by monsters. Monsters are chaos beasts, lurking at the interstices of order, be they conceived as mythical creatures who preceded creation, survivals from an archaic era, creatures who dwell in dangerous lands remote from human habitation, or beings who appear in nightmares. Though the forms and types of monsters are numberless, a single principle holds good for the majority of them: a monster is out of place, conforming to no class or violating existing classes. This is most frequently expressed by the monster's having hybrid form (the result of a mixture of species, attributes, sexes, and other categories), being the result of a transformation, or having dislocated or superfluous parts. Because modes of locomotion and other bodily characteristics are prime modes of classification, the superfluity or lack of organs removes the monster from the ordinary taxonomic divisions. The dragon, for example—perhaps the most widespread monster in myth and folklore—is born through a mixture of species: it is a serpent born asexually from a rooster's egg incubated in manure; by the transformation of an animal; or by the joint generation of a human or worm and a metal. Its form is a compound of species: the body of a serpent or crocodile with the scales of a fish; feet, wings, and occasionally the head of a bird; the forelimbs and occasionally the head of a lion; or, in another dominant type, the ears of an ox, the feet of a tiger, the claws of an eagle, the horns of a deer, the head of a camel, the eyes of a demon, the neck of a snake, the belly of a mollusk, and the scales of a fish. In other types of dragons, organs or attributes of the snake, lizard, fish, mollusk, toad, elephant, horse, pig, ram, deer, eagle, falcon, octopus, or whale predominate. In many traditions, the dragon has the power to transform itself at will. Its possession of superfluous organs is most frequently expressed by its being many headed, and it has both subterranean and aerial characteristics and habits.

The most common hybrid monster generally mixes differing species—e.g., the Centaur (horse-man), the Minotaur (bull-man), Echidna (snake-woman), Pegasus (horse-bird), Sphinx (woman-lion-bird), Siren (bird-woman), and Empusa (animal-metal) of Greek mythology and the griffin (lion-eagle), mermaid (woman-fish), vegetable lamb (plant-animal), barnacle goose (mollusk-bird), and mandrake (plant-man). In other instances, the characteristics are juxtapositions of different species—e.g., the tree that bears human heads as fruit; horses born from eggs; flesh-eating mares; milk-producing birds.

The most extreme form of the fluidity that is characteristic of monsters is the Protean figure who can change into any form or combination of forms at will. In all of these monstrous forms, the central notion appears to be the danger associated with beings that are out of place or are fluid. But some contemporary anthropologists have argued the opposite conclusion; i.e., rather than being threats to the classificatory system, monsters, through their startling combinations and juxtapositions, force people to think more clearly about and distinguish more sharply between the different boundaries of their world. In this interpretation, the monsters are ultimately supportive of order rather than a destructive threat to it.

Relationships of Transformation

One of the largest groups of animal and plant traditions in folklore and religious material is that of transformation. Familiar stories—such as Beauty and the Beast; the transformation of a man into an ass in the Metamorphoses by Apuleius, a Roman writer of the 2nd century CE; the frog king or the swan maiden, as well as such well-known traditions as that of the werewolf, the vampire, or leopard man—testify to the wide dissemination of this theme. Every permutation and combination exists: human into mammal, bird, fish, insect, reptile, amphibian, or plant; animal into human or plant; animal into another species of animal; or plant into animal. There are also partial transformations resulting in hybrid forms as well as alternating transformations—e.g., animal, human, or tree by day and the reverse at night. Another great series of transformations concerns the dead, who either transmigrate into or return in animal and plant forms.

The power to compel another to change form, or to cross boundaries oneself at will, may be judged good or evil depending on the assessment of order in the worldview of the particular culture. In the majority of instances of transformation of another, the transformation is considered to be the result of evil magical powers, and most tales conclude with the disenchantment of the subject, his release from the evil power, and his return to his original form. Many of the instances of self-transformation are for the positive purpose of transcendence.

Several of the motifs present in the folklore of transformation suggest cultic procedures (e.g., transformation into an animal by putting on its skin). Cultic practices probably lie behind and lend credibility to many such tales.

In many societies, ritual change involves a transition period in which boundaries are broken and chaos rules, only to be overcome as order is restored. This is common in festivals in which the social order is temporarily suspended or reversed (as in the ancient Roman Saturnalia and the carnival celebrated in many Roman Catholic countries) and in rites of passage (such as initiation). Animal and plant transformations play a significant role in such ceremonies, both as negative symbols of chaos (e.g., return of the dead in animal form to mingle with the living; ritualized combats against the primordial dragon) and as positive symbols of the breaking through of bounds and the release of the forces of life (e.g., the presence in many of these ceremonies of young males dressed as animals who engage in sacred sexual intercourse). Prominent in such Saturnalian traditions are deities such as the Greek god Dionysus, who can assume vegetable, animal, or human forms at will, who is a god of sudden, dramatic epiphanies (manifestations) and license, and whose devotees, through orgiastic rituals, participate in his freedom to break all bounds in order to recover the boundless vitality and fecundity of primordial chaos. A new life for the cosmos, society, and the individual is supposedly obtained through the abolition of the order of the old.

Initiation ceremonies make use of transformations to a somewhat different end. The initiant receives new birth by the dying of his old self after a series of ordeals. Antagonists, frequently in masked animal form, torment him, and his "death" and rebirth are analogous to the hero's successful fight against monsters. Alternatively, the culmination of initiation is frequently the narration of the myths of the ancestors and the vision of them. Masked men, in mixed animal and plant forms, appear to the initiant to remind him of his true origin as opposed to his biologic origin as a product of his parents. (Other ritual uses of masks achieve the same effect: the ritual transformation of the "actor" into the sacred animal, plant, or deity.)

Frequently, although the nomenclature for plants and animals is learned by a child from birth, the logic of the system is revealed only at initiation, at which point the initiant, as an adult, becomes responsible for the proper observance of all the boundaries required by his society (e.g., among the Senufo of Africa, 58 figurines are presented to the initiant in a carefully prescribed order that provides an inventory of the basic classes of animals, humans and their activities, and social distinctions).

Within many cultures there are religious specialists in the breaking of bounds. Perhaps the most widespread example is that of the shaman who is deemed able to journey at will to heaven or the underworld, mingling with both the gods and the dead. His journey occurs through magical flight (frequently in the form of a bird) with animal psychopomps (soul conductors) or guardians or by ascending the sacred tree that connects heaven and earth. The shaman may transform himself into an animal and know how to converse with animals. Another similar phenomenon is the existence of leopard societies in Africa. In these a practitioner is believed to be able to transform himself into an animal frequently considered to be his incarnate "second self."

Relationships of Identity

Works on the supposedly primitive mentality published in the 19th and early 20th century usually presumed that so-called primitive peoples could not distinguish between plants, animals, and human individuals. This "hazy vision," as it was often called, was believed to lie at the root of religious phenomena such as animism (belief that inanimate objects and natural phenomena have souls) and totemism. More recent studies have demonstrated the presence of complex taxonomies among peoples sometimes described as "primitive," although they do not usually employ the criteria of a modern biologist. Relations of identity, when compared with the other forms of relationship already described, are comparatively rare, occurring most frequently in traditions about the soul. Relations of similarity are more common, usually in literary settings, such as plant or animal fables. The most common expression of identity relates the human soul to that of animals or plants.

Soul-stuff

Although many tend to associate the soul with personal survival or continuity after death, there is an equally ancient view that emphasizes the continuity of life. This view, to which the Dutch anthropologist Albertus Christiaan Kruyt gave the term soul-stuff (a term he contrasted with the postmortem soul), is chiefly found among the rice cultivators of the Indonesian culture area, although it is also witnessed elsewhere. Central to this belief is the circulation of vitality throughout different levels of existence. The soul-stuff is created by the deity as an indestructible reservoir of life. It is eternally reborn—either by returning to its creator, who will redistribute it, or by transmigrating into an embryonic human, animal, or plant. Whatever form it assumes, the same "stuff" is common to all beings.

Death, Post-mortem and Soul

The majority of traditions concerns the postmortem soul, which leaves the body or comes into existence only after death. A number of motifs reflecting different assessments of the nature of life and death occur. The soul may assume an animal or plant form or there may be animal psychopomps, most frequently a winged creature such as a bird or butterfly. The soul may transmigrate into or be reincarnated as an animal or plant. These traditions need to be distinguished from those concerning spirits of the dead who reappear in animal form. Related to these are traditions about the separable soul, which is capable of removing itself or being removed from a person while still living. This most usually occurs in sleep. While detached it may be placed in or assume the form of an animal or, more rarely, a plant. In general, where the notion of soul-stuff predominates, relations of identity are prevalent; where the notion of a death soul is present, the traditions are more closely akin to relations of transformation.

Plural Souls

A more complex pattern, of wide distribution, is that of the plurality of souls. Human vitality and personality are viewed as the result of a complex set of psychic interrelations. A classic example is that of the Apapocuva-Guaraní of Brazil, as described by the anthropologist Curt Nimuendajú: a gentle vegetable soul comes, fully formed, from the dwelling place of the gods and joins with the infant at the moment of birth. To this is joined, shortly after birth, a vigorous animal soul. The type of animal decisively influences the recipient's personality: a gentle person has received a butterfly's soul; a cruel and violent man, that of a jaguar. Upon death, the vegetable soul enters paradise; the animal soul becomes a fierce ghost that plagues the living. The plurality of souls provides a complex taxonomy accounting for and relating the distinctive character traits of plants, animals, and humans.

The Alter Ego or Life Index

Other religious and folkloric traditions view the life of the human individual as bound up with that of a plant or animal: if one is destroyed the other dies as well. In some traditions, this is confined to the familiar or guardian of a witch or shaman; in others, it is a relationship possible for anyone. An example of the latter relationship is nagualism, a phenomenon found among the Indians of Guatemala and Honduras in Central America. Nagualism is the belief that there exists a nagual—an object or, more often, an animal—that stands in a parallel relationship to a person. If the nagual suffers harm or death, the person suffers harm or death as well. According to one story, during the initial hostile encounters between the Indians and the Spaniards, the Indians' naguals fought on their side against the invaders. When the nagual of the Indian chief—which was in the form of a bird—was speared and killed by the Spanish general, the Indian chief died at the same moment.

Nagualism relates the life of each individual to the life of an animal or other object. More rarely, there is a relation between an entire tribe and a particular plant or animal. In some societies, a ritual of identification is performed, usually at birth (e.g., planting a tree or burying the placenta at the roots of a tree). In others, individuals have a vision or undertake a vision quest to identify their alter ego.

Relationships of Similarity

Relations of similarity between human beings and plants or animals usually depend upon the perception of an attribute or aggregate of attributes that they have in common. This process is apparent in colloquial expressions such as when someone is called a "cool cat," a "bitch," a "clumsy ox," a "greedy pig," or "foxy." A similar process appears to lie behind many of the so-called totemic names or theriophoric or phytophoric personal names (e.g., Swift Deer, Bold Eagle) and is concealed in a number of familiar Western names (e.g., Leo, "the lion"; Deborah, "the bee"; and Jonah, "the dove"). The reverse process, the giving of human names to plants or animals, also depends in a majority of instances on the discernment of character similarities. Care must be used, however, in the interpretation of proper names. Every plant or animal name does not necessarily reveal the perception of similarity. For example, the Seminole Indians combine a character name with a shape and animal name in an arbitrary fashion that appears to pay no attention to their meaning, resulting in unusual combinations such as that of a well-known Seminole medicine man whose name translates as "crazy, spherical puma."

The same process is at work in the universal literary form of plant and animal fables. The fable depends for its point upon the association made by the reader or listener between himself and one of a limited number of characteristics possessed by each animal or plant. More complex forms, verging on allegories, such as the beast epic and the debates between various plants and animals as to which are superior, also exist. The popular Physiologus ("Naturalist"), a Greek work from the 2nd century CE, and the medieval bestiary traditions draw morals particularly from monstrous or wondrous animals and plants. Both the fable and the bestiary traditions contributed to the formation of the stereotyped bird, beast, and flower emblems that figure in heraldry and religious iconography.

The process of discovering similarities of personality between plants and animals, on the one hand, and human beings, on the other, also plays a significant role in certain archaic sciences. Physiognomy, which claims to find correspondences between bodily features and psychological characteristics, often makes use of such supposed similarities. The earliest Western systematic treatise, the Aristotelian Physiognomonica, maintains that people with facial characteristics resembling certain animals have the temperaments ascribed to those animals (e.g., persons who have noses with slight notches resemble the crow and are impudent just as the crow is). These views persist in popular figures of speech, such as "bulldog jaw." The same structure underlies the use of plants and animals in archaic healing practices, alchemy, and astrological tables in which animals, plants, and minerals, as well as human personality traits, are associated with the birth signs of the zodiac or planets.

Mythography

"Mythography" is a broad term used to cover what is, in fact, a disparate set of texts from the ancient world, all in prose, all dealing in one way or another with myth, but otherwise not necessarily closely related. Some of them attempt to collect and organize traditional stories some are more concerned with the interpretation and evaluation of them ("interpretive mythography"); and some show a mixture of these tendencies. Even within these general categories, there is wide variation among the surviving examples. Systematic mythography includes attempts at organizing the whole of Greek myth into a single narrative (Pseudo-Apollodorus, which covers everything from the reign of Ouranos and Gaia to the generation after the Trojan War), but also works in which the same material is organized as individual stories (Hyginus's Fabulae), as well as more specialized treatments that focus on a particular subset of myths, such as transformations, love stories, and star myths (Antoninus Liberalis, Parthenius, and Pseudo-Eratosthenes, respectively). Interpretive mythography is likewise varied, but in general it has the aim of making sense of myth in light of other intellectual and philosophical developments, for instance, by attempting to reconcile myth and the observable facts of the real world (Palaephatus) or to explain it as philosophical or religious allegory (Cornutus and others). Many scholars use the term "mythography" solely in reference to the systematic sort. Mythography as a genre is normally seen as a Hellenistic and Imperial phenomenon, but antecedents appear alongside the earliest prose writers of history and philosophy in the 5th century BCE. One area of important investigation remains how to distinguish early mythography from these allied genres, a vexed question because later authorities may often call the same author a historian, genealogist, and mythographer without distinction, and the sources are not well preserved. Mythography remained a continuous activity from these origins until the end of Antiquity, and even beyond. The early Hellenistic examples of the genre, which seem to have been crucial in establishing the central forms and varieties of mythography, are themselves poorly preserved, but we have rather more texts surviving from the 1st century BCE onward, and these often give us our only glimpses of their predecessors. For purposes of convenience, mythographic works here are divided into chronological categories:

- Early (that is, Archaic and Classical).

- Hellenistic.

- Imperial—but it should be remembered that precise chronology is difficult to establish.

Mythopoeia

Mythopoeia is essentially writing about one's personal mythology, or writing in a style of prose and story-telling involving an extensive, deep, rich mythology the author has constructed over many years. It goes beyond protagonists and story arcs. It goes beyond battlefields, crowns, thrones, wars for land, wealth, fame, romance, love, and power. It goes beyond the traditional tropes of dragon-riders, vampire love stories, fairies, and elves. It is not world-building or fantasy maps drawn on a page.

Mythopoeia is purely about the archetypes of the psyche that exist in the self.

Mytho-poetic writing is about constructing the larger themes of life and living life on the page, of grandiose tragedy, redemption, determinism vs. freewill, of the divine nature of the individual versus the Gods, being and non-being, and of the greater themes of the unconscious mind that holds meaning in mythic symbols and imagery hidden in the lower brain. It is existential and profound, played out via characters in story, yet driven by a greater plan beyond a single protagonist or story arc.

How can one character in modern fiction portray all that? They cannot. Therefore, such fiction requires a different perspective and approach, a different prose style, deeper themes, broader tropes, and wilder and more imaginative creative writing tied to the individual and his/her dreams. As such, it is about transposing the world of people, events, struggle, and the nature of this world onto the mythic landscape of the human mind and heart, apart from those ideas. Though we are limited in our play of the larger, more modern world we live in, we are its driver in our own minds and imagination as writers and creators.

The conscious and unconscious mythical mind of the individual writer and artist must remove the shallow projections of our personal needs, desires, and dreams, and replace them with the more sublime and universal themes embedded in the mind, connecting with symbols, mythic images, and archetypes whose purpose and meaning plays into our survival and the very meaning of our lives as human beings in the universe. In that sense, mythopoeia doesn't exist in most modern fiction, simply because modern fiction often derives from our personal desires and frustrations and our "emotional needs", rather than the personal myth of the self and the spirit apart from the flesh.

And so mythopoeia, and really all great fantasy literature, is very much a religious experience, and demands more from us as writers if it is to succeed and stir others. It demands much more.

Mytho-poetic writing is about exploring the archetypes of the unconscious, as Carl Jung has written about. It involves exploring the vast architecture of the self; where Gods, worlds, and tragedy collide, huge landscapes and legions of characters engage in a conflict and struggle that wages fiercely in the author's unconscious mind and psychology, separate from society and modern struggles for money, sex, love, power, and desire. It is writing on a "different level" from traditional modern dystopia.

In many ways it is like writing Bibles, Torah's, or Quran's not as religious expression but as expressions of one's personal connection to the Creator in a respectful way that incorporates one's chosen modern religion into it.

Christopher Tolkien's Silmarillion is a "pure mythopoeia" as it is based on the author's careful study of ancient Western philology, combined with his own psychological symbols. Unlike most modern fantasy today, Tolkien's books appear to be free of modern human "needs" and desires, of modern politics, allegory, fantasy fiction tropes, extreme violence, gratuitous sex, greed, fame, and personal conflict. Its struggles exist ONLY in the author and in his spirit, yet remain outside his personal desires for love, money, fame, family, and other traps of modern fantasy. His mythology existed purely in his psychology, and so was designed around his own metaphysical beliefs about larger themes in literature and religious experience – immortality, Christianity, faith, free will, Greek tragedy, good vs evil – as well as careful studies of pagan Indo-European mythology.

But to embrace the grander themes of mythopoeia in fantasy through a careful study of the Simarillion and the ancient pagan manuscripts that inspired it. Through the exploration of the ancient pagan mythology of our ancestors' ancient symbols and stories (based on the countries our families come from), we can begin to construct extremely rich and diverse story-telling beyond what's being written today in the money-making, pop-culture sphere.

As such it is not pure mythopoeia, but one designed to build on modern expectations, filling in story and character arc where mythopoeia is difficult to grasp or follow over the length of the larger dream-like novels.

The Phantammeron still contains pieces of stories, archetypes, and themes in which the death or transformation of its characters exist purely to drive the larger plot and meaning of the story beyond the myths. As such, it exists, not to serve just the expression of dreams or the psychological development of a few protagonists, but to explore the transcendental meaning of both of the meaning of all life, that transcendental middle-realm between dreams and reality which exists in us and our relationship to the world, to those we love, to global events, and our lives own inner divinity expressed through story and fairy tale. That is mythopoeia. That is myth-making.

Those seeking new fantasy worlds with meaning and depth, will reject the current fiction world of pure entertainment and money, and instead find fulfillment through the more thrilling, imaginative, and expansive realm of private mytho-poetic expression.

Mythopoeia deserves more from writers and readers. It can inspire more young people to challenge themselves beyond modern protagonist literature, and explore the deeper themes of the psychological and cultural mythology that exists in themselves versus their book characters and the modern world of conflict, modern religious demands, and consumeristic desire they live in.

Through this level of personal exploration it is the belief that modern men and women of the future can find psychological fulfillment through mytho-poetic literature beyond modern fiction today, and seek to discover their own symbols, their own meaning, and their spiritual place in the world through its medium.

Comparative Mythology

Comparative mythology is the comparison of myths from different cultures in an attempt to identify shared themes and characteristics. Comparative mythology has served a variety of academic purposes. For example, scholars have used the relationships between different myths to trace the development of religions and cultures, to propose common origins for myths from different cultures, and to support various psychological theories.

Comparativists versus Particularists

The anthropologist C. Scott Littleton defines comparative mythology as "the systematic comparison of myths and mythic themes drawn from a wide variety of cultures". By comparing different cultures' mythologies, scholars try to identify underlying similarities and to reconstruct a "protomythology" from which those mythologies developed. To an extent, all theories about mythology follow a comparative approach: as the scholar of religion Robert Segal notes, "by definition, all theorists of myth seek similarities among myths". However, scholars of mythology can be roughly divided into particularists, who emphasize the differences between myths, and comparativists, who emphasize the similarities. Particularists tend to "maintain that the similarities deciphered by comparativists are vague and superficial".

Comparative approaches to mythology held great popularity among eighteenth- and nineteenth-century scholars. Many of these scholars believed that all myths showed signs of having evolved from a single myth or mythical theme. For example, the nineteenth-century philologist Friedrich Max Müller led a school of thought which interpreted nearly all myths as poetic descriptions of the sun's behavior. According to this theory, these poetic descriptions had become distorted over time into seemingly diverse stories about gods and heroes. However, modern-day scholars lean more toward particularism, feeling suspicious of broad statements about myths. One exception to this trend is Joseph Campbell's theory of the "monomyth".

The myth of Prometheus was first attested by Hesiodus and then constituted the basis for a tragic trilogy of plays, possibly by Aeschylus, consisting of Prometheus Bound, Prometheus Unbound and Prometheus Pyrphoros.

Approaches to Comparative Mythology

Comparative mythologists come from various fields, including folklore, anthropology, history, linguistics, and religious studies, and they have used a variety of methods to compare myths. These are some important approaches to comparative mythology.

Linguistic

Some scholars look at the linguistic relationships between the myths of different cultures—for example, the similarities between the names of gods in different cultures. One particularly successful example of this approach is the study of Indo-European mythology. Scholars have found striking similarities between the mythological and religious terms used in different cultures of Europe and India. For example, the Greek sky-god Zeus Pater, the Roman sky-god Jupiter, and the Indian (Vedic) sky-god Dyauá[1]£ Pitá[1].

2
Concepts in Mythology

There are various concepts that are studied under mythology such as structuralist theory, mythological dances and religion, geomythology, myths and rituals, theology, etc. This chapter closely examines the concepts related to mythology to provide an extensive understanding of the subject.

Religion

Religion is still contentious as a term. For some, it's synonymous with obfuscation and dogmatic beliefs, whereas for others it relates to a core body of values.

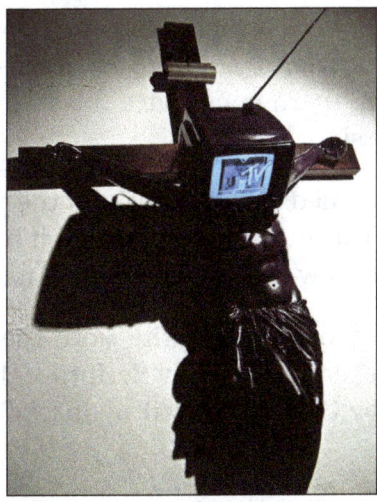

Religion can be seen as a powerful set of cultural practices that offers meaning to a community, and a vision of order in the world. Religions can be used for pernicious ends.

Yet they also have the capacity to generate the virtue of faith or trust, at times when adversity may give cause for despair. Like myth, any religion is capable of a wide range of interpretations. Like Christianity, Islam is much richer as a religion than the caricature offered by extremists.

Only by becoming aware of the diversity of religious practice and understanding, both across time and within contemporary society (in Australia and internationally), can we move beyond naïve assumptions that religion is simply about dogmatism.

The fact that every religion, like every political system, has its own set of myths, does not mean that we should avoid teaching religion within a secular educational structure. Globalisation means that we no longer live in a society dominated by a single religious tradition. Secularisation offers a space for studying how myths and religions enable any culture to question the received truths of the economic and social order.

The term theology has a harder time than religion in the marketplace of ideas. For educated people raised to think of science as based on observation, and theology as based on unquestioned propositions, there is no place for studying theology within secular society, except within a confessional context.

Yet theology is any form of reasoned discussion about the principles of a religious tradition, embodied in its stories. The ancient Greeks used it to refer to poetic stories about the gods or God (for which Hebrew uses a plural word, namely Elohim).

In the Latin West, Augustine avoided using the word theology, because he thought it too pagan. For him, what mattered was Holy Scripture, the sacred stories of the Hebrews, given fresh meaning by Christ, revered by his followers as the living embodiment of Jewish wisdom.

Augustine preferred to think of Christian teaching as first of all about the Scriptures, the ancient songlines, as it were, of the Hebrews, made accessible through Christ to the world.

While Christian theology was shaped at medieval universities by male intellectuals, applying logic to Scripture, mystics (often women) drew on poetry to interpret religious experience. The writing and music of Hildegard of Bingen belongs more to theopoetics than to theology, retrieving an ancient impulse to communicate the spiritual life through song as more powerful than analytic prose.

Religious Literacy

Myth, religion and theology are all rich concepts that defy easy definition. They are terms that are integral to religious literacy, the goal to which any form of religious studies must aspire.

Whether within primary, secondary or tertiary education, students need to be made aware of the variety of ways in which cultures have understood these concepts, as well as of the range of terms they have employed to communicate and discuss such ideas.

Theology is not a word that makes sense in every religion. Within Australian Indigenous communities, the sacred is communicated first of all through song, transmitted orally rather than through written text. In the case of Judaism and Islam, the key notion is that of Law, as a divine principle larger than the individual laws by which it is manifest.

In Buddhism, the cosmic law may be defined in terms of dharma rather than of a transcendent law giver. Myths and religions communicate core values in different ways.

Within a secular society shaped by multiple religious traditions, there is an urgent need for both believers and non-believers to understand the core principles of any religion, to prevent those traditions being taken over by narrow ideologues who preach hate and intolerance.

We need to promote religious literacy, not to enforce commitment to any particular religious tradition, but to better understand religious discourse and imagery. Only through such literacy, can we better understand the meaning of terms like myth, religion and theology.

Theology and Myth

Theology, philosophically oriented discipline of religious speculation and apologetics that is traditionally restricted, because of its origins and format, to Christianity but that may also encompass, because of its themes, other religions, including especially Islam and Judaism. The themes of theology include God, humanity, the world, salvation, and eschatology (the study of last times).

The subject matter of the discipline is treated in a number of other articles. For a survey of systematic interpretations of the divine or sacred, see agnosticism; atheism; deism; dualism; monotheism; nature worship; pantheism; polytheism; theism; and totemism. For a survey of major theological concerns within particular religions, see doctrine and dogma. For treatment of Judeo-Christian theology in the context of other aspects of the tradition, see biblical literature; Christianity; Eastern Orthodoxy; Judaism; Protestantism; and Roman Catholicism.

Nature of Theology

The concept of theology that is applicable as a science in all religions and that is therefore neutral is difficult to distill and determine. The problem lies in the fact that, whereas theology as a concept had its origins in the tradition of the ancient Greeks, it obtained its content and method only within Christianity. Thus, theology, because of its peculiarly Christian profile, is not readily transferable in its narrow sense to any other religion. In its broader thematic concerns, however, theology as a subject matter is germane to other religions.

The Greek philosopher Plato, with whom the concept emerges for the first time, associated with the term theology a polemical intention—as did his pupil Aristotle. For Plato, theology described the mythical, which he allowed may have a temporary pedagogical significance that is beneficial to the state but is to be cleansed from all offensive and abstruse elements with the help of political legislation. This identification of theology and mythology also remained customary in later Greek thought. In contrast to philosophers, "theologians" (e.g., the 8th-century-BCE Greek poets Hesiod and Homer, the cultic servants of the oracle at Delphi, and the rhetoricians of the Roman cult of emperor worship) testified to and proclaimed that which they viewed as divine. Theology thus became significant as the means of proclaiming the gods, of confessing to them, and of teaching and "preaching" this confession. In this practice of "theology" by the Greeks lies the prefiguration of what later would be known as theology in the history of Christianity. In spite of all the contradictions and nuances that were to emerge in the understanding of this concept in various Christian confessions and schools of thought, a formal criterion remains constant: theology is the attempt of adherents of a faith to represent their statements of belief consistently, to explicate them out of the basis (or fundamentals) of their faith, and to assign to such statements their specific place within the context of all other worldly relations (e.g., nature and history) and spiritual processes (e.g., reason and logic).

Here, then, the above indicated difficulty becomes apparent. In the first place, theology is a spiritual or religious attempt of "believers" to explicate their faith. In this sense it is not neutral and is not attempted from the perspective of removed observation—in contrast to a general history of religions. The implication derived from the religious approach is that it does not provide a formal and indifferent scheme devoid of presuppositions within which all religions could be subsumed. In the second place, theology is influenced by its origins in the Greek and Christian traditions, with the implication that the transmutation of this concept to other religions is endangered by the very circumstances of origination. If one attempts, nevertheless, such a transmutation—and if one then speaks of a theology of primitive religions and of a theology of Buddhism—one must be aware of the fact that the concept "theology," which is uncustomary and also inadequate in those spheres, is applicable only to a very limited extent and in a very modified form. This is because some Eastern religions have atheistic qualities and provide no access to the theos ("god") of theology. If one nonetheless speaks of theology in religions other than Christianity or Greek religion, one implies—in formal analogy to what has been observed above—the way in which representatives of other religions understand themselves.

Relationship of Theology to the History of Religions and Philosophy

Relationship to the History of Religions

If theology explicates the way in which the believer understands his faith—or, if faith is not a dominating quality, the way in which a religion's practitioners understand their religion—this implies that it claims to be normative, even if the claim does not, as in Hinduism and Buddhism, culminate in the pretension to be absolutely authoritative. The normative element in these religions arises simply out of the authority of a divine teacher or out of a revelation (e.g., a vision or auditory revelation) or some other kind of spiritual encounter as a result of which one feels committed. The academic study of religion, which encompasses also religious psychology, religious sociology, and the history and phenomenology of religion as well as the philosophy of religion, has emancipated itself from the normative aspect in favour of a purely empirical analysis. This empirical aspect, which corresponds to the modern conception of science, can be applied only if it functions on the basis of objectifiable (empirically verifiable) entities. Revelation of the kind of event that would have to be characterized as transcendent, however, can never be understood as such an objectifiable entity. Only those forms of religious life that are positive and arise out of experience can be objectified. Wherever such forms are given, the religious person is taken as the source of the religious phenomena that are to be interpreted. Understood in this manner, the study of religion represents a necessary step in the process of secularization.

Nevertheless, it cannot be said that theology and the history of religions only contradict one another. The "theologies"—for want of a better term—of the various religions are concerned with religious phenomena, and the adherents of the religions of the more "advanced" cultures are themselves constrained—especially at a time of increasing cultural interdependency—to take cognizance of and to interpret theologically the fact that besides their own religion there are many others. In this regard, then, there are not only analytical but also theological statements concerning religious phenomena, particularly in regard to the manner in which such statements are encountered in specific primitive or high religions. Thus, the objects of the history of religions and those of theology cannot be clearly separated. They are merely approached with different categories and criteria. If the history of religions does not surrender its neutrality—since such a surrender would thereby reduce the discipline to anthropology in an ideological sense (e.g., religion understood as mere projection of the psyche or of societal conditions)—theology will recognize the history of religions as a science providing valuable material and as one of the sciences in the universe of sciences.

Relationship to Philosophy

The relationship of theology to philosophy is much more difficult to determine, because it is much more complicated. The problems can here only be mentioned. If one understands philosophy as the discipline that attempts to explicate the totality of being, the difference between philosophy and theology becomes apparent. If theology is responsible to an authority that initiates its thinking, speaking, and witnessing—e.g., a document containing revealed truth, as well as the spiritual testimony related to it—philosophy bases its arguments on the ground of timeless evidence, an evidence with which autonomous reason understands itself to be confronted. Since, on the other hand, theology also uses reason and systematically develops its tenets—however much its critical reflections are based on religious convictions—there are many common areas that have partly complementary significance but that partly also lead to polemical tensions.

The Significance of Theology

The Religious Significance of Theology

Just as in the case of religions themselves, so also their theological reflections are not limited to a special religious sphere, separated from common life. Whoever speaks of God and the gods speaks at the same time of humanity and of the meaning of existence. He makes therewith statements about the world, its conditions of being created, its estrangement from the purpose of creation (e.g., sin), and its determined goal (eschatology, or view of the last times). Out of these statements result normative directives for life in the world, not only for the purpose of gaining salvation but also for concrete ethical behaviour in the context of the I-Thou (or person to person) relationship, of the clan, of the nation, and of society. In ancient times, all aspects of life (e.g., the relationship between the sexes, hygiene, and work, among others) were determined religiously and permeated by cultic forms and practices. In this regard, every religion contains the totality of being that its "theology" intends to express—if one also includes certain rudiments of reflection in primitive religion in the concept "theology."

In primitive religions the tribe represents the pivot around which all worldly relations turn. The primeval (or mythical) time to which the tribe traces its own origins is also the time of salvation and fulfilment. Therefore, primitive religions primarily concern themselves with the ancestral cult. Involved in tribal concerns in the realm of religious thought are conceptions of mana (spiritual power, or force)—i.e., the teaching that tribal heads, medicine men, and sorcerers are subjects of special charisma (spiritual power or influence) and more potent powers of life. In Eastern religions, as in Western religions, this understanding is infinitely refined, developed, and theologically reflected. In regard to the relationship of humanity to the world, many Eastern religions (especially Hinduism) have a definite sceptically tinged negative view of all reality, which is especially pronounced in contrast to the Christian doctrine of creation. Although this doctrine points to a "happy event" in Christianity, the call to life and reality is understood in Eastern thought in the opposite manner. As the Scottish religious scholar and missionary Stephen Neill wrote:

> "To be man implies being cut off from all true reality. Creation should have never happened, and its faults should be eliminated as soon as possible. The illusion that I am is a calamity. Not death is to be explained, but rather birth."

The Cultural Importance of Theology

Since theology does not remain restricted to transcendent statements and to an esoteric and sacred realm, and since it rather encompasses all worldly dimensions (cosmology, anthropology, historiography, and other areas), it has always had important significance for cultural evolution and general intellectual life. Western historians hardly need to be reminded of the fact that the prophetic theology of history in the Hebrew Bible (Old Testament)—e.g., the 8th-century-BCE Hebrew prophets Amos and Isaiah—decisively influenced the origins of the concept of history and, indeed, made this concept possible in the first place. A Hebrew Bible theology of history is based on the understanding of history as a linear process, as directed to a goal (i.e., the Kingdom of God) and as qualified by the characteristic of singularity. This view of history contrasts with a cyclical understanding of successive events—i.e., the view that history repeats itself. The fact that university and school were originally initiated by the church (as is still very often the case in mission fields) is based on the fact that theology has thematized in its various subjects the various dimensions of life (nature, history, ethics, and other disciplinary areas). Also, much of modern philosophy has emerged out of theological themes and categories; even in the works of Karl Marx remnants of this fact are still observable. Modern philosophy has, by and large, only gradually emancipated itself from this theological origin, but this emancipation also has taken place in a manner that has retained the dialectical relationship of theology and philosophy. That theological questions in the modern age of secularism are less openly posed than in the time of the Middle Ages does not reduce their lasting significance. They always re-emerge, often in disguised form, such as in the quest for the meaning of life and existence or in the nihilistic resignation regarding that quest; furthermore, they re-emerge in the quest for the dignity of human existence, the inviolability of life, the determination of human rights, and many other such questions. The German American theologian Paul Tillich investigated specifically the secular realm in view of the relevance of these latent theological questions.

Theological Themes

The themes discussed by theology are of universal dimensions. They encompass the doctrine of God, of humanity, and of the world. Even when no "doctrine of God" exists in the strict sense of the term, as in the case of what are sometimes called "atheistic" religions (e.g., certain forms of Hinduism and Buddhism), humanity and the world are understood in the context of finality and therefore have religious aspects. The inclusion of the world in theological discussion also implies that behaviour in the world—that is, ethics—is included in theology; in some areas (e.g., Confucianism) this aspect gains a dominating position. Ethical conceptions—derived from theological concepts in the broad meaning of theology—are developed in contradictory forms: they can lead to ascetic world denial but also to a definite world affirmation. The first form is realized in Buddhism and Hinduism, the second in Confucianism. In Christianity both forms are represented. The theological theme of the relation of humanity and the world has been described by the 17th-century French scientist and philosopher Blaise Pascal as the doctrine of the "dignity and poverty of man"—i.e., the doctrine of creation and fall—and, related to this, the proclamation of salvation and the presentation of a path to salvation. This path leads, in the various religions, into greatly diverging directions. It can be placed under the exclusive direction of divine grace (as in Amida Buddhism and in Protestant Christianity); it can be left to the activity and initiative of humanity (as in Confucianism); or it can be characterized by a combination of the two principles (as in Zen Buddhism and in the Roman Catholic combination of grace and merit). Finally, theology also includes among its various themes statements concerning the process and goal of history (eschatology), especially concerning the relation of secular history and the history of salvation.

Functions of Theology

The vastness of theological interests and aspects implies that theology can master the material with which it is confronted only within a broad spectrum of partial disciplines. Since theology is based on authority (revelation), and since this authority is documented in the scriptures (especially in Christianity), it is constrained to engage in philological and historical studies of these sources and, related to these studies, also with herme-neutical (critical interpretive) questions. This historical task broadens into a concern with the history and tradition of the religion that a particular theology represents. In this concern many difficult and controversial questions arise, including whether and to what extent the canon (scriptural standard) of the sources of revelation is glossed over and modified by tradition and what normative value the modifying tradition has or should have. These problems play an important part in the relationship between Prot-estantism and Catholicism, even though the problems are also treated independently by each confession.

The question of truth posed by theology requires the constitution of a discipline that specifically concerns itself with fundamental questions (systematic theology). Its task can be determined in the following manner: (1) It has to develop the totality of religious teachings (dogmatics, or the doctrine of faith). (2) It has to interpret hu-manity's existence in the world and, related to this, to determine the norms (ethics derived from faith) for action in the world—e.g., for one's disposition toward fellow humans and toward societal and political structures and institutions. (3) It further has to represent its claim to truth in the context of confrontation with other claims to truth and with other criteria of verification (apologetics, polemics). As part of this concern, theology's task is to explain reasonably, in view of historical relativism, the absolute claim of the truth that it represents. Related to this is the modern-day task of coordinating its doctrine of creation or its doctrine of the revelation of the tran-scendent (e.g., the Christ event in Christianity) with the worldview of modern natural science and its thesis of the immanency of being—i.e., of being that is self-contained. Another aspect of this task is the confrontation with other religions' claims to truth, which can lead to vastly different results: either—this is noted only as an example—it can lead to the thesis of the complementary positions of individual religions and therefore to tolerance (as, for example, in Hinduism as well as in some schools in the West) or to one's own religion's claim to be absolute (as in Christianity, at least among the most important of its representatives). But also, in the last mentioned situation, such a claim is widely modified. It can manifest itself by a total rejection of other religions as "devil's work," but it can also be expressed in an interpretation of other religions as first steps to and as seeds of a religious development, the comple-tion of which it knows itself to be.

The vast dimension of theological themes implies that theology is, with its many dis-ciplines, a microcosmic image of the university. Even though it is a science in which the believers or the adherents of a particular religion explicate and critically analyze the truth that is represented by them, it nevertheless has to remain free within the frame-work of this commitment, and it has to fulfill the responsibility of its scientific task on the basis of its own autonomy. The opposite of this freedom would arise when an institution (e.g., the church) restricts the range of theological inquiry with normative claims, forcing the discipline therewith to assume ideological functions. The struggle concerning the freedom and limitations of theology—i.e., concerning responsible criticism and author-ity—is a struggle that has accompanied the history of theology from the very beginnings to the present.

According to Hege, both primitive and modern theology is inescapably constrained by its mythical backbone:

> "Hermeneutically, theologians must recognize that mythical thought permeates the biblical texts. Dogmatically, theologians must be aware of the mythological elements of theology and of how extensively theology relies on mythical forms and functions, especially in light of our awareness of the ubiquity of myth."

Structuralist Theory of Mythology

In structural anthropology, Claude Lévi-Strauss, a French anthropologist, makes the claim that "myth is language". Through approaching mythology as language, Lévi-Strauss suggests that it can be approached the same way as language can be approached by the same structuralist methods used to address language. Thus, Lévi-Strauss offers a structuralist theory of mythology; he clarifies, "Myth is language, functioning on an es-pecially high level where meaning succeeds practically at 'taking off' from the linguistic ground on which it keeps rolling."

Lévi-Strauss breaks down his argument into three main parts. Meaning is not isolated within the specific fundamental parts of the myth, but rather within the composition of these parts. Although myth and language are of similar categories, language functions differently in myth. Finally, language in myth exhibits more complex functions than in any other linguistic expression. From these suggestions, he draws the conclusion that myth can be broken down into constituent units, and these units are different from the constituents of language. Finally, unlike the constituents of language, the constituents of a myth, which he labels "mythemes," function as "bundles of relations."

This approach is a break from the "symbolists", such as Carl Jung, who dedicate themselves to find meaning solely within the constituents rather than their relations. For instance, Lévi-Strauss uses the example of the Oedipus myth and breaks it down to its component parts.

Reading it in sequence from left to right, top to bottom, the myth is categorized se-quentially and by similarities. Through analyzing the commonalities between the "mythemes" of the Oedipus story, understandings can be wrought from its categories.

Thus, a structural approach towards myths is to address all of these constituents. Fur-thermore, a structural approach should account for all versions of a myth, as all ver-sions are relevant to the function of the myth as a whole. This leads to what Lévi-Strauss calls a spiral growth of the myth which is continuous while the structure itself is not.

The growth of the myth only ends when the "intellectual impulse which has produced it is exhausted."

From Mythology to Literary Criticism

Myths are primarily acknowledged as oral traditions, while literature is in the form of written text. Still, anthropologists and literary critics would both acknowledge the links between myths and relatively more contemporary literature. Therefore, many literary critics take the same Lévi-Straussian structuralist, as it is coined, approach to literature. This approach is, again, similar to Symbolist critics' approach to literature. There is a search for the lowest constituent of the story. But as with the myth, Lévi-Straussian structuralism then analyzes the relations between these constituent parts in order to compare even greater relations between versions of stories as well as among stories themselves.

Furthermore, Lévi-Strauss suggests that the structural approach and mental processes dedicated towards analyzing the myth are similar in nature to those in science. This connection between myth and science is further elaborated in his books, "Myth and Meaning" and "The Savage Mind". He suggests that the foundation of structuralism is based upon an innate understanding of the scientific process, which seeks to break down complex phenomena into its component parts and then analyze the relations between them. The structuralist approach to myth is precisely the same method, and as a method this can be readily applied to literature.

Dance in Mythology and Religion

Dance is present in mythology and religion globally. Dance has certainly been an important part of ceremony, rituals, celebrations and entertainment since before the birth of the earliest human civilizations. Archaeology delivers traces of dance from prehistoric times such as the 5,000-year-old Bhimbetka rock shelters paintings in India and Egyptian tomb paintings depicting dancing figures from c. 3300 BC.

One of the earliest structured uses of dances may have been in the performance and in the telling of myths. It was also sometimes used to show feelings for one of the opposite gender. It is also linked to the origin of "love making." Before the production of written languages, dance was one of the methods of passing these stories down from generation to generation.

Another early use of dance may have been as a precursor to ecstatic trance states in healing rituals. Dance is still used for this purpose by many cultures from the Brazilian rainforest to the Kalahari Desert.

An early manuscript describing dance is the Natya Shastra on which is based the modern interpretation of classical Indian dance (e.g. Bharathanatyam).

Greek Mythology

In a classical Greek song, Apollo, the god of medicine, music and poetry, one of the twelve greater gods and son of the chief god Zeus, was called The Dancer. In a Greek line Zeus himself is represented as dancing. Terpsichore is one of the nine Muses, representing dancing and dramatic chorus. In Sparta, a province of ancient Greece, the law compelled parents to exercise their children in dancing from the age of five years. They were led by grown men, and sang hymns and songs as they danced. In very early times a Greek chorus, consisting of the whole population of the city, would meet in the market-place to offer up thanksgivings to the god of the country. Their jubilees were always attended with hymn-singing and dancing.

Dance in Scriptures

The Torah, the Psalms, and many other scriptures reference dance:

Old Testament:

- A Time to Dance.

    ◦ Ecclesiastes 3:4.

- Social Dance in celebration of what God has done.

    ◦ Exodus 15:20.

    ◦ Judges 21:21 - 23.

- In celebration before the Lord.

    ◦ 2 Samuel 6:14-16.

    ◦ 1 Chronicles 15:29.

- Social dancing in celebration of a god.

    ◦ Exodus 32:19.

    ◦ 1 Kings 18:26 (The act of celebrating a false god is condemned here).

- A child's dance.

    ◦ Judges 11:34.

    ◦ Job 21:11.

- Celebration of warriors.
  - 1 Samuel 18:6-7.
  - 1 Samuel 21:11.
  - 1 Samuel 29:5.
- As an expression of happiness.
  - Psalm 30:11.
  - Lamentations 5:15.
- In Worship to the Lord.
  - Psalm 149:3.
  - Psalm 150:4.
- Social Dance with Friends.
  - Jeremiah 31:4.
  - Jeremiah 31:13.
- A Lovers Dance.
  - Song of Solomon 6:13.

New Testament:

- Social Dance with Friends.
  - Luke 15:25.
- Jesus uses dance as a metaphor.
  - Matthew 11:17.
- For the king.
  - Matthew 14:6 and Mark 6:22.

Hindu Scriptures

From a Hindu point of view, the whole Universe is being brought into existence as the manifestation of the dance of the Supreme Dancer, Nataraja. In the Hindu scriptures, every god has his or her own style (lasya and tandava respectively represent two aspects of dance) we read about 23 celestial beings called Apsarases who dance to please the gods and express the supreme truths in the magic of movement.

The dance in the Hinduism used to be a part of a sacred temple ritual, especially in South and Eastern India, where the female priestesses devadasi's worshiped different aspects of the Divine through the elaborate language of mime and gestures. Natyashastra is the most ancient and the most elaborate scripture describing every element and aspect of this sacred art-worship.

The temple dance gradually evolved into what is known today as the South Indian Classical Dance that still preserves many ritualistic elements of Hinduism. Some of the classical Indian dancers are believed to be incarnations of apsaras.

Christianity

In the Protoevangelium of James, it is reported that Mary danced before the Ark of the Covenant in the Temple of Jerusalem at the time of her presentation.

Throughout the history of Christianity, several denominations and independent congregations prohibited social dancing for various reasons; however, dance has always been a part of the social life of many Christians. Christian lyrics are found in the sounds of Ballroom, Country, Rock and Roll, Night Club, and other dance music. Ballet originated in Italy at weddings.

Numerous examples of traditional dance can be found in modern Roman Catholic communities. The Brazilian dance and martial art of capoeira (particularly capoeira angola) is regularly performed—including between capoeiristas of different sexes—to lyrics and ladinhas (litanies) praising God, the saints, and the Virgin. In a similar vein, several genres of dance music in Romani people/Romani culture involve religious themes and lyrics. In the Philippines, the Subli—a devotional dance of the Catholic Tagalogs in Batangas Province—honours the True Cross. Finally, the celebrations of Carnival and Mardi Gras feature dance.

Many Charismatic and Pentecostal Protestant denomonations practice dance during worship services. Congregants frequently dance during services as an act of worship. Some Charismatics practice prophetic dance, a religious practice in which practitioners believe they are representing what the Lord is doing through their movements. This is often accompanied with banners, ribbons and, instruments. Bethel Church in Redding, California has a school where people who wished to be trained in prophetic dance can go.

Myth and Ritual

Myth and ritual are two central components of religious practice. Although myth and ritual are commonly united as parts of religion, the exact relationship between them has been a matter of controversy among scholars. One of the approaches to this problem is "the myth and ritual, or myth-ritualist, theory," held notably by the so-called Cambridge Ritualists, which holds that "myth does not stand by itself but is tied to ritual." This theory is still disputed; many scholars now believe that myth and ritual share common paradigms, but not that one developed from the other.

The "myth and ritual school" is the name given to a series of authors who have focused their philological studies on the "ritual purposes of myths." Some of these scholars (e.g., W. Robertson-Smith, James George Frazer, Jane Ellen Harrison, S. H. Hooke) supported the "primacy of ritual" hypothesis, which claimed that "every myth is derived from a particular ritual and that the syntagmatic quality of myth is a reproduction of the succession of ritual act."

Historically, the important approaches to the study of mythological thinking have been those of Vico, Schelling, Schiller, Jung, Freud, Lucien Lévy-Bruhl, Lévi-Strauss, Frye, the Soviet school, and the Myth and Ritual School.

In the 1930s, Soviet researchers such as Jakov E. Golosovker, Frank-Kamenecky, Olga Freidenberg, Mikhail Bakhtin, "grounded the study of myth and ritual in folklore and in the world view of popular culture."

Following World War II, the semantic study of myth and ritual, particularly by Bill Stanner and Victor Turner, has supported a connection between myth and ritual. However, it has not supported the notion that one preceded and produced the other, as supporters of the "primacy of ritual" hypothesis would claim. According to the currently dominant scholarly view, the link between myth and ritual is that they share common paradigms.

Ritual from Myth

One possibility immediately presents itself: perhaps ritual arose from myth. Many religious rituals—notably Passover among Jews, Christmas and Easter among Christians, and the Hajj among Muslims—commemorate, or involve commemoration of, events in religious literature.

E. B. Tylor

Leaving the sphere of historical religions, the ritual-from-myth approach often sees the relationship between myth and ritual as analogous to the relationship between science and technology. The pioneering anthropologist Edward Burnett Tylor is the classic exponent of this view. He saw myth as an attempt to explain the world: for him, myth was a sort of proto-science. Ritual is secondary: just as technology is an application of science, so ritual is an application of myth—an attempt to produce certain effects, given the supposed nature of the world: "For Tylor, myth functions to explain the world as an end in itself. Ritual applies that explanation to control the world." A ritual always presupposes a pre-existing myth: in short, myth gives rise to ritual.

Myth from Ritual (Primacy of Ritual)

Against the intuitive idea that ritual re-enacts myth or applies mythical theories, many 19th-century anthropologists supported the opposite position: that myth and religious doctrine result from ritual. This is known as the "primacy of ritual" hypothesis.

William Robertson Smith

This view was asserted for the first time by the bible scholar William Robertson Smith. The scholar Meletinsky notes that Smith introduced the concept "dogmatically." In his Lectures on the Religion of the Semites, Smith draws a distinction between ancient and modern religion: in modern religion, doctrine is central; in ancient religion, ritual is central. On the whole, Smith argues, ancients tended to be conservative with regard to rituals, making sure to pass them down faithfully. In contrast, the myths that justified those rituals could change. In fact, according to Smith, many of the myths that have come down to us arose "after the original, nonmythic reason for the ritual had somehow been forgotten."

As an example, Smith gives the worship of Adonis. Worshipers mourned Adonis's mythical death in a ritual that coincided with the annual withering of the vegetation. According to Smith, the ritual mourning originally had a nonmythical explanation: with the annual withering of plants, "the worshippers lament out of natural sympathy just as modern man is touched with melancholy at the falling of autumn leaves. "Once worshipers forgot the original, nonmythical reason for the mourning ritual, they created "the myth of Adonis as the dying and rising god of vegetation to account for the ritual."

Stanley Edgar Hyman

In his essay "The Ritual View of Myth and the Mythic," Stanley Edgar Hyman makes an argument similar to Smith's:

"In Fiji, the physical peculiarities of an island with only one small patch of fertile soil are explained by a myth telling how Mberewalaki, a culture hero, flew into a passion at the misbehavior of the people of the island and hurled all the soil he was bringing them in a heap, instead of laying it out properly. Hocart points out that the myth is used aetiologically to explain the nature of the island, but did not originate in that attempt. The adventures of Mberewalaki originated, like all mythology, in ritual performance, and most of the lore of Hocart's Fijian informants consisted of such ritual myths. When they get interested in the topology of the island or are asked about it, Hocart argues, they do precisely what we would do, which is ransack their lore for an answer."

Here Hyman argues against the etiological interpretation of myth, which says that myths originated from attempts to explain the origins (etiologies) of natural phenomena. If true, the etiological interpretation would make myth older than, or at least independent of, ritual—as E.B. Tylor believes it is. But Hyman argues that people use myth for etiological purposes only after myth is already in place: in short, myths didn't originate as explanations of natural phenomena. Further, Hyman argues, myth originated from ritual performance. Thus, ritual came before myth, and myth depends on ritual for its existence until it gains an independent status as an etiological story.

James Frazer

The famous anthropologist Sir James George Frazer claimed that myth emerges from ritual during the natural process of religious evolution. Many of his ideas were inspired by those of Robertson Smith. In The Golden Bough, Frazer famously argues that man progresses from belief in magic (and rituals based on magic), through belief in religion, to science. His argument is as follows:

Man starts out with a reflexive belief in a natural law. He thinks he can influence nature by correctly applying this law: "In magic man depends on his own strength to meet the difficulties and dangers that beset him on every side. He believes in a certain established order of nature on which he can surely count, and which he can manipulate for his own ends."

However, the natural law man imagines—namely, magic—does not work. When he sees that his pretended natural law is false, man gives up the idea of a knowable natural law and "throws himself humbly on the mercy of certain great invisible beings behind the veil of nature, to whom he now ascribes all those far-reaching powers which he once arrogated to himself." In other words, when man loses his belief in magic, he justifies his formerly magical rituals by saying that they re-enact myths or honor mythical beings. According to Frazer:

"Myth changes while custom remains constant; men continue to do what their fathers did before them, though the reasons on which their fathers acted have been long forgotten. The history of religion is a long attempt to reconcile old custom with new reason, to find a sound theory for an absurd practice."

Jane Ellen Harrison and S. H. Hooke

The classicist Jane Ellen Harrison and the biblical scholar S. H. Hooke regarded myth as intimately connected to ritual. However, "against Smith," they "vigorously deny" that myth's main purpose is to justify a ritual by giving an account of how it first arose (e.g., justifying the Adonis worshipers' ritual mourning by attributing it to Adonis's mythical death). Instead, these scholars think a myth is largely just a narrative description of a corresponding ritual: according to Harrison, "the primary meaning of myth is the spoken correlative of the acted rite, the thing done."

Harrison and Hooke gave an explanation for why ancients would feel the need to describe the ritual in a narrative form. They suggest that the spoken word, like the acted ritual, was considered to have magical potency: "The spoken word had the efficacy of an act."

Like Frazer, Harrison believed that myths could arise as the initial reason a ritual was forgotten or became diluted. As an example, she cited rituals that center on the annual renewal of vegetation. Such rituals often involve a participant who undergoes a staged death and resurrection. Harrison argues that the ritual, although "performed annually, was exclusively initiatory"; it was performed on people to initiate them into their roles as full-standing members of society. At this early point, the "god" was simply "the projection of the euphoria produced by the ritual." Later, however, this euphoria became personified as a distinct god, and this god later became the god of vegetation, for "just as the initiates symbolically died and were reborn as fully fledged members of society, so the god of vegetation and in turn crops literally died and were reborn." In time, people forgot the ritual's initiatory function and only remembered its status as a commemoration of the Adonis myth.

Myth and Ritual as Non-coextensive

Not all students of mythology think ritual emerged from myth or myth emerged from ritual: some allow myths and rituals a greater degree of freedom from one another. Although myths and rituals often appear together, these scholars do not think every myth has or had a corresponding ritual, or vice versa.

Walter Burkert

The classicist Walter Burkert believes myths and rituals were originally independent. When myths and rituals do come together, he argues, they do so to reinforce each other. A myth that tells how the gods established a ritual reinforces that ritual by giving it divine status: "Do this because the gods did or do it." A ritual based on a mythical event makes the story of that event more than a mere myth: the myth becomes more important because it narrates an event whose imitation is considered sacred.

Furthermore, Burkert argues that myth and ritual together serve a "socializing function." As an example, Burkert gives the example of hunting rituals. Hunting, Burkert argues, took on a sacred, ritualistic aura once it ceased to be necessary for survival: "Hunting lost its basic function with the emergence of agriculture some ten thousand years ago. But hunting ritual had become so important that it could not be given up." By performing the ritual of hunting together, an ancient society bonded itself together as a group, and also provided a way for its members to vent their anxieties over their own aggressiveness and mortality.

Bronisław Malinowski

Like William Smith, the anthropologist Bronisław Malinowski argued in his essay Myth in Primitive Psychology that myths function as fictitious accounts of the origin of rituals, thereby providing a justification for those rituals: myth "gives rituals a hoary past and thereby sanctions them." However, Malinowski also points out that many cultural practices besides ritual have related myths: for Malinowski, "myth and ritual are therefore not coextensive." In other words, not all myths are outgrowths of ritual, and not all rituals are outgrowths of myth.

Mircea Eliade

Like Malinowski, the religious scholar Mircea Eliade thinks one important function of myth is to provide an explanation for ritual. Eliade notes that, in many societies, rituals are considered important precisely because they were established by the mythical gods or heroes. Eliade approvingly quotes Malinowski's claim that a myth is "a narrative resurrection of a primeval reality." Eliade adds: "Because myth relates the gesta (deeds) of Supernatural Beings, it becomes the exemplary model for all significant human actions." Traditional man sees mythical figures as models to be imitated. Therefore, societies claim that many of their rituals were established by mythical figures, thereby making the rituals seem all the more important. However, also like Malinowski, Eliade notes that societies use myths to sanction many kinds of activities, not just rituals: "For him, too, then, myth and ritual are not coextensive."

Eliade goes beyond Malinowski by giving an explanation for why myth can confer such an importance upon ritual: according to Eliade, "when (ritually) reenacted myth acts as a time machine, carrying one back to the time of the myth and thereby bringing one closer to god." But, again, for Eliade myth and ritual are not coextensive: the same return to the mythical age can be achieved simply by retelling a myth, without any ritual reenactment. According to Eliade, traditional man sees both myths and rituals as vehicles for "eternal return" to the mythical age:

"In imitating the exemplary acts of a god or of a mythic hero, or simply by recounting their adventures, the man of an archaic society detaches himself from profane time and magically re-enters the Great Time, the sacred time."

Recital of myths and enactment of rituals serve a common purpose: they are two different means to remain in sacred time.

Geomythology

Geomythology is the study of alleged references to geological events in mythology. Dorothy Vitaliano, a geologist coined the term in 1968.

"Geomythology indicates every case in which the origin of myths and legends can be shown to contain references to geological phenomena and aspects, in a broad sense including astronomical ones (comets, eclipses, meteor impacts, etc.). As indicated by Vitaliano 'primarily, there are two kinds of geologic folklore, that in which some geologic feature or the occurrence of some geologic phenomenon has inspired a folklore explanation, and that which is the garbled explanation of some actual geologic event, usually a natural catastrophe'."

The claim is that oral traditions about nature are often expressed in mythological language and may contain genuine and perceptive natural knowledge based on careful observation of physical evidence. Geomythology alleges to provide valuable information about past earthquakes, tsunamis, floods, impact events, fossil discoveries, and other events, which are otherwise scientifically unknown or difficult to trace.

To be distinguished from this are plainly aitiological tales that account for geological features without any connection to their formation; for example: the Native American legend of a giant bear chasing a couple who were saved when the land rose beneath their feet; the bear's claws left gouge marks on the sides of the uplift known today as Devils Tower, Wyoming.

In August 2004 the 32nd International Geological Congress held a session on "Myth and Geology", which resulted in the first peer-reviewed collection of papers on the subject.

Similarities between Different Religious Mythologies

Many eighteenth and nineteenth century scholars believed that all world mythologies showed signs of having evolved from a single mythical theme.

There are over a hundred different world mythologies that we know of today. Among these are the Greek, Roman, Norse, Etruscan, Celtic, Slavic, Egyptian, Mesopotamian, Babylonian, Arabian, Islamic, Hindu, Buddhist, Chinese, and many more myths.

Anyone with the knowledge of more than one of these world mythologies would realize that there are some glaring similarities between them.

Have a look at the five major themes forming the common ground for world mythologies:

- Creation: from Chaos or Nothingness: It is natural that the most common question early humans tried to answer was of how we came into being. How was the world created? According to Hindu mythology, in the beginning, only Vishnu was there. When Vishnu thought about creation, Brahma was created from a lotus that came from his navel. It was Brahma who finally created the world.

  Similar creation myths involving the world being created out of chaos or a vast, empty, nothingness can be found in the myths of ancient Babylon (the Enûma

Eliš myth), ancient Greece (the golden egg laid by Nyx or Night), the Book of Genesis (Elohim creating the heavens and earth in six days), and in Norse mythology (the yawning void named Ginnungagap), among numerous others.

The Hindu god Brahma creating the world.

- Sacrifice for Creation: Many cultures have stories about divine figures whose death creates an essential part of reality. In Indian Vedic mythology, the Purusha Sukta narrates that all things were made out of the mangled limbs of Purusha, a magnified non-natural man, who was sacrificed by the gods.

  Similarly, the Chinese myth of Pangu and the Norse myth of Ymir both tell of a cosmic giant who was killed to create the world. A myth from the Wemale people of Seram Island, Indonesia, tells of a miraculously-conceived girl named Hainuwele, whose murdered corpse sprouts into the people's staple food crops.

Norse gods Odin, Vili and Vé slew the primaeval giant Ymir
and created the world from his flesh and bones.

- The Great Flood: A flood myth is a narrative in which a great flood, usually sent by a deity or deities, destroys civilization, often in an act of divine retribution. In the Genesis mythology of the Hebrew Bible, Yahweh (God) decides to flood the earth because of the depth of the sinful state of mankind. That's where we get Noah's ark.

The Hindu myth of Manu (found in the Satapatha Brahmana and the Puranas) is similar to that of Noah's story, albeit less popularly known today.

A similar theme is seen in the Babylonian Epic of Gilgamesh, Mesopotamian flood stories, Deucalion's story in Greek mythology, and Bergelmir in Norse Mythology.

Genesis mythology: Male-female pairs from all species queueing up to board Noah's Ark.

- Centre of the World: Many world mythologies mention a place that sits at the center of the world and acts as a point of contact between different levels of the universe. Vedic India, ancient China, and the ancient Germans all had myths featuring a "Cosmic Tree" whose branches reach heaven and whose roots reach hell.

Mount Meru is a sacred mountain with five peaks in Hindu, Jain and Buddhist cosmology and is considered to be the center of all the physical, metaphysical and spiritual universes. Yggdrasil is the tree connecting the nine worlds in Norse cosmology. In Greek mythology, Omphalos stones are considered to be the "navel" of the world.

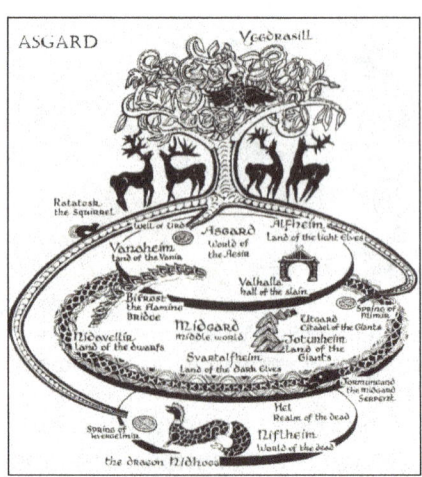

Yggdrasil connecting the nine worlds, according to Norse Mythology.

- Younger Gods Defeating Older Gods: Many cultures have a creation myth in which a group of younger, more civilized gods conquers and struggles against a group of older gods who represent the forces of chaos.

The Greek Titanomachy: Zeus, king of the Olympian gods, fighting Cronus, king of the Titans.

In Hindu mythology, the younger devas (gods) battle the older asuras (demons). In the Greek myth of the Titanomachy, the Olympian go Structuralist theory of mythology Geomythologyds defeat the Titans, an older and more primitive divine race, and establish cosmic order. Similarly, the Celtic gods of life and light struggle against the Fomorians, ancient gods of death and darkness.

These are but a few of the various similarities that exist in the myths of different cultures.

References

- Get-literate-in-myth-religion-and-theology-38283: theconversation.com, Retrieved 13 July, 2020

- Functions-of-theology, theology: britannica.com, Retrieved 27 March, 2020

- Meletinsky, Eleazar Moiseevich The Poetics of Myth (Translated by Guy Lanoue and Alexandre Sadetsky, foreword by Guy Lanoue) 2000 Routledge ISBN 0-415-92898-2

- Compare: Piccardi, Luigi (2007). "Preface". In Piccardi, Luigi; Masse, W. Bruce (eds.). Myth and Geology. Special publication - Geological Society of London. 273. London: Geological Society of London. p. vii. ISBN 9781862392168. Retrieved 2017-10-10

- Massive-similarities-between-different-world-mythologies: edtimes.in, Retrieved 16 April, 2020

3
European Mythology

European mythology is the collection of stories and myths associated with Christian mythologies, proto-Indo-European mythologies, Lithuanian mythologies, English mythologies, etc. This chapter sheds light on the subject of European mythology for an in-depth understanding of it.

Norse Mythology

Norse or Scandinavian mythology comprises the pre-Christian legends and religious beliefs of the Scandinavian people and Northern Germanic tribes, which tend to reflect a focus on physical prowess and military might. These myths were originally orally transmitted in the form of odes, sagas, and poetic epics. Knowledge of them is primarily based on two works called the Eddas and other medieval texts written down during and after the Christianization of the Norse peoples. The vast majority of written sources were assembled from accounts recorded in Iceland in the eleventh century C.E.

The Norse gods were mortal, and only through Iðunn's apples could they hope to live until Ragnarök.

In Scandinavian folklore, Norse mythology has long held cultural currency, and some traditions have been maintained until the present day. This rich mythological tradition also remains as an inspiration in modern literature, as well as for other forms of artwork (including visual representations, films, comic books and stage productions).

Given that Norse myths and texts were repressed and persecuted under Christian rule, relatively few have survived into the modern day. However, some of these tales were recorded by Christian scholars, particularly in the Prose Edda and the Heimskringla by Snorri Sturluson, who believed that pre-Christian deities were men and women rather than devils (and would thus reveal elements of their respective culture's histories). Sturluson, who was a leading poet, chieftain, and diplomat in Iceland, condensed the extensive sagas into prose retellings that made the various tales of Norse mythology systematic and coherent. An additional source for the modern understanding of Norse mythology is the Poetic Edda (also known as the Elder Edda), which contains versions of many tales, some of which are also found in the Prose Edda. More specifically, it consists of 29 long poems, of which 11 deal with the Germanic deities, the rest with legendary heroes like Sigurd the Volsung (the Siegfried of the German version, Nibelungenlied).

Although scholars think it was transcribed later than the other Edda, the language and poetic forms involved in the tales appear to have been composed centuries earlier than their transcription. Over and above the Eddas, there is also the Danish Gesta Danorum by Saxo Grammaticus, which is unfortunately of lesser utility due to the author's more extensive editorial alterations.

Besides these sources, there are surviving legends in Scandinavian poetry and folklore. In the first case, mythological reference and allusion abounds in traditional Nordic (skaldic) poetry, some of which survives in runic inscriptions and in books (many of which were redacted after the golden age of this poetic form had passed). Some of these poetic and folkloric references can be corroborated with legends appearing in other Germanic literatures, for example the tale related in the Anglo-Saxon Battle of Finnsburgh and the many allusions to mythological tales in the Old English poem Deor. When several partial references and tellings survive, scholars can often reconstruct the underlying tale.

Finally, the archaeological record can also be seen to provide useful clues concerning the nature of these beliefs. For instance, scholars have discovered and translated some runic inscriptions, such as the Rök Runestone and the Kvinneby amulet, that make reference to Nordic mythology. Likewise, there are also numerous runestones and image stones that depict scenes from Norse mythology, such as Thor's fishing trip, scenes from the Völsunga saga, Odin and Sleipnir, Loki with curled dandy-like mustaches and lips that are sewn together, Odin being devoured by Fenrir, and Hyrrokkin riding to Balder's funeral (the last of these is depicted on one of the surviving stones from the Hunnestad Monument).

Cosmology

Scandinavians believed that the cosmos was divided into nine interrelated realms, some of which attracted considerably greater mythological attention. Of primary importance was the threefold separation of the universe into the realms of the gods (Asgard and Vanaheim, homes of the Aesir and Vanir, respectively), the realm of mortals (Midgard) and the frigid underworld (Niflheim), which housed Hel (queen of the underworld). These three realms were supported by an enormous tree (Yggdrasil), with the realm of the gods ensconced among the upper branches, the realm of mortals approximately halfway up the tree (and surrounded by an impassable sea), and the underworld nestled among its roots.

Asgard could be reached by traversing Bifrost, a magical rainbow bridge guarded by Heimdall, the mute god of vigilance who could see and hear a thousand miles. Valhalla, Odin's hall (which is located within Asgard), can be seen as the Norse Heaven, as it is the final resting place for the souls of the greatest human warriors. To earn one's place among them, it was required that one's bravery be observed by the Valkyries, Odin's mounted female messengers whose sparkling armor supposedly created the famed Aurora Borealis (northern lights).

Other less important realms include Muspell, world of burning heat and home of Surt, a giant whose skin was lava and who had hair of fire; Alfheim, world of the elves; Svartálfheim, home of the dark elves; Nidavellir, world of the dwarves, tiny men who were incomparable miners and goldsmiths; and Jotunheim, world of the Jotun or giants.

The cosmology of Norse mythology also involves certain elements of duality. For example, the night and the day have their own mythological counterparts - Dagr/Skinfaxi and Nótt/Hrímfaxi, the sun (Sol) and the chasing wolf (Skoll), the moon (Mani) and its chasing wolf (Hati), and the total opposites of Niflheim and Muspell in the origin of the world and its cosmic composition.

Supernatural Beings

Norse cosmology postulates three separate "clans" of deities: the Aesir, the Vanir, and the Jotun. The distinction between Aesir and Vanir is relative, for the two are said to have made peace, exchanged hostages, intermarried and reigned together after a prolonged war. In fact, the most major divergence between the two groups is in their respective areas of influence, with the Aesir representing war and conquest, and the Vanir representing exploration, fertility and wealth. Some of the most important of these deities include Odin, the father god who rules the pantheon; Frigg, Odin's wife and queen of the gods; Thor, a storm god and warrior/hero; Freya, the goddess of beauty and sexual attraction; Heimdall, the far-seeing sentry of Asgard; Tyr, the god of combat; Balder, the god of spring and renewal; and, Loki, the devious trickster deity.

The relative peace between the Aesir and the Vanir presents a profound contrast to their permanently stormy relations with the Jotun (Old English: Eotenas or Entas). This group, whose name is often translated as "giants" (although "trolls" and "demons" have been suggested as suitable alternatives), are generally depicted as foul, monstrous beings, comparable to the Titans and Gigantes of Greek mythology. Despite these negative associations, the gods were still seen to be relatively closely related to the Jotun, as both Æsir and Vanir continued to intermarry with the Giants (not to mention the fact that many of the gods were descendants of them). For example, Loki was the child of two giants, and Hel was half-giantess. Some of the giants are mentioned by name in the Eddas and they seem to be representations of natural forces.

In addition, there are many other supernatural beings, including elves, dwarves, and monsters (including Fenrir, the gigantic wolf, and Jörmungandr, the sea-serpent (or "worm") that is coiled around Midgard). These two creatures are described as the progeny of Loki, the trickster-god, and a giantess.

Along with many other polytheistic religions, this mythology lacks the predominant good-evil dualism of the monotheistic Middle Eastern traditions. Thus, Odin and Hel are not seen as pure opposites; Loki is not primarily an adversary of the gods, though he is seen to delight in causing Thor's plans to go awry. Likewise, the giants are not so much fundamentally evil, as they are rude, boisterous, and uncivilized. Thus, the dualism that exists is not an opposition of good versus evil, but order versus chaos.

Völuspá: The Origin and End of the World

The origin and eventual fate of the world are described in Völuspá ("The völva's prophecy" or "The sybil's prophecy"), one of the most striking poems in the Poetic Edda. These haunting verses contain one of the most vivid creation accounts in all of religious history and a representation of the eventual destruction of the world that is unique in its combination of the themes of apocalypse and rebirth.

In the Völuspá, Odin, the chief god of the Norse pantheon, has conjured up the spirit of a dead Völva (shaman or sybil) and commanded this spirit to reveal the past and the future. She is reluctant, and asks: "What do you ask of me? Why tempt me?" but since she is already dead, she shows no fear of Odin. In fact, as she begins to detail the collapse of the universe, she continually taunts him: "Well, would you know more?" Despite his evident despair, Odin insists, reasoning that if he is to fulfill his function as king of the gods, he must possess all knowledge. The poem ends when the sybil finishes revealing the secrets of creation and dissolution, at which point she returns to the underworld, leaving Odin to contemplate the traumatic future that he and the other Aesir will eventually face.

The Beginning

According to the Scandinavians, the universe in its primordial state was a realm of fire (Muspell) and ice (Niflheim). When the warm air of Muspell hit the cold ice of Niflheim, the outline of a giant (Ymir) and the icy cow (Audhumla) were created. Slowly, the giant cow began to lick the frost off of the sleeping giant's skin, eventually freeing him from his icy prison. As Ymir slept, the continuing heat from Muspell made him sweat. He sweat out Surt, a flaming giant who went to Muspell, whose fire made him feel welcome. Later, Ymir woke and drank Audhumla's milk. But each drop of milk he spilled became a god: Odin, Vili and Ve, who proceeded to create seven more worlds and their inhabitants.

The Norns spin the threads of fate at the foot of Yggdrasil, the tree of the world.

The sybil then describes Yggdrasil (the world tree that supports the realms of gods, giants and humans) and the three norns (female symbols of inexorable fate, whose names indicate the past, present, and future), who spin the threads of fate amid the tree's enormous roots. Next, she describes the additional past events, including the primeval war between Aesir and Vanir, and the murder of Baldr, Odin's handsome son. Completing this chronicle, she then turns her attention to the future.

End Times (Eschatological Beliefs)

The Old Norse vision of the future is bleak. Norse mythology's vision of the end times is uniquely stark and pessimistic: not only are the Norse gods capable of being defeated by residents of Yggdrasil's other branches, but they are in fact destined to be defeated, and have always lived with this knowledge. In the end, it was believed the forces of chaos will outnumber and overcome the divine and human guardians of order. Loki and his monstrous children will burst their bonds; the dead will sail from Niflheim to attack the living. Heimdall, the watchman of the gods, will summon the heavenly host with a blast on his horn, which will precipitate the final doomed battle between order and chaos (Ragnarök). The gods, aware of the futility of their plight, will nevertheless gather the finest warriors (the Einherjar) from Valhalla to fight on their side when the day comes, but in the end they will be powerless to prevent the world from descending into the chaos out of which it had once emerged; the gods and their world will be destroyed. Odin will be swallowed by Fenrir. Thor will kill Jörmungandr, but will drown in its venom. Loki, the quintessentially liminal figure (embodying both the chaos of the giants and the order of the gods) will be the last to die, after having taken a wound from Heimdall. Following these titanic struggles, the earth itself succumbs:

> "The sun shall be darkened, earth sinks in the sea,
>
> Glide from the heaven the glittering stars.
>
> Smoke-reek rages and reddening fire,
>
> The high heat licks against heaven itself."

However, some traditions (including Snorri's Edda) manage to reach an optimistic conclusion. Though the Aesir will fall, their demise will also cause chaos to be defeated and will usher in a new world from the ashes of the old one, as "in that time the earth shall emerge out of the sea, and shall then be green and fair; then shall the fruits of it be brought forth unsown." Further, many of these accounts state that the death of the Aesir frees the world and allows for the rebirth of Balder, the god of spring who returns from the dead to usher in an era of peace and plenitude.

Kings and Heroes

The Ramsund carving depicting passages from the Völsunga saga.

In addition to its concentration on supernatural creatures and divine realms, Norse mythological literature also relates many legends concerning human heroes and kings. These tales, often told about the founders of clans and kingdoms, possessed great importance as illustrations of national origins and as models of proper action. Thus, Norse literature may have fulfilled the same function as the national epic in other European literatures or it may have been more closely related to tribal identity. Many of the legendary figures probably existed, leading generations of Scandinavian scholars to attempt to extract history from myth in the sagas.

Sometimes, the same hero resurfaces in several forms depending on which part of the Germanic world the epics survived (such as Weyland/Völund and Siegfried/Sigurd, and probably Beowulf/Bödvar Bjarki). Other notable heroes are Hagbard, Starkad, Ragnar Lodbrok, Sigurd Ring, Ivar Vidfamne and Harald Hildetand. Renowned also are the shield-maidens, who were "ordinary" women who had chosen the path of the warrior.

Norse Worship

Centers of Faith

The Germanic tribes rarely constructed large temples because the form of worship practiced by the ancient Germanic and Scandinavian people, called the Blót, were often celebrated outdoors, in sacred groves. This worship could also take place at home and at simple altars of piled stones known as horgr.

Gamla Uppsala, the center of worship in Sweden until the temple was destroyed the late eleventh century.

However, the Scandinavian world did have a few important ritual centers, such as Skiringsal, Lejre and Uppsala, where more formalized worship was carried out. For example, Adam of Bremen, an important chronicler of the Christianization of Scandinavia, claims that there was a relatively impressive temple in Uppsala with three wooden statues of Thor, Odin and Freyr.

Priests

While religious professionals seem to have existed in Norse culture, they never took on the professional and semi-hereditary character of the Celtic druidical class. This was because the shamanistic aspect of the tradition was maintained by women, the Völvas, meaning that the male ritual specialists played a more restricted role than their druidic counterparts.

It is often said that the Germanic tradition of kingship evolved out of a priestly office, as the priestly role of the king was congruent with the general role of godi, who was the head of a kindred group of families and who administered the sacrifices.

Human Sacrifice

A unique eye-witness account of Germanic human sacrifice survives in Ibn Fadlan's account of a Rus ship burial, where a slave-girl had volunteered to accompany her lord to the next world. More indirect accounts are given by Tacitus, Saxo Grammaticus and Adam of Bremen.

However, the Ibn Fadlan account is actually a burial ritual. Current understanding of Norse mythology suggests an ulterior motive to the slave-girl's "sacrifice." It is believed that in Norse mythology a woman who joined the corpse of a man on the funeral pyre would be that man's wife in the next world. For a slave girl to become the wife of a lord was an obvious increase in status.

Carl Larsson, Midwinter Sacrifice: the sacrifice of King Domalde at Gamla Uppsala.

The Heimskringla tells of Swedish King Aun who sacrificed nine of his sons in an effort to prolong his life until his subjects stopped him from killing his last son (Egil). According to Adam of Bremen, the Swedish kings sacrificed male slaves every ninth year during the Yule sacrifices at the Temple at Uppsala. The Swedes had the right not only to elect kings but also to depose them, and both King Domalde and King Olof Trätälja are said to have been sacrificed after years of famine.

Finally, as Odin was associated with death by hanging, a possible practice of Odinic sacrifice by strangling has some archeological support in the existence of bodies perfectly preserved by the acid of the Jutland (later taken over by Danish people) peat bogs, into which they were cast after having been strangled. An example is Tollund Man. However, as we possess no written accounts that explicitly interpret the cause of these stranglings, they could have other explanations.

Interactions with Christianity

An important problem in interpreting Norse mythology is that often the closest accounts that we have to "pre-contact" times were written by Christians. The Younger Edda and the Heimskringla were written by Snorri Sturluson in the thirteenth century, over two hundred years after Iceland became Christianized. Thus, Snorri's works likely carry a large amount of Christian bias in their interpretation of Norse myths.

Virtually all of the saga literature came out of Iceland, a relatively small and remote island, and even in the climate of religious tolerance there, Snorri was guided by an essentially Christian viewpoint. The Heimskringla provides some interesting insights into this issue. Snorri introduces Odin as a mortal warlord in Asia who acquires magical powers, settles in Sweden, and becomes a demi-god following his death. Having undercut Odin's divinity, Snorri then provides the story of a pact of Swedish King Aun with Odin to prolong his life by sacrificing his sons. Later in the Heimskringla, Snorri records in detail how converts to Christianity such as Saint Olaf Haraldsson brutally converted Scandinavians to Christianity.

An 1830 portrayal of Ansgar, a Christian missionary invited to Sweden by its king Björn at Hauge in 829.

Trying to avert civil war, the Icelandic parliament voted in Christianity, but for some years tolerated heathenry in the privacy of one's home. Sweden, on the other hand, had a series of civil wars in the eleventh century, which ended with the burning of the Temple at Uppsala. In England, on the other hand, Christianization occurred earlier and sporadically, rarely by force. Conversion by coercion was sporadic throughout the areas where Norse gods had been worshipped. However, the conversion did not happen overnight. Christian clergy did their utmost to teach the populace that the Norse gods were demons, but their success was limited and the gods never became evil in the popular mind in most of Scandinavia.

One gruesome form of execution occurred during the Christianization of Norway. King Olaf Tryggvason had male völvas (practitioners of traditional forms of Viking shamanism, sorcery, prophecy) bound in stout ropes and left on a tidal skerry to drown.

Two centrally located and far from isolated settlements can illustrate how long the Christianization took. Archaeological studies of graves at the Swedish island of Lovön have shown that the Christianization took 150-200 years, which was a fairly extended period, given that this was a location in close proximity to both secular and religious authorities. Otherwise there are few accounts from the fourteenth to the eighteenth century, but the clergy, such as Olaus Magnus wrote about the difficulties of extinguishing the old beliefs. In the nineteenth and early twentieth century Swedish folklorists documented what commoners believed, and what surfaced were many surviving traditions of the gods of Norse mythology. By then, however, the traditions had been sufficiently decontextualized as to have lost the cohesiveness attested to in Snorri's accounts. Most gods had been forgotten and only the hunting Odin and the giant-slaying Thor figured in numerous legends. Freyja was mentioned a few times and Baldr only survived in legends about place names.

Modern Influences

The gods of Norse and Germanic mythology have left numerous traces in elements of everyday life in most Western countries (especially those who use a Germanic language). An example of this is found in some of the names of the days of the week, which were formerly modeled after the planets (e.g. Sun, Moon, Mars, Mercury, Jupiter, Venus, Saturn) but eventually some of the names (i.e. for Tuesday through to Friday) were replaced with the names of divine Germanic equivalents.

Other elements of Norse mythology survived into modern times such as the Norse belief in destiny has been very firm until modern times. Since the Christian hell resembled the abode of the dead in Norse mythology one of the names was borrowed from the old faith, Helvíti i.e. Hel's punishment. Some elements of the Yule traditions were also preserved, such as the Swedish tradition of slaughtering the pig at Christmas (Christmas ham), which originally was part of the sacrifice to Freyr.

Day	Origin
Monday	Moon's day
Tuesday	Tyr's (Tiw's) day
Wednesday	Odin's (Wodin's) day
Thursday	Thor's day
Friday	Frigg's or Freyja's day
Sunday	Sun's day

Germanic Neopaganism

The nineteenth and twentieth centuries have seen attempts to revive the old Germanic religion in both Europe and the United States under various names, including Ásatrú ("Aesir Faith"), Odinism, Wotanism, Forn Sed ("Old Custom") or Heathenry. In Iceland, Ásatrú was recognized by the state as an official religion in 1973, which legalized its various ceremonies (e.g. marriage and child-naming). It has also become an official and legal religion in all the Nordic countries.

Christian Mythology

Christian mythology is the body of myths associated with Christianity and the Bible. The term encompasses a broad variety of legends and stories, especially those considered sacred narratives. Mythological themes and elements occur throughout Christian literature, including recurring myths such as ascending to a mountain, the axis mundi, myths of combat, descent into the Underworld, accounts of a dying-and-rising god, flood stories, stories about the founding of a tribe or city, and myths about great heroes (or saints) of the past, paradises, and self-sacrifice.

Various authors have also used it to refer to other mythological and allegorical elements found in the Bible, such as the story of the Leviathan. The term has been applied to myths and legends from the Middle Ages, such as the story of Saint George and the Dragon, the stories of King Arthur and his Knights of the Round Table, and the legends of the Parsival. Multiple commentators have classified John Milton's epic poem Paradise Lost as a work of Christian mythology. The term has also been applied to modern stories revolving around Christian themes and motifs, such as the writings of C. S. Lewis, J. R. R. Tolkien, Madeleine L'Engle, and George MacDonald.

Over the centuries, Christianity has divided into many denominations. Not all of these denominations hold the same set of sacred traditional narratives. For example, the books of the Bible accepted by the Roman Catholic Church and the Eastern Orthodox churches include a number of texts and stories (such as those narrated in the Book of Judith and Book of Tobit) that many Protestant denominations do not accept as canonical.

Saint George and the Dragon by Gustave Moreau.

Attitudes

Christian theologian and professor of New Testament, Rudolf Bultmann wrote that:

The cosmology of the New Testament is essentially mythical in character. The world is viewed as a three storied structure, with the earth in the center, the heaven above, and the underworld beneath. Heaven is the abode of God and of celestial beings -- the angels. The underworld is hell, the place of torment. Even the earth is more than the scene of natural, everyday events, of the trivial round and common task. It is the scene of the supernatural activity of God and his angels on the one hand, and of Satan and his de-mons on the other. These supernatural forces intervene in the course of nature and in all that men think and will and do. Miracles are by no means rare. Man is not in control of his own life. Evil spirits may take possession of him. Satan may inspire him with evil thoughts. Alternatively, God may inspire his thought and guide his purposes. He may grant him heavenly visions. He may allow him to hear his word of succor or demand. He may give him the supernatural power of his Spirit. History does not follow a smooth unbroken course; it is set in motion and controlled by these supernatural powers. This æon is held in bondage by Satan, sin, and death (for "powers" is precisely what they are), and hastens towards its end. That end will come very soon, and will take the form of a cosmic catastrophe. It will be inaugurated by the "woes" of the last time. Then the Judge will come from heaven, the dead will rise, the last judgment will take place, and men will enter into eternal salvation or damnation.

Myths as Traditional or Sacred Stories

In its broadest academic sense, the word myth simply means a traditional story. How-ever, many scholars restrict the term "myth" to sacred stories. Folklorists often go fur-ther, defining myths as "tales believed as true, usually sacred, set in the distant past or other worlds or parts of the world, and with extra-human, inhuman, or heroic charac-ters".

In classical Greek, muthos, from which the English word myth derives, meant "story, narrative." By the time of Christ, muthos had started to take on the connotations of "fable, fiction," and early Christian writers often avoided calling a story from canonical scripture a "myth". Paul warned Timothy to have nothing to do with "godless and silly myths" (bebēthous kai graōdeis muthous). This negative meaning of "myth" passed into popular usage. Some modern Christian scholars and writers have attempted to re-habilitate the term "myth" outside academia, describing stories in canonical scripture (especially the Christ story) as "true myth"; examples include C. S. Lewis and Andrew Greeley. Several modern Christian writers, such as C.S. Lewis, have described elements of Christianity, particularly the story of Christ, as "myth" which is also "true" ("true myth"). Others object to associating Christianity with "myth" for a variety of reasons: the association of the term "myth" with polytheism, the use of the term "myth" to indi-cate falsehood or non-historicity, and the lack of an agreed-upon definition of "myth". As examples of Biblical myths, every cites the creation account in Genesis 1 and 2 and the story of Eve's temptation. Many Christians believe parts of the Bible to be symbolic or metaphorical (such as the Creation in Genesis).

Christian tradition contains many stories that do not come from canonical Christian texts yet still illustrate Christian themes. These non-canonical Christian myths in-clude legends, folktales, and elaborations on canonical Christian mythology. Chris-tian tradition has produced a rich body of legends that were never incorporated into the official scriptures. Legends were a staple of medieval literature. Examples include hagiographies such as the stories of Saint George or Saint Valentine. A case in point is the historical and canonized Brendan of Clonfort, a 6th-century Irish churchman and founder of abbeys. Round his authentic figure was woven a tissue that is arguably legendary rather than historical: the Navigatio or "Journey of Brendan". The legend discusses mythic events in the sense of supernatural encounters. In this narrative, Brendan and his shipmates encounter sea monsters, a paradisal island and a floating ice islands and a rock island inhabited by a holy hermit: literal-minded devotés still seek to identify "Brendan's islands" in actual geography. This voyage was recreated by Tim Severin, suggesting that whales, icebergs and Rockall were encountered.

Folktales form a major part of non-canonical Christian tradition. Folklorists define folktales (in contrast to "true" myths) as stories that are considered purely fictitious by their tellers and that often lack a specific setting in space or time. Christian-themed folktales have circulated widely among peasant populations. One widespread folktale genre is that of the Penitent Sinner (classified as Type 756A, B, C, in the Aarne-Thompson index of tale types); another popular group of folktales describe a clever mortal who outwits the Devil. Not all scholars accept the folkloristic convention of applying the terms "myth" and "folktale" to different categories of traditional narrative.

Christian tradition produced many popular stories elaborating on canonical scripture. According to an English folk belief, certain herbs gained their current healing power from having been used to heal Christ's wounds on Mount Calvary. In this case, a non-canonical story has a connection to a non-narrative form of folklore — namely, folk medicine. Arthurian legend contains many elaborations upon canonical mythology. For example, Sir Balin discovers the Lance of Longinus, which had pierced the side of Christ. According to a tradition widely attested in early Christian writings, Adam's skull lay buried at Calvary; when Christ was crucified, his blood fell over Adam's skull, symbolizing humanity's redemption from Adam's sin.

Saint Brendan's voyage, from a German manuscript.

Christt

- The Gospel accounts of Jesus Christ, his life and death. Here the narrative is combined by the author with a story of how all Christian theology "came to be". For example, the story of Jesus as the "word" or "Logos" (John 1:1), the Incarnation of the Logos or Son of God as the man Jesus (e.g., Luke 1:35), and Christ's atonement for humanity's sins (e.g., Matthew 26:28). Important narratives within the Gospel accounts include:

  - Christ's miraculous conception and birth from the Virgin Mary.

  - The baptism of Jesus.

  - Satan's temptation of Christ.

  - The Transfiguration of Jesus.

  - Parables of Jesus.

  - The Last Supper.

  - The death and resurrection of Jesus.

  - The Ascension.

- The Acts of the Apostles - the story of the Early Christian church, the ministry of the Twelve Apostles and of Paul the Apostle.

  - The descent of the Holy Spirit on Jesus' disciples after the Ascension.

Eschatology

- The coming of the Antichrist.

- The Second Coming.

- The resurrection of the dead.

- Judgement Day.

- The final and total establishment of the Kingdom of God on earth.

Examples of Christian myths not mentioned in canon and literary and traditional elaborations on canonical Christian mythology:

- Versions of Christian mythology used by Gnostic Christianity:

  - The Valentinian creation myth involving Sophia and the demiurge.

  - The Manichaean creation myth.

- The Gnostic accounts of Jesus, some of which present a Docetic view of Jesus.

- Literary treatments of Christian canon or theology:

  - John Milton's Paradise Lost, which describes Satan's revolution against God and the Fall of Man, and his Paradise Regained, which describes Satan's temptation of Christ.

  - Dante Alighieri's Divine Comedy, a literary allegory that describes a visit to Hell, Purgatory, and Heaven.

  - John Bunyan's Pilgrim's Progress, a Christian spiritual allegory.

  - C.S. Lewis's The Pilgrim's Regress, a more modern Christian spiritual allegory.

  - According to some interpretations, C.S. Lewis's The Lion, the Witch, and the Wardrobe allegorically represents Christ's death and resurrection (although Lewis denies that the story is a direct allegory;).

- Legends about Christian saints and heroes. Examples include Abgarus of Edessa, John the Dwarf, and Saint George. Legends about saints are commonly called hagiographies. Some such stories are heavily miraculous, such as those found in Jacobus de Voragine's Golden Legend; others, less so.

Dante and Beatrice gaze upon the highest Heaven (The Empyrean).

- Stories about artifacts such as the Holy Grail, Holy Lance and Shroud of Turin.

- Names and biographical details supplied for unnamed Biblical characters.

- The legends of King Arthur and Charlemagne as Christian kings, notably the Quest for the Holy Grail.

- Legendary history of the Christian churches, such as the tales from the Crusades or the paladins in medieval romance.

- Legends of the Knights Templar and the Priory of Sion.

- Medieval Christian stories about angels and guardian angels.

- Non-canonical elaborations or amendments to Biblical tales, such as the tales of Salomé, the Three Wise Men, or St. Dismas.

Connections to other Belief Systems

Jewish Mythology

- Cosmogony:

  ○ The 7-day creation week narrative (Genesis 1-2:3).

  ○ The Eden narrative (Genesis 2:4-3:24).

- Origins:

  ○ The Fall of Man: Although the Book of Genesis does not mention original sin, many Christians interpret the Fall as the origin of original sin.

  ○ Noah's Ark.

  ○ The Tower of Babel: the origin and division of nations and languages.

- The life of Abraham.

- The Exodus of the Hebrews from Egypt.

- The Hebrews' conquest of the Promised Land.

- The period of the Hebrew prophets. One example is the apocryphal part of the Book of Daniel (14:1-30; excluded from the Hebrew and Protestant canon) that tells the story of Bel and the dragon.

Zoroastrianism

Some scholars believe that many elements of Christian mythology, particularly its linear portrayal of time, originated with the Persian religion of Zoroastrianism. Mary Boyce, an authority on Zoroastrianism, writes:

> "Zoroaster was thus the first to teach the doctrines of an individual judgment, Heaven and Hell, the future resurrection of the body, the general Last Judgment, and life everlasting for the reunited soul and body. These doctrines were to become familiar articles of faith to much of mankind, through borrowings by Judaism, Christianity and Islam."

Mircea Eliade believes the Hebrews had a sense of linear time before Zoroastrianism influenced them. However, he argues, "a number of other (Jewish) religious ideas were discovered, revalorized, of systematized in Iran". These ideas include a dualism between good and evil, belief in a future savior and resurrection, and "an optimistic eschatology, proclaiming the final triumph of Good".

The concept of Amesha Spentas and Daevas probably gave rise to the Christian understanding of angels and demons.

Other Connections

In Buddhist mythology, the demon Mara tries to distract the historical Buddha, Siddhartha Gautama, before he can reach enlightenment. Huston Smith, a professor of philosophy and a writer on comparative religion, notes the similarity between Mara's temptation of the Buddha before his ministry and Satan's temptation of Christ before his ministry.

In the Book of Revelation, the author sees a vision of a pregnant woman in the sky being pursued by a huge red dragon. The dragon tries to devour her child when she gives birth, but the child is "caught up to God and his throne". This appears to be an allegory for the triumph of Christianity: the child presumably represents Christ; the woman may represent God's people of the Old and New Testaments (who produced Christ); and the Dragon symbolizes Satan, who opposes Christ.

According to Catholic scholars, the images used in this allegory may have been inspired by pagan mythology:

"This corresponds to a widespread myth throughout the ancient world that a goddess pregnant with a savior was pursued by a horrible monster; by miraculous intervention, she bore a son who then killed the monster."

Mythical Themes and Types

Academic studies of mythology often define mythology as deeply valued stories that explain a society's existence and world order: those narratives of a society's creation, the society's origins and foundations, their god(s), their original heroes, mankind's connection to the "divine", and their narratives of eschatology (what happens in the "after-life"). This is a very general outline of some of the basic sacred stories with those themes.

Cosmogonic Myths

The Christian texts use the same creation myth as Jewish mythology as written in the Old Testament. According to the Book of Genesis, the world was created out of a darkness and water in seven days. (Unlike a Jew, a Christian might include the miracle of

Jesus' birth as a sort of second cosmogonic event) Canonical Christian scripture incorporates the two Hebrew cosmogonic myths found in Genesis 1-2:2 and Genesis 2:

Genesis 1–2:3

In the first text on the creation (Genesis 1-2:3), the Creator is called Elohim (translated "God"). He creates the universe over a six-day period, creating a new feature each day: first he creates day and night; then he creates the firmament to separate the "waters above" from the "waters below"; then he separates the dry land from the water; then he creates plants on the land; then he places the sun, moon, and stars in the sky; then he creates swimming and flying animals; then he creates land animals; and finally he creates man and woman together, "in his own image". On the seventh day, God rests, providing the rationale for the custom of resting on Sabbath.

Genesis 2:4–3:24

The second creation myth in Genesis differs from the first in a number of important elements. Here the Creator is called Yahweh elohim (commonly translated "Lord God", although Yahweh is in fact the personal name of the God of Israel and does not mean Lord).

This myth begins with the words, "When the LORD God made the earth and the heavens, and no shrub of the field was yet in the earth, and no plant of the field had yet sprouted, for the LORD God had not sent rain upon the earth" (Genesis 2:4-5 NASB). It then proceeds to describe Yahweh creating a man called Adam out of dust. Yahweh creates the Garden of Eden as a home for Adam, and tells Adam not to eat the fruit of the Tree of Knowledge of Good and Evil in the center of the Garden (next to the Tree of Life).

Yahweh also creates animals, and shows them to man, who names them. Yahweh sees that there is no suitable companion for the man among the beasts, and he subsequently puts Adam to sleep and takes out one of Adam's ribs, creating from it a woman whom Adam names Eve.

A serpent tempts Eve to eat from the Tree of Knowledge of Good and Evil, and she succumbs, offering the fruit to Adam as well. As a punishment, Yahweh banishes the couple from the Garden and "placed on the east side of the Garden of Eden the cherubim with a fiery revolving sword to guard the way to the Tree of Life". The Lord says he must banish humans from the Garden because they have become like him, knowing good and evil (because of eating the forbidden fruit), and now only immortality (which they could get by eating from the Tree of Life) stands between them and godhood:

"The man has now become like one of us, knowing good and evil. He must not be allowed to reach out his hand and take also from the tree of life and eat, and live forever" (Genesis 3:22).

Although the text of Genesis does not identify the tempting serpent with Satan, Christian tradition equates the two. This tradition has made its way into non-canonical Christian "myths" such as John Milton's Paradise Lost.

Ascending the Mountain

According to Lorena Laura Stookey, many myths feature sacred mountains as "the sites of revelations": "In myth, the ascent of the holy mountain is a spiritual journey, promising purification, insight, wisdom, or knowledge of the sacred". As examples of this theme, Stookey includes the revelation of the Ten Commandments on Mount Sinai, Christ's ascent of a mountain to deliver his Sermon on the Mount, and Christ's ascension into Heaven from the Mount of Olives.

Axis Mundi

Many mythologies involve a "world center", which is often the sacred place of creation; this center often takes the form of a tree, mountain, or other upright object, which serves as an axis mundi or axle of the world. A number of scholars have connected the Christian story of the crucifixion at Golgotha with this theme of a cosmic center. In his Creation Myths of the World, David Leeming argues that, in the Christian story of the crucifixion, the cross serves as "the axis mundi, the center of a new creation".

According to a tradition preserved in Eastern Christian folklore, Golgotha was the summit of the cosmic mountain at the center of the world and the location where Adam had been both created and buried. According to this tradition, when Christ is crucified, his blood falls on Adam's skull, buried at the foot of the cross, and redeems him. George Every discusses the connection between the cosmic center and Golgotha in his book Christian Mythology, noting that the image of Adam's skull beneath the cross appears in many medieval representations of the crucifixion.

In Creation Myths of the World, Leeming suggests that the Garden of Eden may also be considered a world center.

Combat Myth

Many Near Eastern religions include a story about a battle between a divine being and a dragon or other monster representing chaos—a theme found, for example, in the Enuma Elish. A number of scholars call this story the "combat myth". A number of scholars have argued that the ancient Israelites incorporated the combat myth into their religious imagery, such as the figures of Leviathan and Rahab, the Song of the Sea, Isaiah 51:9-10's description of God's deliverance of his people from Babylon, and the portrayals of enemies such as Pharaoh and Nebuchadnezzar. The idea of Satan as God's opponent may have developed under the influence of the combat myth. Scholars have also suggested that the Book of Revelation uses combat myth imagery in its descriptions of cosmic conflict.

Descent to the Underworld

According to David Leeming, writing in The Oxford Companion to World Mythology, the harrowing of hell is an example of the motif of the hero's descent to the underworld, which is common in many mythologies. According to Christian tradition, Christ descended to hell after his death in order to free the souls there; this event is known as the Harrowing of Hell. This story is narrated in the Gospel of Nicodemus and may be the meaning behind 1 Peter 3:18-22.

The Harrowing of Hell, depicted in the Petites Heures de Jean de Berry, 14th-century illuminated manuscript.

Dying God

Many myths, particularly from the Near East, feature a god who dies and is resurrected; this figure is sometimes called the "dying god". An important study of this figure is James George Frazer's The Golden Bough, which traces the dying god theme through a large number of myths. The dying god is often associated with fertility. A number of scholars, including Frazer, have suggested that the Christ story is an example of the "dying god" theme. In the topic "Dying god" in The Oxford Companion to World Mythology, David Leeming notes that Christ can be seen as bringing fertility, though of a spiritual as opposed to physical kind.

In his 2006 homily for Corpus Christi, Pope Benedict XVI noted the similarity between the Christian story of the resurrection and pagan myths of dead and resurrected gods: "In these myths, the soul of the human person, in a certain way, reached out toward that God made man, who, humiliated unto death on a cross, in this way opened the door of life to all of us."

Flood Myths

Many cultures have myths about a flood that cleanses the world in preparation for rebirth. Such stories appear on every inhabited continent on earth. An example is the biblical story of Noah. In The Oxford Companion to World Mythology, David Leeming notes that, in the Bible story, as in other flood myths, the flood marks a new beginning and a second chance for creation and humanity.

Founding Myths

According to Sandra Frankiel, the records of "Jesus' life and death, his acts and words" provide the "founding myths" of Christianity. Frankiel claims that these founding myths are "structurally equivalent" to the creation myths in other religions, because they are "the pivot around which the religion turns to and which it returns", establishing the "meaning" of the religion and the "essential Christian practices and attitudes". Tom Cain uses the expression "founding myths" more broadly, to encompass such stories as those of the War in Heaven and the fall of man; according to Cain, "the disastrous consequences of disobedience" is a pervasive theme in Christian founding myths.

Christian mythology of their society's founding would start with Jesus and his many teachings, and include the stories of Christian disciples starting the Christian Church and congregations in the 1st century. This might be considered the stories in the four canonical gospels and the Acts of the Apostles. The heroes of the first Christian society would start with Jesus and those chosen by Jesus, the twelve apostles including Peter, John, James, as well as Paul and Mary (mother of Jesus).

Hero Myths

In his influential 1909 work Der Mythus von der Geburt des Helden (The Myth of the Birth of the Hero), Otto Rank argued that the births of many mythical heroes follow a common pattern. Rank includes the story of Christ's birth as a representative example of this pattern.

According to Mircea Eliade, one pervasive mythical theme associates heroes with the slaying of dragons, a theme which Eliade traces back to "the very ancient cosmogonico-heroic myth" of a battle between a divine hero and a dragon. He cites the Christian legend of Saint George as an example of this theme. An example from the Late Middle Ages comes from Dieudonné de Gozon, third Grand Master of the Knights of Rhodes, famous for slaying the dragon of Malpasso. Eliade writes:

"Legend, as was natural, bestowed upon him the attributes of St. George, famed for his victorious fight with the monster. In other words, by the simple fact that he was regarded as a hero, de Gozon was identified with a category, an archetype, which equipped him with a mythical biography from which it was impossible to omit combat with a reptilian monster."

In the Oxford Companion to World Mythology David Leeming lists Moses, Jesus, and King Arthur as examples of the heroic monomyth, calling the Christ story "a particularly complete example of the heroic monomyth". Leeming regards resurrection as a common part of the heroic monomyth, in which the resurrected heroes often become sources of "material or spiritual food for their people"; in this connection, Leeming notes that Christians regard Jesus as the "bread of life".

In terms of values, Leeming contrasts "the myth of Jesus" with the myths of other "Christian heroes such as St. George, Roland, el Cid, and even King Arthur"; the later hero myths, Leeming argues, reflect the survival of pre-Christian heroic values—"values of military dominance and cultural differentiation and hegemony"—more than the values expressed in the Christ story.

Paradise

Many religious and mythological systems contain myths about a paradise. Many of these myths involve the loss of a paradise that existed at the beginning of the world. Some scholars have seen in the story of the Garden of Eden an instance of this general motif.

In illustrations of the Book of Genesis, Pomors often(quantify) depicted sirins as birds sitting in paradise trees.

Sacrifice

Sacrifice is an element in many religious traditions and often represented in myths. In The Oxford Companion to World Mythology, David Leeming lists the story of Abraham and Isaac and the story of Christ's death as examples of this theme. Wendy Doniger describes the gospel accounts as a "meta-myth" in which Jesus realizes that he is part of a "new myth of a man who is sacrificed in hate" but "sees the inner myth, the old myth of origins and acceptance, the myth of a god who sacrifices himself in love".

Eucharist

Related to the doctrine of transubstantiation, the Christian practice of eating the flesh and blood of Jesus Christ during the Eucharist is an instance of theophagy.

Transference of Evil

The theological concept of Jesus being born to atone for original sin is central to the Christian narrative. According to Christian theology, by Adam disobeying God in the Garden of Eden, humanity acquired an ingrained flaw that keeps humans in a state of moral imperfection, generally called "original sin". According to Paul the Apostle, Adam's sin brought sin and death to all humanity: "Through one man, sin entered the world, and through sin, death" (Romans 5:12).

According to the orthodox Christian view, Jesus saved humanity from final death and damnation by dying for them. Most Christians believe that Christ's sacrifice supernaturally reversed death's power over humanity, proved when he was resurrected, and abolished the power of sin on humanity. According to Paul, "if the many died by the trespass of the one man, how much more did God's grace and the gift that came by the grace of the one man, Jesus Christ, overflow to the many" (Romans 5:15). For many Christians, atonement doctrine leads naturally into the eschatological narratives of Christian people rising from the dead and living again, or immediately entering heaven to join Jesus.

Atonement in Canonical Scripture

Paul's theological writings lay out the basic framework of the atonement doctrine in the New Testament. However, Paul's letters contain relatively little mythology (narrative). The majority of narratives in the New Testament are in the Gospels and the Book of Revelation.

Although the Gospel stories do not lay out the atonement doctrine as fully as does Paul, they do have the story of the Last Supper, crucifixion, death and resurrection. Atonement is also suggested in the parables of Jesus in his final days. According to Matthew's gospel, at the Last Supper, Jesus calls his blood "the blood of the new covenant, which will be poured out for the forgiveness of many" (Matthew 26:28). John's gospel is especially rich in atonement parables and promises: Jesus speaks of himself as "the living bread that came down from heaven"; "and the bread that I shall give is My flesh, which I shall give for the life of the world" (John 6:51); "Truly, truly, I say to you, unless a grain of wheat falls to the ground and dies, it remains alone; but if it dies, it bears much fruit" (John 12:24).

Atonement in Non-canonical Literature

The sacrifice and atonement narrative appears explicitly in many non-canonical writings as well. For instance, in Book 3 of Milton's Paradise Lost, the Son of God offers to become a man and die, thereby paying mankind's debt to God the Father.

The Harrowing of Hell is a non-canonical myth extrapolated from the atonement doctrine. According to this story, Christ descended into the land of the dead after his crucifixion, rescuing the righteous souls that had been cut off from heaven due to the taint of original sin. The story of the harrowing was popular during the Middle Ages. An Old English poem called "The Harrowing of Hell" describes Christ breaking into Hell and rescuing the Old Testament patriarchs. (The Harrowing is not the only explanation that Christians have put forth for the fate of the righteous who died before Christ accomplished the atonement).

In modern literature, atonement continues to be theme. In the first of C. S. Lewis's Narnia novels, The Lion, the Witch and the Wardrobe, a boy named Edmund is condemned to death by a White Witch, and the magical lion-king Aslan offers to die in Edmund's place, thereby saving him. Aslan's life is sacrificed on an altar, but returns to life again. Aslan's self-sacrifice for Edmund is often interpreted as an allegory for the story of Christ's sacrifice for humanity; although Lewis denied that the novel is a mere allegory.

Witches

In the early modern period, distinguished Christian theologians developed elaborated witch mythologies which contributed to the intensification of witch hunts. Major works in Christian demonology, such as Malleus Maleficarum, were dedicated to the implementation of Exodus 22:18 of the Old Testament: "You shall not permit a sorceress to live." The concept of witches' sabbath was well articulated by the 17th century. Theologian Martin Delrio was one of the first to provide a vivid description in his influential Disquisitiones magicae:

A witch departing for Witches' Sabbath on a broomstick — a motif included in Errores Gazariorum ("Errors of the Gazarii") written in 1437, probably by a Savoyard inquisitor.

There, on most occasions, once a foul, disgusting fire has been lit, an evil spirit sits on a throne as president of the assembly. His appearance is terrifying, almost always that of a male goat or a dog. The witches come forward to worship him in different ways. Sometimes they supplicate him on bended knee; sometimes they stand with their back turned to him. They offer candles made of pitch or a child's umbilical cord, and kiss him on the anal orifice as a sign of homage. Sometimes they imitate the sacrifice of the Mass (the greatest of all their crimes), as well as purifying with water and similar Catholic ceremonies. After the feast, each evil spirit takes by the hand the disciple of whom he has charge, and so that they may do everything with the most absurd kind of ritual, each person bends over backwards, joins hands in a circle, and tosses his head as frenzied fanatics do. Then they begin to dance. They sing very obscene songs in his (Satan's) honour. They behave ridiculously in every way, and in every way contrary to accepted custom. Then their demon-lovers copulate with them in the most repulsive fashion.

Eschatological Myths

Christian eschatological myths include stories of the afterlife: the narratives of Jesus Christ rising from the dead and now acting as a saviour of all generations of Christians, and stories of heaven and hell. Eschatological myths would also include the prophesies of end of the world and a new millennium in the Book of Revelation, and the story that Jesus will return to earth someday.

The major features of Christian eschatological mythology include afterlife beliefs, the Second Coming, the resurrection of the dead, and the final judgment.

Immediate Afterlife (Heaven and Hell)

Most Christian denominations hold some belief in an immediate afterlife when people die. Christian scripture gives a few descriptions of an immediate afterlife and a heaven and hell; however, for the most part, both New and Old Testaments focus much more on the myth of a final bodily resurrection than any beliefs about a purely spiritual afterlife away from the body.

Much of the Old Testament does not express a belief in a personal afterlife of reward or punishment:

"All the dead go down to Sheol, and there they lie in sleep together—whether good or evil, rich or poor, slave or free (Job 3:11-19). It is described as a region "dark and deep," "the Pit," and "the land of forgetfulness," cut off from both God and human life above (Pss. 6:5; 88:3-12). Though in some texts Yahweh's power can reach down to Sheol (Ps. 139:8), the dominant idea is that the dead are abandoned forever. This idea of Sheol is negative in contrast to the world of life and light above, but there is no idea of judgment or of reward and punishment."

Later Old Testament writings, particularly the works of the Hebrew prophets, describe a final resurrection of the dead, often accompanied by spiritual rewards and punishments:

"Many who sleep in the dust of the earth shall awake. Some shall live forever; others shall be in everlasting contempt. But the wise shall shine brightly like the splendor of the firmament, and those who lead the many to justice shall be like the stars forever" (Daniel 12:2).

However, even here, the emphasis is not on an immediate afterlife in heaven or hell, but rather on a future bodily resurrection.

The New Testament also devotes little attention to an immediate afterlife. Its primary focus is the resurrection of the dead. Some New Testament passages seem to mention the (non-resurrected) dead experiencing some sort of afterlife (for example, the parable of Lazarus and Dives); yet the New Testament includes only a few myths about heaven and hell. Specifically, heaven is a place of peaceful residence, where Jesus goes to "prepare a home" or room for his disciples (John 14:2). Drawing on scriptural imagery (John 10:7, John 10:11-14), many Christian narratives of heaven include a nice green pasture land and a meeting with a benevolent God. Some of the earliest Christian art depicts heaven as a green pasture where people are sheep led by Jesus as "the good shepherd" as in interpretation of heaven.

As the doctrines of heaven and hell and (Catholic) purgatory developed, non-canonical Christian literature began to develop an elaborate mythology about these locations. Dante's three-part Divine Comedy is a prime example of such afterlife mythology, describing Hell (in Inferno), Purgatory (in Purgatorio), and Heaven (in Paradiso). Myths of hell differ quite widely according to the denomination.

Jesus as the Good Shepherd, painting on ceiling of S. Callisto catacomb, early Christian art, mid 3rd century A.D. Example of earliest Christian art showing a pastoral scene in the afterlife.

Second Coming

The Second Coming of Christ holds a central place in Christian mythology. The Second Coming is the return of Christ to earth during the period of transformation preceding the end of this world and the establishment of the Kingdom of Heaven on earth. According to Matthew's gospel, when Jesus is on trial before the Roman and Jewish authorities, he claims, "In the future you will see the Son of Man sitting at the right hand of the Mighty One and coming on the clouds of heaven." The legend of the Wandering Jew concerns a Jew who taunted Jesus on the way to the Crucifixion and was then cursed to walk the earth until the Second Coming.

The Wandering Jew by Gustave Doré.

Resurrection and Final Judgment

Christian mythology incorporates the Old Testament's prophecies of a future resurrection of the dead. Like the Hebrew prophet Daniel (e.g., Daniel 12:2), the Christian Book of Revelation (among other New Testament scriptures) describes the resurrection: "The sea gave up the dead that were in it, and death and Hades gave up the dead that were in them; and they were judged, every one of them according to their deeds." The righteous and faithful enjoy bliss in the earthly Kingdom of Heaven, but the evil and non-Christian are "cast into the lake of fire".

The Kingdom of Heaven on Earth

Christian eschatological myths feature a total world renovation after the final judgment. According to the Book of Revelation, God "will wipe every tear from their eyes, and there will be no more death or mourning, wailing or pain, for the old order has passed away". According to Old and New Testament passages, a time of perfect peace and happiness is coming:

"They will beat their swords into plowshares and their spears into pruning hooks. One nation will not raise the sword against another; nor will they train for war again."

Certain scriptural passages even suggest that God will abolish the current natural laws in favor of immortality and total peace:

- "Then the wolf will be a guest of the lamb, and the leopard will lie down with the kid. The calf and the young lion will browse together, with a little child to guide them. There will be no harm or ruin on all my holy mountain, for the earth will be filled with knowledge of the Lord as water fills the sea."

- "On this mountain, (God) will destroy the veil that veils all peoples, the web that is woven over all nations: he will destroy Death forever."

- "The trumpet will sound, and the dead will be raised imperishable, and we will be changed."

- "Night will be no more, nor will they need light from lamp or sun, for the Lord God shall give them light, and they shall reign forever and ever."

Millennialism and Amillennialism

When Christianity was a new and persecuted religion, many Christians believed the end times were imminent. Scholars debate whether Jesus was an apocalyptic preacher; however, his early followers, "the group of Jews who accepted him as messiah in the years immediately after his death, understood him in primarily apocalyptic terms". Prevalent in the early church and especially during periods of persecution, this Christian belief in an imminent end is called "millennialism". (It takes its name from the thousand-year ("millennial") reign of Christ that, according to the Book of Revelation, will precede the final world renovation; similar beliefs in a coming paradise are found in other religions, and these phenomena are often also called "millennialism")

Millennialism comforted Christians during times of persecution, for it predicted an imminent deliverance from suffering. From the perspective of millennialism, human action has little significance: millennialism is comforting precisely because it predicts that happiness is coming no matter what humans do: "The seeming triumph of Evil made up the apocalyptic syndrome which was to precede Christ's return and the millennium."

However, as time went on, millennialism lost its appeal. Christ had not returned immediately, as earlier Christians had predicted. Moreover, many Christians no longer needed the comfort that millennialism provided, for they were no longer persecuted: "With the triumph of the Church, the Kingdom of Heaven was already present on earth, and in a certain sense the old world had already been destroyed." (Millennialism has revived during periods of historical stress, and is currently popular among Evangelical Christians).

In the Roman Church's condemnation of millennialism, Eliade sees "the first manifestation of the doctrine of (human) progress" in Christianity. According to the amillennial view, Christ will indeed come again, ushering in a perfect Kingdom of Heaven on earth, but "the Kingdom of God is (already) present in the world today through the presence of the heavenly reign of Christ, the Bible, the Holy Spirit and Christianity". Amillennialists do not feel "the eschatological tension" that persecution inspires; therefore, they interpret their eschatological myths either figuratively or as descriptions of far-off events rather than imminent ones. Thus, after taking the amillennial position, the Church not only waited for God to renovate the world (as millennialists had) but also believed itself to be improving the world through human action.

Attitudes toward Time

According to Mircea Eliade, many traditional societies have a cyclic sense of time, periodically reenacting mythical events. Through this re-enactment, these societies achieve an "eternal return" to the mythical age. According to Eliade, Christianity retains a sense of cyclical time, through the ritual commemoration of Christ's life and the imitation of Christ's actions; Eliade calls this sense of cyclical time a "mythical aspect" of Christianity.

However, Judeo-Christian thought also makes an "innovation of the first importance", Eliade says, because it embraces the notion of linear, historical time; in Christianity, "time is no longer (only) the circular Time of the Eternal Return; it has become linear and irreversible Time". Summarizing Eliade's statements on this subject, Eric Rust writes, "A new religious structure became available. In the Judaeo-Christian religions—Judaism, Christianity, Islam—history is taken seriously, and linear time is accepted. The Christian myth gives such time a beginning in creation, a center in the Christ-event, and an end in the final consummation."

In contrast, the myths of many traditional cultures present a cyclic or static view of time. In these cultures, all the "(important) history is limited to a few events that took place in the mythical times". In other words, these cultures place events into two categories, the mythical age and the present, between which there is no continuity. Everything in the present is seen as a direct result of the mythical age:

One traditional depiction of the cherubim and chariot vision, based on the description by Ezekiel.

"Just as modern man considers himself to be constituted by (all of) History, the man of the archaic societies declares that he is the result of only a certain number of mythical events."

Because of this view, Eliade argues, members of many traditional societies see their lives as a constant repetition of mythical events, an "eternal return" to the mythical age:

"In imitating the exemplary acts of a god or of a mythical hero, or simply by recounting their adventures, the man of an archaic society detaches himself from profane time and magically re-enters the Great Time, the sacred time."

According to Eliade, Christianity shares in this cyclic sense of time to an extent. "By the very fact that it is a religion", he argues, Christianity retains at least one "mythical aspect" — the repetition of mythical events through ritual. Eliade gives a typical church service as an example:

"Just as a church constitutes a break in plane in the profane space of a modern city, so the service celebrated inside (the church) marks a break in profane temporal duration. It is no longer today's historical time that is present—the time that is experienced, for example, in the adjacent streets—but the time in which the historical existence of Jesus Christ occurred, the time sanctified by his preaching, by his passion, death, and resurrection."

Heinrich Zimmer also notes Christianity's emphasis on linear time; he attributes this emphasis specifically to the influence of Augustine of Hippo's theory of history. Zimmer does not explicitly describe the cyclical conception of time as itself "mythical" per se, although he notes that this conception "underlies Hindu mythology".

Neil Forsyth writes that "what distinguishes both Jewish and Christian religious systems is that they elevate to the sacred status of myth narratives that are situated in historical time".

Political and Philosophical Ideas

According to Mircea Eliade, the medieval "Gioacchinian myth of universal renovation in a more or less imminent future" has influenced a number of modern theories of history, such as those of Lessing (who explicitly compares his views to those of medieval "enthusiasts"), Fichte, Hegel, and Schelling; and has also influenced a number of Russian writers.

Calling Marxism "a truly messianic Judaeo-Christian ideology", Eliade writes that Marxism "takes up and carries on one of the great eschatological myths of the Middle Eastern and Mediterranean world, namely: the redemptive part to be played by the Just (the 'elect', the 'anointed', the 'innocent', the 'missioners', in our own days the proletariat), whose sufferings are invoked to change the ontological status of the world".

"The Christian Mythology of Socialism", Will Herberg argues that socialism inherits the structure of its ideology from the influence of Christian mythology upon western thought.

In The Oxford Companion to World Mythology, David Leeming claims that Judeo-Christian messianic ideas have influenced 20th-century totalitarian systems, citing the state ideology of the Soviet Union as an example.

According to Hugh S. Pyper, the biblical "founding myths of the Exodus and the exile, read as stories in which a nation is forged by maintaining its ideological and racial purity in the face of an oppressive great power", entered "the rhetoric of nationalism throughout European history", especially in Protestant countries and smaller nations.

Christmas Stories in Popular Culture

Christmas stories have become prevalent in Western literature and culture.

The Bible

Old Testament

Mythic patterns such as the primordial struggle between good and evil appear in passages throughout the Hebrew Bible, including passages that describe historical events. A distinctive characteristic of the Hebrew Bible is the reinterpretation of myth on the basis of history, as in the Book of Daniel, a record of the experience of the Jews of the Second Temple period under foreign rule, presented as a prophecy of future events and expressed in terms of "mythic structures" with "the Hellenistic kingdom figured as a terrifying monster that cannot but recall the Near Eastern pagan myth of the dragon of chaos".

Destruction of Leviathan. 1865 engraving by Gustave Doré.

Mircea Eliade argues that the imagery used in some parts of the Hebrew Bible reflects a "transfiguration of history into myth". For example, Eliade says, the portrayal of Nebuchadnezzar as a dragon in Jeremiah 51:34 is a case in which the Hebrews "interpreted contemporary events by means of the very ancient cosmogonico-heroic myth" of a battle between a hero and a dragon.

According to scholars including Neil Forsyth and John L. McKenzie, the Old Testament incorporates stories, or fragments of stories, from extra-biblical mythology. According to the New American Bible, a Catholic Bible translation produced by the Confraternity of Christian Doctrine, the story of the Nephilim in Genesis 6:1-4 "is apparently a fragment of an old legend that had borrowed much from ancient mythology", and the "sons of God" mentioned in that passage are "celestial beings of mythology". The New American Bible also says that Psalm 93 alludes to "an ancient myth" in which God battles a personified Sea. Some scholars have identified the biblical creature Leviathan as a monster from Canaanite mythology. According to Howard Schwartz, "the myth of the fall of Lucifer" existed in fragmentary form in Isaiah 14:12 and other ancient Jewish literature; Schwartz claims that the myth originated from "the ancient Canaanite myth of Athtar, who attempted to rule the throne of Ba'al, but was forced to descend and rule the underworld instead".

Some scholars have argued that the calm, orderly, monotheistic creation story in Genesis 1 can be interpreted as a reaction against the creation myths of other Near Eastern cultures. In connection with this interpretation, David and Margaret Leeming describe Genesis 1 as a "demythologized myth" and John L. McKenzie asserts that the writer of Genesis 1 has "excised the mythical elements" from his creation story.

Perhaps the most famous topic in the Bible that could possibly be connected with mythical origins is the topic of Heaven (or the sky) as the place where God (or angels, or the saints) resides, with stories such as the ascension of Elijah (who disappeared in the sky), war of man with an angel, flying angels. Even in the New Testament Paul the Apostle is said to have visited the third heaven, and Jesus was portrayed in several books as going to return from Heaven on a cloud, in the same way he ascended thereto. The official text repeated by the attendees during Roman Catholic mass (the Apostles' Creed) contains the words "He ascended into Heaven, and is Seated at the Right Hand of God, The Father. From thence He will come again to judge the living and the dead". Medieval cosmology adapted its view of the Cosmos to conform with these scriptures, in the concept of celestial spheres.

New Testament and Early Christianity

According to a number of scholars, the Christ story contains mythical themes such as descent to the underworld, the heroic monomyth, and the "dying god.

Some scholars have argued that the Book of Revelation incorporates imagery from ancient mythology. According to the New American Bible, the image in Revelation 12:1-6 of a pregnant woman in the sky, threatened by a dragon, "corresponds to a widespread myth throughout the ancient world that a goddess pregnant with a savior was pursued by a horrible monster; by miraculous intervention, she bore a son who then killed the monster". Bernard McGinn suggests that the image of the two Beasts in Revelation stems from a "mythological background" involving the figures of Leviathan and Behemoth.

The Pastoral Epistles contain denunciations of "myths" (muthoi). This may indicate that Rabbinic or Gnostic mythology was popular among the early Christians to whom the epistles were written and that the epistles' author was attempting to resist that mythology.

The Sibylline oracles contain predictions that the dead Roman Emperor Nero, infamous for his persecutions, would return one day as an Antichrist-like figure. According to Bernard McGinn, these parts of the oracles were probably written by a Christian and incorporated "mythological language" in describing Nero's return.

From Roman Empire to Europe

After Christian theology was accepted by the Roman Empire, promoted by St. Augustine in the 5th century, Christian mythology began to predominate the Roman Empire. Later the theology was carried north by Charlemagne and the Frankish people, and Christian themes began to weave into the framework of European mythologies. The pre-Christian Germanic and Celtic mythology that were native to the tribes of Northern Europe were denounced and submerged, while saint myths, Mary stories, Crusade myths, and other Christian myths took their place. However, pre-Christian myths never went entirely away, they mingled with the (Roman Catholic) Christian framework to form new stories, like myths of the mythological kings and saints and miracles, for example. Stories such as that of Beowulf and Icelandic, Norse, and Germanic sagas were reinterpreted somewhat, and given Christian meanings. The legend of King Arthur and the quest for the Holy Grail is a striking example. The thrust of incorporation took on one of two directions. When Christianity was on the advance, pagan myths were Christianized; when it was in retreat, Bible stories and Christian saints lost their mythological importance to the culture.

Middle Ages

According to Mircea Eliade, the Middle Ages witnessed "an upwelling of mythical thought" in which each social group had its own "mythological traditions". Often a profession had its own "origin myth" which established models for members of the profession to imitate; for example, the knights tried to imitate Lancelot or Parsifal. The medieval trouveres developed a "mythology of woman and Love" which incorporated Christian elements but, in some cases, ran contrary to official church teaching.

George Every includes a discussion of medieval legends in his book Christian Mythology. Some medieval legends elaborated upon the lives of Christian figures such as Christ, the Virgin Mary, and the saints. For example, a number of legends describe miraculous events surrounding Mary's birth and her marriage to Joseph.

In many cases, medieval mythology appears to have inherited elements from myths of pagan gods and heroes. According to Every, one example may be "the myth of St. George" and other stories about saints battling dragons, which were "modelled no doubt in many cases on older representations of the creator and preserver of the world in combat with chaos". Eliade notes that some "mythological traditions" of medieval knights, namely the Arthurian cycle and the Grail theme, combine a veneer of Christianity with traditions regarding the Celtic Otherworld. "many scholars" see a link between stories in "Irish-Celtic mythology" about journeys to the Otherworld in search of a cauldron of rejuvenation and medieval accounts of the quest for the Holy Grail.

According to Eliade, "eschatological myths" became prominent during the Middle Ages during "certain historical movements". These eschatological myths appeared "in the Crusades, in the movements of a Tanchelm and an Eudes de l'Etoile, in the elevation of Fredrick II to the rank of Messiah, and in many other collective messianic, utopian, and prerevolutionary phenomena". One significant eschatological myth, introduced by Gioacchino da Fiore's theology of history, was the "myth of an imminent third age that will renew and complete history" in a "reign of the Holy Spirit"; this "Gioacchinian myth" influenced a number of messianic movements that arose in the late Middle Ages.

Renaissance and Reformation

During the Renaissance, there arose a critical attitude that sharply distinguished between apostolic tradition and what George Every calls "subsidiary mythology"—popular legends surrounding saints, relics, the cross, etc.—suppressing the latter.

Unicorn mosaic on a 1213 church floor in Ravenna.

The works of Renaissance writers often included and expanded upon Christian and non-Christian stories such as those of creation and the Fall. Rita Oleyar describes these writers as "on the whole, reverent and faithful to the primal myths, but filled with their own insights into the nature of God, man, and the universe". An example is John Milton's Paradise Lost, an "epic elaboration of the Judeo-Christian mythology" and also a "veritable encyclopedia of myths from the Greek and Roman tradition".

According to Cynthia Stewart, during the Reformation, the Protestant reformers used "the founding myths of Christianity" to critique the church of their time.

Every argues that "the disparagement of myth in our own civilization" stems partly from objections to perceived idolatry, objections which intensified in the Reformation, both among Protestants and among Catholics reacting against the classical mythology revived during the Renaissance.

Enlightenment

The philosophes of the Enlightenment used criticism of myth as a vehicle for veiled criticisms of the Bible and the church. According to Bruce Lincoln, the philosophes "made irrationality the hallmark of myth and constituted philosophy—rather than the Christian kerygma—as the antidote for mythic discourse. By implication, Christianity could appear as a more recent, powerful, and dangerous instance of irrational myth".

Since the end of the 18th century, the biblical stories have lost some of their mythological basis to western society, owing to the scepticism of the Enlightenment, 19th-century freethinking, and 20th century modernism. Most westerners no longer found Christianity to be their primary imaginative and mythological framework by which they understand the world. However other scholars believe mythology is in our psyche, and that mythical influences of Christianity are in many of our ideals, for example the Judeo-Christian idea of an after-life and heaven. The book Virtual Faith: The Irreverent Spiritual Quest of Generation X by Tom Beaudoin explores the premise that Christian mythology is present in the mythologies of pop-culture, such as Madonna's Like a Prayer or Soundgarden's Black Hole Sun. Modern myths are strong in comic book stories (as stories of culture heroes) and detective novels as myths of good versus evil.

Modern Period

Some commentators have categorized a number of modern fantasy works as "Christian myth" or "Christian mythopoeia". Examples include the fiction of C.S. Lewis, Madeleine L'Engle, J.R.R. Tolkien, and George MacDonald.

In The Eternal Adam and the New World Garden, written in 1968, David W. Noble argued that the Adam figure had been "the central myth in the American novel since 1830". As examples, he cites the works of Cooper, Hawthorne, Melville, Twain, Hemingway, and Faulkner.

English Mythology

English mythology is the collection of myths that have emerged throughout the history of England, sometimes being elaborated upon by successive generations, and at other times being rejected and replaced by other explanatory narratives. These narratives consist of folk traditions developed in England after the Norman Conquest, integrated with traditions from Anglo-Saxon mythology, Christian mythology, and Celtic mythology. Elements of the Matter of Britain and Welsh mythology which relate directly to England are included, such as the foundation myth of Brutus of Troy and the Arthurian legends, but these are combined with narratives from the Matter of England and traditions from English folklore.

King Arthur and the Knights of the Round Table.

Notable Figures and Legends

- Alfred the Great: In 878 burns the cakes in Athelney, Somerset before defeating the Great Heathen Army at the Battle of Edington.

- King Arthur: Legendary leader who, according to medieval histories and romances, led the Knights of the Round Table in the defence of Britain against Saxon invaders. A central figure in the legends making up the Matter of Britain.

- Athelston: Anonymous Middle English verse romance, often classified as a Matter of England text. Its themes of kingship, justice and the rule of law relate to the politics of Richard II's reign.

- Beowulf: Epic poem in Old English. The original manuscript has no title, but the story it tells has become known by the name of its protagonist. Beowulf may be the oldest surviving long poem in Old English and is commonly cited as one of the most important works of Anglo-Saxon literature.

- Sir Bevis of Hampton: Legendary English hero; the subject of medieval metrical romances which bear his name.

- Brutus of Troy, or Brute of Troy: Legendary descendant of the Trojan hero Aeneas, known in medieval British history as the eponymous founder and first king of Britain. Brutus first appears in the Historia Brittonum, but is best known from Geoffrey of Monmouth's Historia Regum Britanniae.

- Fulk FitzWarin: Subject of the medieval legend Fouke le Fitz Waryn, which relates the story of Fulk's life as an outlaw and his struggle to regain his familial right to Whittington Castle from King John.

- The Tale of Gamelyn: Romance taking place during the reign of King Edward I, telling the story of Gamelyn and the various obstacles he must overcome in order to retrieve his rightful inheritance from his older brother. Written in a dialect of Middle English and considered part of the Matter of England.

- Guy of Warwick: Legendary English hero of Romance popular in England and France from the 13th to 17th centuries; considered to be part of the Matter of England.

- Havelok the Dane, or Lay of Havelok the Dane: Middle English Romance considered to be part of the Matter of England; the story derives from two earlier Anglo-Norman texts.

- Hengist and Horsa: Legendary brothers said to have led the Angles, Saxons and Jutes in their invasion of Britain in the 5th century; Horsa was killed fighting the Britons, but Hengist successfully conquered Kent, becoming the forefather of its Jutish kings. A figure named Hengest appears in the Finnesburg Fragment and in Beowulf.

- King Horn: Chivalric romance in Middle English; considered part of the Matter of England. Believed to be the oldest extant romance in Middle English.

- Lady Godiva: English noblewoman who, according to legend, rode naked – covered only in her long hair – through the streets of Coventry to gain a remission of the oppressive taxation that her husband imposed on his tenants. The term "Peeping Tom" originates from later versions of this legend, in which a man named Thomas watched her ride and was struck blind or dead.

- Robin Hood: Heroic outlaw of English folklore who, according to legend, was a highly skilled archer and swordsman. Traditionally depicted dressed in Lincoln green, he is said to rob from the rich and give to the poor. Alongside his band of Merry Men in Sherwood Forest and against the Sheriff of Nottingham, he became a popular folk figure in the Late Middle Ages, and continues to be represented in literature, film and television.

- Sceafa: Ancient Lombardic king in English legend. The story has Sceafa appearing mysteriously as a child, coming out of the sea in an empty skiff. The name has historically been modernized Shava.

- Waltheof of Melrose: 12th century English abbot and saint; born to the English nobility, Waltheof is noted for his severe, self-imposed austerities and kindness to the poor.

- Wayland the Smith: Legendary master blacksmith who appears in Deor, Waldere, and Beowulf; the legend is depicted on the Franks Casket.

Lithuanian Mythology

Lithuanian mythology is the mythology of Lithuanian polytheism, the religion of pre-Christian Lithuanians. Like other Indo-Europeans, ancient Lithuanians maintained a polytheistic mythology and religious structure. In pre-Christian Lithuania, mythology was a part of polytheistic religion; after the Christianisation mythology survived mostly in folklore, customs and festive rituals. Lithuanian mythology is very close to the mythology of other Baltic nations and tribes and is being considered a part of the Baltic mythology.

Baltic religion.

Early Lithuanian religion and customs were based on oral tradition. Therefore the very first records about Lithuanian mythology and beliefs were made by travellers, Christian missionaries, chronicle writers and historians. Original Lithuanian oral tradition partially survived in national ritual and festive songs and legends which were started to write down in 18th century. The first bits about Baltic religion were written down by Herodotus and Tacitus. In the 9th century there is one attestation about Prussian funeral traditions by Wulfstan.

An old sacrificial stone in Lithuania.

Relations with other Mythological Systems

Lithuanian mythology is perhaps closest to Latvian mythology, and according to the prevalent point of view, Lithuanians shared the same myths and basic features of their religion with the Old Prussians. On the other hand, individual elements have much in common with other mythological systems, and especially with those of neighbouring cultures.

There is a Finnic Mordvin/Erza thunder god named Pur'ginepaz which in folklore has themes resembling Lithuanian Perkunas. "Sparks fly from the cartwheels and the hooves of fiery-red horses of Pur'ginepaz, the Erza thunder god, when he drives across the sky". In several mythical songs the thunder god Pur'ginepaz marries an earthly girl Litova (Lituva, Syrzha, etc.). These also closely resemble the Vedic Parjanya.

The Periods of Lithuanian Mythology

Pre-Christian mythology is known mainly through speculation and reconstruction, although the existence of some mythological elements, known from later sources, has been confirmed by archaeological findings. It is reflected in folk tales, such as Jūratė and Kastytis, Eglė the Queen of Serpents and the Myth of Sovijus.

The next period of Lithuanian mythology started in the 15th century, and lasted till approximately the middle of the 17th century. The myths of this period are mostly heroic, concerning the founding of the state of Lithuania. Perhaps two the best known stories are those of the dream of the Grand Duke Gediminas and the founding of Vilnius, the capital of Lithuania, and of Šventaragis' Valley, which also concerns the history of Vilnius. Many stories of this kind reflect actual historical events. In general, these myths are coloured by patriotism. Already by the 16th century, there existed a non-unified pantheon; data from different sources did not correspond one with another, and local spirits, especially those of the economic field, became mixed up with more general gods and ascended to the level of gods.

The third period began with the growing influence of Christianity and the activity of the Jesuits, roughly since the end of the 16th century. The earlier confrontational approach to the pre-Christian Lithuanian heritage among common people was abandoned, and attempts were made to use popular beliefs in missionary activities. This also led to the inclusion of Christian elements in mythic stories.

The last period of Lithuanian mythology began in the 19th century, when the importance of the old cultural heritage was admitted, not only by the upper classes, but by the nation more widely. The mythical stories of this period are mostly reflections of the earlier myths, considered not as being true, but as the encoded experiences of the past. They concentrated on moral problems, and on a heroic vision of the past, rather than on individual heroes, who very often even lacked proper names, being referred to as "a duke", "the ruler of the castle", etc.

Flag of Vaidevutis.

Elements of Lithuanian Mythology

Gods and Nature

Stories, songs, and legends of this kind describe laws of nature and such natural processes as the change of seasons of the year, their connections with each other and with the existence of human beings. Nature is often described in terms of the human family; in one central example (found in many songs and stories), the sun is called the mother, the moon the father, and stars the sisters of human beings. Lithuanian mythology is rich in gods and minor gods of water, sky and earth.

Samogitian Sanctuary, a reconstruction of paleoastronomic observatory.

Legacy

Lithuanian mythology serves as a constant inspiration for Lithuanian artists. Many interpretations of Eglė - the Queen of Serpents were made in poetry and visual art. In modern Lithuanian music polytheistic rituals and sutartinės songs were source of inspiration for Bronius Kutavičius. Old Lithuanian names, related to nature and mythology are often given to the children.

Sculpture of Eglė the Queen of Serpents in Palanga, Lithuania.

Proto-Indo-European Mythology

Proto-Indo-European myths may be defined as narratives which have certain elements in common, such as a God/person X who does Y in connection with a God/person/being Z, where X and Z are cognates, respectively, in several Indo-European languages, and Y is something specific like "kills monster." Many Indo-European myths have at their core some simple observation of nature or life, such as that the sun is "born" each morning and "dies" each night, or that wheat must be cut and threshed ("killed and tortured") before it can be used to make bread.

Types of Sources for the Reconstruction of Indo-european Myths

- Actual mythological tales in which Gods act like Gods.

- Legends or histories. Many foundation myths of a country or city, including sometimes bare king-lists, consist of a reprise of the nature myths.

- Folktales which are highly subject to borrowing but some examples can be determined to conserve native myths based on the forms of the names which modern storytellers are not always able to interpret correctly.

Jacob Grimm gives a more complete list of types of sources including riddles and proverbs, but they must be used with care. In areas where the original religion has been replaced by hostile monotheistic religions, many Indo-European myths persist in the form of fairy tales, romances and saints' tales, and sometimes as the "history" of the Gods or heroes in the monotheistic religions themselves, a point of which they do not like to be reminded.

Proto-Indo-European Myths: Although many myths might be considered "Indo-European myths" on the grounds that they are told in some Indo-European language, the very brief list of myths which follows can be shown by the cognate names to descend from a common ancestor in the Indo-European languages and therefore qualify as Proto-Indo-European myths. Most of these were identified and described as early as 1887 by George Cox, in The Mythology of the Aryan Nations, and they have been discussed by many other authors with a better understanding of linguistics since that time. There are in fact some 28 myths that can be reconstructed to a Proto-Indo-European original based on this very high linguistic standard, but most of these have not been recognized by Indo-European linguists. In the list that follows, the numbers after each myth, such as 5 of 11 language families, are used to indicate that a certain myth is known in cognate forms in at least five of the eleven major language families among the Indo-European languages. Three examples of a cognate myth in widely separated languages represent a minimum criterion for inclusion.

Creation Myths

- Primal Cow Creation Myth ("World made from the Body of a Giant Bovine", attested in 5 of the 11 language families).

- Birth of the Horse Twins from the grain/horse mother (found in 7 of the 11 language groups).

- Danu killed and cut open to produce a river (a Partition Creation myth; found in at least 3 of the 11 language families).

- Time gives birth to the Sun and the Moon.

Cyclic or Seasonal Myths

- Perkunos, a Storm God loses his "weapon of power" then uses it to kill winter (found in 5 of the 11 language groups).

- Cloud/cows stolen from the Sun God by the Wind God and then returned (found in 4 of the 11 language groups).

- Dying Corn God, dies and is reborn, causes seasons (Frazer, Vol. 8 and 9 of the Golden Bough, esp. Vol. 9, found in 4 of the 11 language families.) The John Barleycorn song is widely recognized as a form of this myth.

- Uncle Water (Apam Napat or Neptune) melts the ice and releases the water causing flooding (Gamkrelidze and Ivanov, found in 5 of the 11 language families).

Others

- Quest of the golden apples of immortality, usually by a Wind God.

Culture Myths

Stories in which some godlike being teaches culture or the "arts of civilization" (actually technologies) to humans are found in all cultures. The culture myths of the Indo-Europeans tell how the Culture Gods taught humans how to make fire, the proper way to kill and butcher an animal (sacrifice), religious rituals and law codes, smithing, weaving, ploughing and healing. Culture Gods (e.g. Prometheus and Loki) sometimes have an intermediate position between Gods and humans. They are certainly supernatural, but they often die or are tortured by other Gods for their beneficence to humans; nevertheless they are often revived and worshiped like regular Gods. Mallory and Adams call them Craft Gods and argue that they are not linguistically reconstructible; however Cox compares Greek Prometheus with Hindu Pramanthu. Smith Gods, a subset of the Culture Gods, are slightly reconstructible according to Mallory and Adams.

Religious uses of Myths

Many texts state specifically that telling or listening to a myth confers a blessing on the listeners. For example the text of the Táin Bó Cúailnge has a colophon that reads "A blessing be upon all such as shall faithfully keep the Táin in memory as it stands here and shall not add any other form to it." Telling myths is also considered a way to praise and honor the Gods so myths are often recited or sung especially at festivals for a particular God, or as Tacitus puts it "The praises of their Gods, and the achievements of their heroes, are usually chanted at their festival meetings" (Germania c.ii). This behavior is extremely widespread among the Indo-Europeans and it is important for understanding the Proto-Indo-European religion, but scholars have generally ignored it. The telling or performance of myths was apparently the original impetus for the tradition of Greek drama at the festivals of Dionysus, although by the time we have a written record of the dramas, they are not restricted in subject matter to the myths of any particular God according to Moulton, (The Ancient Classical Drama).

Interestingly, for what it says about humans, myths are very often used to present ideas about social or political conditions or concerns, usually in an indirect manner. It might be thought that in the "old days" myths were told because people actually believed in them, but when the myths are no longer believed, they are just told for entertainment value, since they now appear in comic books, operas, movies and other modern works of fiction. But it can be shown that in the time of classical Greek drama, for example, many myths were told as a commentary on Greek society, which is a way in which myths are often used now. And people were not more credulous in the old days. There are people now, as there were in the past, who believe in all sorts of nonsense in a simple-minded way, and then there always were and still are people who have a more sophisticated understanding of the world and of the nature of the information that is presented to them. The character of myths that allows them to be bent to any use has allowed them to be of continuous interest and utility and it is probably this very factor that is responsible for their preservation.

References

- Norse-Mythology: newworldencyclopedia.org, Retrieved 28 January, 2020

- H. James Birx Encyclopedia of Time: Science, Philosophy, Theology, & Culture, Band 1 SAGE, 13.01.2009 ISBN 9781412941648 p. 303

- Jūrate Baranova; et al., eds. (2001). "Chapter iv Lithuanian mythology by Gintaras Beresnev-ičius". Lithuanian philosophy: persons and ideas Lithuanian philosophical studies, ii. Cultural heritage and contemporary change series IVa, Eastern and Central Europe, volume 17. The Council For Research In Values And Philosophy. ISBN 1-56518-137-9. Archived from the original on 28 September 2007. Retrieved 7 September 2007

- Piemyth: piereligion.org, Retrieved 15 May, 2020

4
Greek and Roman Mythology

Greek mythology refers to the study of myths of ancient Greeks and legendary Greek genres. Roman mythology refers to the study of myths and culture of ancient Romans and legendary Roman genres. This chapter includes the origin, lives, deities, mythological creatures, ritual practices and the significance of ancient Greeks and Romans for a thorough understanding of the subject.

Greek Mythology

Greek mythology is the body of stories concerning the gods, heroes, and rituals of the ancient Greeks. That the myths contained a considerable element of fiction was recognized by the more critical Greeks, such as the philosopher Plato in the 5th–4th century BCE. In general, however, in the popular piety of the Greeks, the myths were viewed as true accounts. Greek mythology has subsequently had extensive influence on the arts and literature of Western civilization, which fell heir to much of Greek culture.

Electra and Orestes killing Aegisthus in the presence of their mother, Clytemnestra; detail of a Greek vase, 5th century BC.

Although people of all countries, eras, and stages of civilization have developed myths that explain the existence and workings of natural phenomena, recount the deeds of gods or heroes, or seek to justify social or political institutions, the myths of the Greeks have remained unrivaled in the Western world as sources of imaginative and appealing ideas. Poets and artists from ancient times to the present have derived inspiration from Greek mythology and have discovered contemporary significance and relevance in Classical mythological themes.

Orestes being purified by Apollo after his acquittal by the court of the Areopagus, detail of a 5th-century-BCE Greek vase; in the Louvre.

Sources of Myths: Literary and Archaeological

The Homeric Poems: The Iliad and the Odyssey

Homer, copy of a lost bust from the 2nd century from Baiae, Italy.

The 5th-century-BCE Greek historian Herodotus remarked that Homer and Hesiod gave to the Olympian gods their familiar characteristics. Few today would accept this literally. In the first book of the Iliad, the son of Zeus and Leto (Apollo, line 9) is as instantly identifiable to the Greek reader by his patronymic as are the sons of Atreus (Agamemnon and Menelaus, line 16). In both cases, the audience is expected to have knowledge of the myths that preceded their literary rendering. Little is known to suggest that the Greeks treated Homer, or any other source of Greek myths, as mere entertainment, whereas there are prominent Greeks from Pindar to the later Stoa for whom myths, and those from Homer in particular, are so serious as to warrant bowdlerization or allegorization.

The Works of Hesiod: Theogony and Works and Days

The fullest and most important source of myths about the origin of the gods is the Theogony of Hesiod. The elaborate genealogies mentioned above are accompanied by folktales and etiological myths. The Works and Days shares some of these in the context of a farmer's calendar and an extensive harangue on the subject of justice addressed to Hesiod's possibly fictitious brother Perses. The orthodox view treats the two poems as quite different in theme and treats the Works and Days as a theodicy (a natural theology). It is possible, however, to treat the two poems as a diptych, each part dependent on the other. The Theogony declares the identities and alliances of the gods, while the Works and Days gives advice on the best way to succeed in a dangerous world, and Hesiod urges that the most reliable—though by no means certain—way is to be just.

Hesiod, detail of a mosaic by Monnus, 3rd century; in the Rhenish State Museum, Trier, Ger.

Other Literary Works

Fragmentary post-Homeric epics of varying date and authorship filled the gaps in the accounts of the Trojan War recorded in the Iliad and Odyssey; the so-called Homeric Hymns (shorter surviving poems) are the source of several important religious myths. Many of the lyric poets preserved various myths, but the odes of Pindar of Thebes are particularly rich in myth and legend. The works of the three tragedians—Aeschylus, Sophocles, and Euripides, all of the 5th century BCE—are remarkable for the variety of the traditions they preserve.

In Hellenistic times Callimachus, a 3rd-century-BCE poet and scholar in Alexandria, recorded many obscure myths; his contemporary, the mythographer Euhemerus, suggested that the gods were originally human, a view known as Euhemerism. Apollonius of Rhodes, another scholar of the 3rd century BCE, preserved the fullest account of the Argonauts in search of the Golden Fleece.

Achilles killing Penthesilea during the Trojan War, interior of an
Attic cup, c. 460 BCE; in the Museum of Antiquities, Munich.

In the period of the Roman Empire, the Geography of Strabo, the Library of the pseudo-Apollodorus (attributed to a 2nd-century-CE scholar), the antiquarian writings of the Greek biographer Plutarch, and the works of Pausanias, a 2nd-century-CE historian, as well as the Latin Genealogies of Hyginus, a 2nd-century-CE mythographer, have provided valuable sources in Latin of later Greek mythology.

Archaeological Discoveries

The discovery of the Mycenaean civilization by Heinrich Schliemann, a 19th-century German amateur archaeologist, and the discovery of the Minoan civilization in Crete (from which the Mycenaean ultimately derived) by Sir Arthur Evans, a 20th-century English archaeologist, are essential to the 21st-century understanding of the development of myth and ritual in the Greek world. Such discoveries illuminated aspects of Minoan culture from about 2200 to 1450 BCE and Mycenaean culture from about 1600 to 1200 BCE; those eras were followed by a Dark Age that lasted until about 800 BCE. Unfortunately, the evidence about myth and ritual at Mycenaean and Minoan sites is entirely monumental, because the Linear B script (an ancient form of Greek found in both Crete and Greece) was mainly used to record inventories.

Geometric designs on pottery of the 8th century BCE depict scenes from the Trojan cycle, as well as the adventures of Heracles. The extreme formality of the style, however, renders much of the identification difficult, and there is no inscriptional evidence accompanying the designs to assist scholars in identification and interpretation. In the succeeding Archaic, Classical, and Hellenistic periods, Homeric and various other mythological scenes appear to supplement the existing literary evidence.

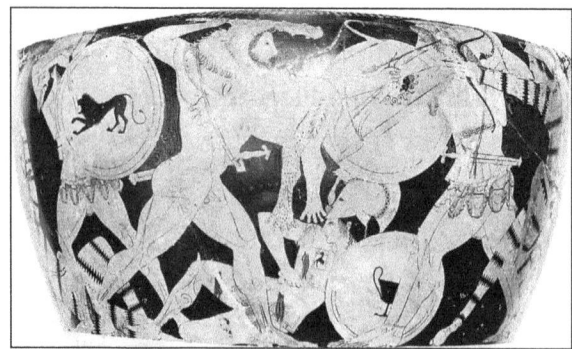

Heracles fighting with the Amazons, detail from a volute krater attributed to Euphronius, c. 500 BCE; in the Archaeological Museum, Arezzo, Italy.

Forms of Myth in Greek Culture

To distinguish between myth, legend, and folktale can be useful, provided it is remembered that the Greeks themselves did not do so.

Religious Myths

Greek religious myths are concerned with gods or heroes in their more serious aspects or are connected with ritual. They include cosmogonical tales of the genesis of the gods and the world out of Chaos, the successions of divine rulers, and the internecine struggles that culminated in the supremacy of Zeus, the ruling god of Olympus (the mountain that was considered the home of the gods). They also include the long tale of Zeus's amours with goddesses and mortal women, which usually resulted in the births of younger deities and heroes. The goddess Athena's unique status is implicit in the story of her motherless birth (she sprang full-grown from Zeus's forehead); and the myths of Apollo explain that god's sacral associations, describe his remarkable victories over monsters and giants, and stress his jealousy and the dangers inherent in immortal alliances.

The gods on Olympus: Athena, Zeus, Dionysus, Hera, and Aphrodite. Detail of a painting on a Greek cup; in the National Archaeological Museum, Tarquinia, Italy.

Myths of Dionysus, on the other hand, demonstrate the hostility aroused by a novel faith. Some myths are closely associated with rituals, such as the account of the drowning of the infant Zeus's cries by the Curetes, attendants of Zeus, clashing their weapons, or Hera's annual restoration of her virginity by bathing in the spring Canathus. Some myths about heroes and heroines also have a religious basis. The tale of creation and moral decline forms part of the myth of the Four Ages. The subsequent destruction of humanity by flood and regeneration of humans from stones is partly based on folktale.

Leucothea giving Dionysus a drink from the Horn of Plenty, antique bas-relief; in the Lateran Museum, Rome.

Legends

Theseus killing the Minotaur, detail of a vase painting by the Kleophrades Painter, 6th century BC; in the British Museum.

Myths were viewed as embodying divine or timeless truths, whereas legends (or sagas) were quasi-historical. Hence, famous events in epics, such as the Trojan War, were generally regarded as having really happened, and heroes and heroines were believed to have actually lived. Earlier sagas, such as the voyage of the Argonauts, were accepted in a similar fashion. Most Greek legends were embellished with folktales and fiction, but some certainly contain a historical substratum. Such are the tales of more than one sack of Troy, which are supported by archaeological evidence, and the labours of Heracles, which might suggest Mycenaean feudalism. Again, the legend of the Minotaur (a being part human, part bull) could have arisen from exaggerated accounts of bull leaping in ancient Crete.

In another class of legends, heinous offenses—such as attempting to rape a goddess, deceiving the gods grossly by inculpating them in crime, or assuming their prerogatives—were punished by everlasting torture in the underworld. The consequences of social crimes, such as murder or incest, were also described in legend (e.g., the story of Oedipus, who killed his father and married his mother). Legends were also sometimes employed to justify existing political systems or to bolster territorial claims.

Folktales

Folktales, consisting of popular recurring themes and told for amusement, inevitably found their way into Greek myth. Such is the theme of lost persons—whether husband, wife, or child (e.g., Odysseus, Helen of Troy, or Paris of Troy)—found or recovered after long and exciting adventures. Journeys to the land of the dead were made by Orpheus (a hero who went to Hades to restore his dead wife, Eurydice, to the realm of the living), Heracles, Odysseus, and Theseus (the slayer of the Minotaur). The victory of the little man by means of cunning against impossible odds, the exploits of the superman (e.g., Heracles), or the long-delayed victory over enemies are still as popular with modern writers as they were with the Greeks.

The abduction of Helen, Greek bas-relief; in the Lateran Museum, Rome.

The successful countering of the machinations of cruel sires and stepmothers, the rescue of princesses from monsters, and temporary forgetfulness at a crucial moment are also familiar themes in Greek myth. Recognition by tokens, such as peculiarities of dress or Odysseus's scar, is another common folktale motif. The babes-in-the-woods theme of the exposure of children and their subsequent recovery is also found in Greek myth. The Greeks, however, also knew of the exposure of children as a common practice.

Types of Myths in Greek Culture

Myths of Origin

Myths of origin represent an attempt to render the universe comprehensible in human terms. Greek creation myths (cosmogonies) and views of the universe (cosmologies) were more systematic and specific than those of other ancient peoples. Yet their very artistry serves as an impediment to interpretation, since the Greeks embellished the myths with folktale and fiction told for its own sake. Thus, though the aim of Hesiod's Theogony is to describe the ascendancy of Zeus (and, incidentally, the rise of the other gods), the inclusion of such familiar themes as the hostility between the generations, the enigma of woman (Pandora), the exploits of the friendly trickster (Prometheus), and the struggles against powerful beings or monsters like the Titans (and, in later tradition, the Giants) enhances the interest of an epic account.

According to Hesiod, four primary divine beings first came into existence: the Gap (Chaos), Earth (Gaea), the Abyss (Tartarus), and Love (Eros). The creative process began with the forcible separation of Gaea from her doting consort Heaven (Uranus) in order to allow her progeny to be born. The means of separation employed, the cutting off of Uranus's genitals by his son Cronus, bears a certain resemblance to a similar story recorded in Babylonian epic. The crudity is relieved, however, in characteristic Greek fashion, by the friendly collaboration of Uranus and Gaea, after their divorce, on a plan to save Zeus from the same Cronus, his cannibalistic sire.

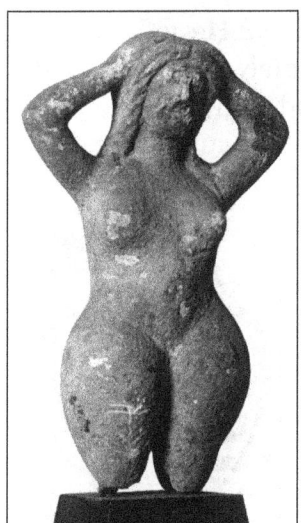

Gaea, terra-cotta statuette from Tanagra, Greece; in the Musée Borély, Marseille.

According to Greek cosmological concepts, the Earth was viewed as a flat disk afloat on the river of Ocean. The Sun (Helios) traversed the heavens like a charioteer and sailed around the Earth in a golden bowl at night. Natural fissures were popularly regarded as entrances to the subterranean house of Hades—i.e., the home of the dead.

Helios in his chariot, relief sculpture excavated at Troy in 1872; in the National Museums in Berlin.

Myths of the Ages of the World

From a very early period, Greek myths seem to have been open to criticism and alteration on grounds of morality or of misrepresentation of known facts. In the Works and Days, Hesiod makes use of a scheme of Four Ages (or Races): Golden, Silver, Bronze, and Iron. "Race" is the more accurate translation, but "Golden Age" has become so established in English that both terms should be mentioned. These races or ages are separate creations of the gods, the Golden Age belonging to the reign of Cronus and the subsequent races being the creation of Zeus. Those of the Golden Age never grew old, were free from toil, and passed their time in jollity and feasting. When they died, they became guardian spirits on Earth.

Why the Golden Age came to an end Hesiod failed to explain, but it was succeeded by the Silver Age. After an inordinately prolonged childhood, the men of the Silver Age began to act presumptuously and neglected the gods. Consequently, Zeus hid them in the Earth, where they became spirits among the dead.

Hector donning his breastplate, amphora by Euthymides, c. 500
BC; in the National Museum of Antiquities, Munich.

Zeus next created the men of the Bronze Age, men of violence who perished by mutual destruction. At this point the poet intercalates the Age (or Race) of Heroes. He thereby destroys the symmetry of the myth, in the interests of history: what is now known as the Minoan-Mycenaean period was generally believed in antiquity to have been a good time to live. (This subjection of myth to history is not universal in Greece, but it is found in writers such as Hesiod, Xenophanes, Pindar, Aeschylus, and Plato.) Of these heroes the more-favoured (who were related to the gods) reverted to a kind of restored Golden Age existence under the rule of Cronus (forced into honourable exile by his son Zeus) in the Isles of the Blessed.

The final age, the antithesis of the Golden Age, was the Iron Age, during which the poet himself had the misfortune to live. But even that was not the worst, for he believed that a time would come when infants would be born old and there would be no recourse left against the universal moral decline. The presence of evil was explained by Pandora's rash action in opening the fatal jar.

Elsewhere in Greek and Roman literature, the belief in successive periods or races is found with the belief that by some means, when the worst is reached, the system gradually (Plato, Politikos) or quickly (Virgil, Fourth Eclogue) returns to the Golden Age. Hesiod may have known this version; he wishes to have been born either earlier or later. There is also a myth of progress, associated with Prometheus, god of craftsmen, but the progress is limited, for the 19th-century concept of eternal advancement is absent from Greek thought.

Myths of the Gods

The "judgment of Paris," Hermes leading Athena, Hera, and Aphrodite to Paris, detail of a red-figure kylix by Hieron, 6th century BC; in the Collection of Classical Antiquities of the National Museums in Berlin.

Myths about the gods described their births, victories over monsters or rivals, love affairs, special powers, or connections with a cultic site or ritual. As these powers tended to be wide, the myths of many gods were correspondingly complex. Thus, the Homeric Hymns to Demeter, a goddess of agriculture, and to the Delian and Pythian Apollo describe how these deities came to be associated with sites at Eleusis, Delos, and Delphi, respectively. Similarly, myths about Athena, the patroness of Athens, tend to emphasize the goddess's love of war and her affection for heroes and the city of Athens, and those concerning Hermes (the messenger of the gods), Aphrodite (goddess of love), or Dionysus describe Hermes' proclivities as a god of thieves, Aphrodite's lovemaking, and Dionysus's association with wine, frenzy, miracles, and even ritual death. Poseidon (god of the sea) was unusually atavistic in that his union with Earth, and his equine adventures appear to hark back to his pre-marine status as a horse or earthquake god.

Many myths are treated as trivial and lighthearted, but this judgment rests on the suppressed premise that any divine behaviour that seems inappropriate for a major religion must have seemed absurd and fictitious to the Greeks. Homer barely mentions the judgment of Paris, but he knew the far from trivial consequences for Troy of the favour of Aphrodite and the bitter enmity of Hera and Athena, which the "judgment of Paris" was composed to explain.

Dionysus and Ariadne with an Eros figure, fragmentary Apulian red-figure
pelike, terra-cotta from Apulia, Italy, about 360–350 BCE.

As time went on, an accretion of minor myths continued to supplement the older and more authentic ones. Thus, the loves of Apollo, virtually ignored by Homer and Hesiod, explained why the bay (or laurel) became Apollo's sacred tree and how he came to father Asclepius, a healing god. Similarly, the presence of the cuckoo on Hera's sceptre at Hermione or the invention of the panpipe were explained by fables. Such etiological myths proliferated during the Hellenistic era, though in the earlier periods genuine examples are harder to detect.

Parthenon frieze: Poseidon, Apollo, and Artemis..

Of folk deities, the nymphs (nature goddesses) personified nature or the life in water or trees and were said to punish unfaithful lovers. Water nymphs (Naiads) were reputed to drown those with whom they fell in love, such as Hylas, a companion of Heracles. Even the gentle Muses (goddesses of the arts and sciences) blinded their human rivals, such as the bard Thamyris. Satyrs (youthful folk deities with bestial features) and sileni (old and drunken folk deities) were the nymphs' male counterparts. Like sea deities, sileni possessed secret knowledge that they would reveal only under duress. Charon, the grisly ferryman of the dead, was also a popular figure of folktale.

Myths of Heroes

Hero myths included elements from tradition, folktale, and fiction. The saga of the Argonauts, for example, is highly complex and includes elements from folktale and fiction. Episodes in the Trojan cycle, such as the departure of the Greek fleet from Aulis or Theseus's Cretan expedition and death on Scyros, may belong to traditions dating from the Minoan-Mycenaean world. On the other hand, events described in the Iliad probably owe far more to Homer's creative ability than to genuine tradition. Even heroes like Achilles, Hector, or Diomedes are largely fictional, though doubtlessly based on legendary prototypes. The Odyssey is the prime example of the wholesale importation of folktales into epic. All the best-known Greek hero myths, such as the labours of Heracles and the adventures of Perseus, Cadmus, Pelops, or Oedipus, depend more for their interest on folktales than on legend.

Reverse side of a silver denarius showing Odysseus walking with a staff and being greeted by his dog, Argus, in a fine narrative illustration of Homer's Odyssey. Coin was struck in the Roman Republic, 82 BCE. Diameter 19 mm.

Certain heroes—Heracles, the Dioscuri (the twins Castor and Pollux), Amphiaraus (one of the Argonauts), and Hyacinthus (a youth whom Apollo loved and accidentally killed)—may be regarded as partly legend and partly religious myth. Thus, whereas Heracles, a man of Tiryns, may originally have been a historical character, the myth of his demise on Oeta and subsequent elevation to full divinity is closely linked with a cult. In time, Heracles' popularity was responsible for connecting his story with the Argonauts, an earlier attack on Troy, and with Theban myth. Similarly, the exploits of the Dioscuri are those of typical heroes: fighting, carrying off women, and cattle rustling.

After their death they passed six months alternately beneath the Earth and in the world above, which suggests that their worship, like that of Persephone (the daughter of Zeus and Demeter), was connected with fertility or seasonal change.

Attic red-figure kylix by Epictetus showing Heracles slaying Busiris, c. 520 BC; in the British Museum, London.

Myths of Seasonal Renewal

Certain myths, in which goddesses or heroes were temporarily incarcerated in the underworld, were allegories of seasonal renewal. Perhaps the best-known myth of this type is the one that tells how Hades, the god of the underworld, carried Persephone off to be his consort, causing her mother, Demeter, the goddess of grain, to allow the earth to grow barren out of her grief. Because of her mother's grief, Zeus permitted Persephone to spend four months of the year in the house of Hades and eight in the light of day. In less benign climates, she was said to spend six months of the year in each. Some scholars hold that Persephone's time belowground represents the summer months, when Greek fields are parched and bare, but the Hymn to Demeter, the earliest source for the myth, states explicitly that Persephone returns when the spring flowers are flourishing (line 401). Myths of seasonal renewal, in which the deity dies and returns to life at particular times of the year, are plentiful. An important Greek example is the Cretan Zeus, mentioned above.

Hades and Persephone in the underworld, interior of a red-figure cup, Greek, from Vulci, c. 430 BC; in the British Museum.

Myths Involving Animal Transformations

Many Greek myths involve animal transformations, though there is no proof that theriolatry (animal worship) was ever practiced by the Greeks. Gods sometimes assumed the form of beasts in order to deceive goddesses or women. Zeus, for example, assumed the form of a bull when he carried off Europa, a Phoenician princess, and he appeared in the guise of a swan in order to attract Leda, wife of a king of Sparta. Poseidon took the shape of a stallion to beget the wonder horses Arion and Pegasus.

Europa being abducted by Zeus disguised as a bull, detail from an Attic krater, 5th century BC; in the National Archaeological Museum, Tarquinia, Italy.

These myths do not suggest theriolatry. No worship is offered to the deity concerned. The animals serve other purposes in the narratives. Bulls were the most powerful animals known to the Greeks and may have been worshipped in the remote past. But, for the Greeks, in even the earliest sources there is no indication that Zeus or Poseidon were once bulls or horses or that Hera was ever "ox-eyed" other than metaphorically or that "gray-eyed" Athena was ever "owl-faced."

Other Types

Other types of myth exemplified the belief that the gods sometimes appeared on Earth disguised as men and women and rewarded any help or hospitality offered them. Baucis, an old Phrygian woman, and Philemon, her husband, for example, were saved from a flood by offering hospitality to Zeus and Hermes, both of whom were in human form.

The punishment of mortals' presumption in claiming to be the gods' superiors, whether in musical skill or even the number of their children, is described in several myths. The gods' jealousy of mortals' musical talents appears in the beating and flaying of the aulos-playing satyr, Marsyas, by Athena and Apollo, as well as in the attaching of ass's ears to King Midas for failing to appreciate the superiority of Apollo's music to that of the god Pan. Jealousy was the motive for the slaying of Niobe's many children, because Niobe flaunted her fecundity to the goddess Leto, who had only two offspring. Similar to such stories are the moral tales about the fate of Icarus, who flew too high on homemade wings, or the myth about Phaethon, the son of Helios, who failed to perform a task too great for him (controlling the horses of the chariot of the Sun).

Transformation into a flower or tree—whether to escape a god's embrace (as with Daphne, a nymph transformed into a laurel tree), as the result of an accident (as with Hyacinthus, a friend of Apollo, who was changed into a flower), or because of pride (as with the beautiful youth Narcissus, who fell in love with his own reflection and was changed into a flower)—was a familiar theme in Greek myth.

Daedalus and Icarus, antique bas-relief; in the Villa Albani, Rome.

Also popular were myths of fairylands, such as the Garden of the Hesperides (in the far west) or the land of the Hyperboreans (in the far north), or encounters with unusual creatures, such as the Centaurs, or distinctive societies, such as the Amazons.

Atlas Brings Heracles the Apples of the Hesperides in the Presence of Athena.

Roman Mythology

Roman mythology is the body of traditional stories pertaining to ancient Rome's legendary origins and religious system, as represented in the literature and visual arts of the Romans. "Roman mythology" may also refer to the modern study of these representations, and to the subject matter as represented in the literature and art of other cultures in any period.

The Romans usually treated their traditional narratives as historical, even when these have miraculous or supernatural elements. The stories are often concerned with politics and morality, and how an individual's personal integrity relates to his or her responsibility to the community or Roman state. Heroism is an important theme. When the stories illuminate Roman religious practices, they are more concerned with ritual, augury, and institutions than with theology or cosmogony.

The study of Roman religion and myth is complicated by the early influence of Greek religion on the Italian peninsula during Rome's protohistory, and by the later artistic imitation of Greek literary models by Roman authors. The Romans were curiously eager to identify their own gods with those of the Greeks, and reinterpret stories about Greek deities under the names of their Roman counterparts. Rome's early myths and legends also have a dynamic relationship with Etruscan religion, less documented than that of the Greeks.

While Roman mythology may lack a body of divine narratives as extensive as that found in Greek literature, Romulus and Remus suckling the she-wolf is as famous as any image from Greek mythology except for the Trojan Horse. Because Latin literature was more widely known in Europe throughout the Middle Ages and into the Renaissance, the interpretations of Greek myths by the Romans often had the greater influence on narrative and pictorial representations of "classical mythology" than Greek sources. In particular, the versions of Greek myths in Ovid's Metamorphoses, written during the reign of Augustus, came to be regarded as canonical.

The Nature of Roman Myth

Because ritual plays the central role in Roman religion that myth held for the Greeks, it is sometimes doubted that the Romans had much of a native mythology. This perception is a product of Romanticism and the classical scholarship of the 19th century, which valued Greek civilization as more "authentically creative." From the Renaissance to the 18th century, however, Roman myths were an inspiration particularly for European painting.

The Roman tradition is rich in historical myths, or legends, concerning the foundation and rise of the city. These narratives focus on human actors, with only occasional intervention from deities but a pervasive sense of divinely ordered destiny.

In Rome's earliest period, history and myth have a mutual and complementary relationship. Major sources for Roman myth include the Aeneid of Vergil and the first few books of Livy's history. Other important sources are the Fasti of Ovid, a six-book poem structured by the Roman religious calendar, and the fourth book of elegies by Propertius. Scenes from Roman myth also appear in Roman wall painting, coins, and sculpture, particularly reliefs.

Founding Myths

The founding of Rome can be investigated through archaeology, but traditional stories handed down by the ancient Romans themselves explain the earliest history of their city in terms of legend and myth. The most familiar of these myths, and perhaps the most famous of all Roman myths, is the story of Romulus and Remus, the twins who were suckled by a she-wolf. This story had to be reconciled with a dual tradition, set earlier in time, that had the Trojan refugee Aeneas escaped to Italy and founded the line of Romans through his son Iulus, the namesake of the Julio-Claudian dynasty.

Romulus and Remus

Roman Icon Actually Younger Than the City.

The icon of Rome's foundation, a life-size bronze statue of a she-wolf with two human infants suckling her, is about 1,700 years younger than its city, Rome's officials admitted on Saturday. The official announcement, made at the Capitoline Museums, where the 30 inch-high bronze is the centrepiece of a dedicated room, quashes the belief that the sculpture was adopted by the earliest Romans as a symbol for their city.

There are several variations on the basic legendary tale. Plutarch presents Romulus and Remus' ancient descent from prince Aeneas, fugitive from Troy after its destruction by the Achaeans. Their maternal grandfather is his descendant Numitor, who inherits the kingship of Alba Longa. NumitorÕs brother Amulius inherits its treasury, including the gold brought by Aeneas from Troy. Amulius uses his control of the treasury to dethrone Numitor, but fears that Numitor's daughter, Rhea Silvia, will bear children who could overthrow him.

Amulius forces Rhea Silvia into perpetual virginity as a Vestal priestess, but she bears children anyway. In one variation of the story, Mars, god of war, seduces and impregnates her: in another, Amulius himself seduces her, and in yet another, Hercules.

The king sees his niece's pregnancy and confines her. She gives birth to twin boys of remarkable beauty; her uncle orders her death and theirs. One account holds that he has Rhea buried alive - the standard punishment for Vestal Virgins who violated their vow of celibacy - and orders the death of the twins by exposure; both means would avoid his direct blood-guilt. In another, he has Rhea and her twins thrown into the River Tiber.

In every version, a servant is charged with the deed of killing the twins, but cannot bring himself to harm them. He places them in a basket and leaves it on the banks of the Tiber. The river rises in flood and carries the twins downstream, unharmed.

The river deity Tiberinus makes the basket catch in the roots of a fig tree that grows in the Velabrum swamp at the base of the Palatine Hill. The twins are found and suckled by a she-wolf (Lupa) and fed by a woodpecker (Picus). A shepherd of Amulius named Faustulus discovers them and takes them to his hut, where he and his wife Acca Larentia raise them as their own children.

In another variant, Hercules impregnates Acca Larentia and marries her off to the shepherd Faustulus. She has twelve sons; when one of them dies, Romulus takes his place to found the priestly college of Arval brothers Fratres Arvales. Acca Larentia is therefore identified with the Arval goddess Dea Dia, who is served by the Arvals. In later Republican religious tradition, a Quirinal priest (flamen) impersonated Romulus (by then deified as Quirinus) to perform funerary rites for his foster mother (identified as Dia).

Another and probably late tradition has Acca Larentia as a sacred prostitute (one of many Roman slangs for prostitute was lupa (she-wolf).

Yet another tradition relates that Romulus and Remus are nursed by the Wolf-Goddess Lupa or Luperca in her cave-lair (lupercal). Luperca was given cult for her protection of sheep from wolves and her spouse was the Wolf-and-Shepherd-God Lupercus, who brought fertility to the flocks. She has been identified with Acca Larentia.

In all versions of the founding myth, the twins grew up as shepherds. They came into conflict with the shepherds of Amulius, leading to battles in which Remus was captured and taken to Amulius, under the accusation of being a thief. Their identity was discovered. Romulus raised a band of shepherds to liberate his brother; Amulius was killed and Romulus and Remus were conjointly offered the crown. They refused it while their grandfather lived, and refused to live in the city as his subjects. They restored Numitor as king, paid due honours to their mother Rhea and left to found their own city, accompanied by a motley band of fugitives, runaway slaves, and any who want a second chance in a new city with new rulers.

The brothers argued over the best site for the new city. Romulus favored the Palatine Hill; Remus wanted the Aventine Hill. They agreed to select the site by divine augury, took up position on their respective hills and prepared a sacred space; signs were sent to each in the form of vultures, or eagles. Remus saw six; Romulus saw twelve, and claimed superior augury (foresight) as the basis of his right to decide.

Remus made a counterclaim: he saw his six vultures first. Romulus set to work with his supporters, digging a trench (or building a wall, according to Dionysius) around the Palatine to define his city boundary. Remus criticized some parts of the work and obstructed others. At last, Remus leaped across the boundary, as an insult to the city's defenses and their creator. For this, he was killed. The Roman ab urbe condita begins from the founding of the city, and places that date as 21 April 753 BC.

Livy gives two versions of Remus' death. In the one "more generally received", Remus criticizes and belittles the new wall, and in a final insult to the new city and its founder alike, he leaps over it. Romulus kills him, saying "So perish every one that shall hereafter leap over my wall". In the other version, Remus is simply stated as dead; no murder is alleged. Two other, lesser known accounts have Remus killed by a blow to the head with a spade, wielded either by Romulus' commander Fabius (according to St. Jerome's version) or by a man named Celer. Romulus buries Remus with honor and regret.

Romulus completes his city and names it Roma after himself. Then he divides his fighting men into regiments of 3000 infantry and 300 cavalry, which he calls "legions". From the rest of the populace he selects 100 of the most noble and wealthy fathers to serve as his council. He calls these men Patricians: they are fathers of Rome, not only because they care for their own legitimate citizen-sons but because they have a fatherly care for Rome and all its people. They are also its elders, and are therefore known as Senators. Romulus thereby inaugurates a system of government and social hierarchy based on the patron-client relationship.

Rome draws exiles, refugees, the dispossessed, criminals and runaway slaves. The city expands its boundaries to accommodate them; five of the seven hills of Rome are settled: the Capitoline Hill, the Aventine Hill, the Caelian Hill, the Quirinal Hill, and the Palatine Hill. As most of these immigrants are men, Rome finds itself with a shortage of marriageable women.

At the suggestion of his grandfather Numitor, Romulus holds a solemn festival in honor of Neptune (according to another tradition the festival was held in honor of the God Consus) and invites the neighboring Sabines and Latins to attend; they arrive en masse, along with their daughters. The Sabine and Latin women who happen to be virgins - 683 according to Livy - are kidnapped and brought back to Rome where they are forced to marry Roman men.

Other Myths

The characteristic myths of Rome are often political or moral, that is, they deal with the development of Roman government in accordance with divine law, as expressed by Roman religion, and with demonstrations of the individual's adherence to moral expectations (mos maiorum) or failures to do so.

Rape of the Sabine women, explaining the importance of the Sabines in the formation of Roman culture, and the growth of Rome through conflict and alliance.

The Rape of the Sabine Women is an episode in the legendary history of Rome in which the first generation of Roman men acquired wives for themselves from the neighboring Sabine families. The English word "rape" is a conventional translation of Latin raptio, which in this context means "abduction" rather than its prevalent modern meaning in English language of sexual violation. Recounted by Livy and Plutarch (Parallel Lives II, 15 and 19), it provided a subject for Renaissance and post-Renaissance works of art that combined a suitably inspiring example of the hardihood and courage of ancient Romans with the opportunity to depict multiple figures, including heroically semi-nude figures, in intensely passionate struggle. Comparable themes from Classical Antiquity are the Battle of the Lapiths and Centaurs and the theme of Amazonomachy, the battle of Theseus with the Amazons. A comparable opportunity drawn from Christian scripture was the Massacre of the Innocents.

Numa Pompilius, the Sabine second king of Rome who consorted with the nymph Egeria and established many of Rome's legal and religious institutions.

Servius Tullius, the sixth king of Rome, whose mysterious origins were freely mythologized and who was said to have been the lover of the goddess Fortuna.

The Tarpeian Rock, and why it was used for the execution of traitors.

The Tarpeian Rock (Latin, Rupes Tarpeia or Saxum Tarpeium) was a steep cliff of the southern summit of the Capitoline Hill, overlooking the Roman Forum in Ancient Rome. It was used during the Roman Republic as an execution site. Murderers, traitors, perjurors, and larcenous slaves, if convicted by the quaestores parricidii, were flung from the cliff to their deaths. Those who had a mental or significant physical disability also suffered the same fate as they were thought to have been cursed by the gods.

Lucretia, whose self-sacrifice prompted the overthrow of the early Roman monarchy and led to the establishment of the Republic.

Horatius at the bridge, on the importance of individual valor.

Mucius Scaevola ("Lefty"), who thrust his right hand into the fire to prove his loyalty to Rome.

Caeculus was a son of Vulcan and the founder of Praeneste.

Manlius and the geese, about divine intervention at the Gallic siege of Rome.

During the Gallic siege of Rome in 390 BC, the account of which became partly mythologized, Marcus Manlius held out for months with a small garrison on the citadel (arx), while the rest of Rome was abandoned. When Gauls under the command of Brennus were attempting to scale the Capitoline, Manlius was roused by the cackling of the sacred geese, rushed to the spot, and threw down the foremost assailants.

After the sack of Rome left the plebeians in pitiful condition, they were forced to borrow large sums of money from the patricians, and once again became the poor debtor class of Rome. Manlius, the hero of Rome, fought for them. Livy says, with some inaccuracy, that he was the first patrician to act as a populist (popularis). Seeing a centurion led to prison for debt, he freed him with his own money, and even sold his estate to relieve other poor debtors, while he accused the Senate of embezzling public money. He was charged with aspiring to kingly power, and condemned by the comitia, but not until the assembly had adjourned to a place outside the walls, where they could no longer see the Capitol which he had saved. The Senate condemned him to death in 385 BC, and he was thrown from the Tarpeian Rock one year later. He is considered the second martyr in the cause of social reform at Rome.

His house on the Capitoline Hill was razed, and the Senate decreed that no patrician should live there henceforth. The Manlii themselves resolved that no patrician Manlius should bear the name of Marcus. According to Mommsen, the story of the saving of the

Capitol was a later invention to justify his cognomen, which may be better explained by his domicile.

Stories pertaining to the Nonae Caprotinae and Poplifugia festivals.

Coriolanus, a story of politics and morality.

The Etruscan city of Corythus as the "cradle" of Trojan and Italian civilization.

The arrival of the Great Mother (Cybele) in Rome.

Religion in Ancient Rome.

Religion and Myth

Divine narrative played a more important role in the system of Greek religious belief than among the Romans, for whom ritual and cult were primary. Although Roman religion was not based on scriptures and exegesis, priestly literature was one of the earliest written forms of Latin prose.

The books (libri) and commentaries (commentarii) of the College of Pontiffs and of the augurs contained religious procedures, prayers, and rulings and opinions on points of religious law. Although at least some of this archived material was available for consultation by the Roman senate, it was often occultum genus litterarum, an arcane form of literature to which by definition only priests had access.

Prophecies pertaining to world history and Rome's destiny turn up fortuitously at critical junctures in history, discovered suddenly in the nebulous Sibylline books, which according to legend were purchased by Tarquin the Proud in the late 6th century BC from the Cumaean Sibyl. Some aspects of archaic Roman religion were preserved by the lost theological works of the 1st-century BC scholar Varro, known through other classical and Christian authors.

At the head of the earliest pantheon were the so-called Archaic Triad of Jupiter, Mars, and Quirinus, whose flamens were of the highest order, and Janus and Vesta. According to tradition, the founder of Roman religion was Numa Pompilius, the Sabine second king of Rome, who was believed to have had as his consort and adviser a Roman goddess or nymph of fountains and prophecy, Egeria.

The Etruscan-influenced Capitoline Triad of Jupiter, Juno and Minerva later became central to official religion, replacing the Archaic Triad - an unusual example within Indo-European religion of a supreme triad formed of two female deities and only one male. The cult of Diana was established on the Aventine Hill, but the most famous Roman manifestation of this goddess may be Diana Nemorensis, owing to the attention paid to her cult by J.G. Frazer in the mythographical classic The Golden Bough.

The gods represented distinctly the practical needs of daily life, and they were scrupulously accorded the rites and offerings considered proper. Early Roman divinities included a host of "specialist gods" whose names were invoked in the carrying out of various specific activities. Fragments of old ritual accompanying such acts as plowing or sowing reveal that at every stage of the operation a separate deity was invoked, the name of each deity being regularly derived from the verb for the operation. Tutelary deities were particularly important in ancient Rome.

Thus, Janus and Vesta guarded the door and hearth, the Lares protected the field and house, Pales the pasture, Saturn the sowing, Ceres the growth of the grain, Pomona the fruit, and Consus and Ops the harvest. Even the majestic Jupiter, the ruler of the gods, was honored for the aid his rains might give to the farms and vineyards. In his more encompassing character he was considered, through his weapon of lightning, the director of human activity and, by his widespread domain, the protector of the Romans in their military activities beyond the borders of their own community. Prominent in early times were the gods Mars and Quirinus, who were often identified with each other. Mars was a god of war; he was honored in March and October. Quirinus is thought by modern scholars to have been the patron of the armed community in time of peace.

Roman Gods and Goddesses.

The 19th-century scholar Georg Wissowa thought that the Romans distinguished two classes of gods, the di indigetes and the di novensides or novensiles: the indigetes were the original gods of the Roman state, their names and nature indicated by the titles of the earliest priests and by the fixed festivals of the calendar, with 30 such gods honored by special festivals; the novensides were later divinities whose cults were introduced to the city in the historical period, usually at a known date and in response to a specific crisis or felt need. Arnaldo Momigliano and others, however, have argued that this distinction cannot be maintained. During the war with Hannibal, any distinction between "indigenous" and "immigrant" gods begins to fade, and the Romans embraced diverse gods from various cultures as a sign of strength and universal divine favor.

Foreign Gods

The absorption of neighboring local gods took place as the Roman state conquered the surrounding territory. The Romans commonly granted the local gods of the conquered territory the same honors as the earlier gods of the Roman state religion. In addition to Castor and Pollux, the conquered settlements in Italy seem to have contributed to the Roman pantheon Diana, Minerva, Hercules, Venus, and deities of lesser rank, some of whom were Italic divinities, others originally derived from the Greek culture of Magna Graecia.

In 203 BC, the cult object embodying Cybele was brought from Pessinus in Phrygia and welcomed with due ceremony to Rome, centuries before the territory was annexed formally. Both Lucretius and Catullus, poets contemporary in the mid-1st century BC, offer disapproving glimpses of her wildly ecstatic cult.

In some instances, deities of an enemy power were formally invited through the ritual of evocatio to take up their abode in new sanctuaries at Rome.

Communities of foreigners (peregrini) and former slaves (libertini) continued their own religious practices within the city. In this way Mithras came to Rome and his popularity within the Roman army spread his cult as far afield as Roman Britain. The important Roman deities were eventually identified with the more anthropomorphic Greek gods and goddesses, and assumed many of their attributes and myths.

Greek mythology is known today primarily from Greek literature and representations on visual media dating from the Geometric period from c. 900 BC to c. 800 BC onward. In fact, literary and archaeological sources integrate, sometimes mutually supportive and sometimes in conflict; however, in many cases, the existence of this corpus of data is a strong indication that many elements of Greek mythology have strong factual and historical roots.

Literary Sources

Mythical narration plays an important role in nearly every genre of Greek literature. Nevertheless, the only general mythographical handbook to survive from Greek antiquity was the Library of Pseudo-Apollodorus. This work attempts to reconcile the contradictory tales of the poets and provides a grand summary of traditional Greek mythology and heroic legends. Apollodorus of Athens lived from c. 180 BC to c. 125 BC and wrote on many of these topics. His writings may have formed the basis for the collection; however the "Library" discusses events that occurred long after his death, hence the name Pseudo-Apollodorus.

Among the earliest literary sources are Homer's two epic poems, the Iliad and the Odyssey. Other poets completed the "epic cycle", but these later and lesser poems now are lost almost entirely. Despite their traditional name, the "Homeric Hymns" have no direct connection with Homer. They are choral hymns from the earlier part of the so-called Lyric age. Hesiod, a possible contemporary with Homer, offers in his Theogony (Origin of the Gods) the fullest account of the earliest Greek myths, dealing with the creation of the world; the origin of the gods, Titans, and Giants; as well as elaborate genealogies, folktales, and etiological myths. Hesiod's Works and Days, a didactic poem about farming life, also includes the myths of Prometheus, Pandora, and the Five Ages. The poet gives advice on the best way to succeed in a dangerous world, rendered yet more dangerous by its gods.

Achilles and Penthesileia by Exekias, c. 540 BC, British Museum, London.

Lyrical poets often took their subjects from myth, but their treatment became gradually less narrative and more allusive. Greek lyric poets, including Pindar, Bacchylides and

Simonides, and bucolic poets such as Theocritus and Bion, relate individual mythological incidents. Additionally, myth was central to classical Athenian drama. The tragic playwrights Aeschylus, Sophocles, and Euripides took most of their plots from myths of the age of heroes and the Trojan War. Many of the great tragic stories (e.g. Agamemnon and his children, Oedipus, Jason, Medea, etc.) took on their classic form in these tragedies. The comic playwright Aristophanes also used myths, in The Birds and The Frogs.

Historians Herodotus and Diodorus Siculus, and geographers Pausanias and Strabo, who traveled throughout the Greek world and noted the stories they heard, supplied numerous local myths and legends, often giving little-known alternative versions. Herodotus in particular, searched the various traditions presented him and found the historical or mythological roots in the confrontation between Greece and the East. Herodotus attempted to reconcile origins and the blending of differing cultural concepts.

The myth of Prometheus first was attested by Hesiod and then constituted the basis for a tragic trilogy of plays, possibly by Aeschylus, consisting of Prometheus Bound, Prometheus Unbound, and Prometheus Pyrphoros.

The poetry of the Hellenistic and Roman ages was primarily composed as a literary rather than cultic exercise. Nevertheless, it contains many important details that would otherwise be lost. This category includes the works of:

- The Roman poets Ovid, Statius, Valerius Flaccus, Seneca and Virgil with Servius's commentary.

- The Greek poets of the Late Antique period: Nonnus, Antoninus Liberalis, and Quintus Smyrnaeus.

- The Greek poets of the Hellenistic period: Apollonius of Rhodes, Callimachus, Pseudo-Eratosthenes, and Parthenius.

Prose writers from the same periods who make reference to myths include Apuleius, Petronius, Lollianus, and Heliodorus. Two other important non-poetical sources are the Fabulae and Astronomica of the Roman writer styled as Pseudo-Hyginus, the Imagines of Philostratus the Elder and Philostratus the Younger, and the Descriptions of Callistratus.

Finally, a number of Byzantine Greek writers provide important details of myth, much derived from earlier now lost Greek works. These preservers of myth include Arnobius, Hesychius, the author of the Suda, John Tzetzes, and Eustathius. They often treat mythology from a Christian moralizing perspective.

Archaeological Sources

The discovery of the Mycenaean civilization by the German amateur archaeologist Heinrich Schliemann in the nineteenth century, and the discovery of the Minoan civilization in Crete by the British archaeologist Sir Arthur Evans in the twentieth century, helped to explain many existing questions about Homer's epics and provided archaeological evidence for many of the mythological details about gods and heroes. Unfortunately, the evidence about myths and rituals at Mycenaean and Minoan sites is entirely monumental, as the Linear B script (an ancient form of Greek found in both Crete and mainland Greece) was used mainly to record inventories, although certain names of gods and heroes have been tentatively identified.

The Roman poet Virgil, here depicted in the fifth-century manuscript, the Vergilius Romanus, preserved details of Greek mythology in many of his writings.

Geometric designs on pottery of the eighth century BC depict scenes from the Trojan cycle, as well as the adventures of Heracles. These visual representations of myths are important for two reasons. Firstly, many Greek myths are attested on vases earlier than in literary sources: of the twelve labors of Heracles, for example, only the Cerberus adventure occurs in a contemporary literary text. Secondly, visual sources sometimes represent myths or mythical scenes that are not attested in any extant literary source. In some cases, the first known representation of a myth in geometric art predates its first known representation in late archaic poetry, by several centuries. In the Archaic, Classical, and Hellenistic periods, Homeric and various other mythological scenes appear, supplementing the existing literary evidence.

Greek mythology has changed over time to accommodate the evolution of their culture, of which mythology, both overtly and in its unspoken assumptions, is an index of the changes. In Greek mythology's surviving literary forms, as found mostly at the end of the progressive changes, it is inherently political, as Gilbert Cuthbertson has argued.

The earlier inhabitants of the Balkan Peninsula were an agricultural people who, using Animism, assigned a spirit to every aspect of nature. Eventually, these vague spirits assumed human forms and entered the local mythology as gods. When tribes from the north of the Balkan Peninsula invaded, they brought with them a new pantheon of gods, based on conquest, force, prowess in battle, and violent heroism. Other older gods of the agricultural world fused with those of the more powerful invaders or else faded into insignificance.

After the middle of the Archaic period, myths about relationships between male gods and male heroes became more and more frequent, indicating the parallel development of pedagogic pederasty (eros paidikos), thought to have been introduced around 630 BC. By the end of the fifth century BC, poets had assigned at least one eromenos, an adolescent boy who was their sexual companion, to every important god except Ares and to many legendary figures. Previously existing myths, such as those of Achilles and Patroclus, also then were cast in a pederastic light. Alexandrian poets at first, then more generally literary mythographers in the early Roman Empire, often re-adapted stories of Greek mythological characters in this fashion.

The achievement of epic poetry was to create story-cycles and, as a result, to develop a new sense of mythological chronology. Thus Greek mythology unfolds as a phase in the development of the world and of humans. While self-contradictions in these stories make an absolute timeline impossible, an approximate chronology may be discerned. The resulting mythological "history of the world" may be divided into three or four broader periods:

- The myths of origin or age of gods (Theogonies, "births of gods"): myths about the origins of the world, the gods, and the human race.

- The age when gods and mortals mingled freely: stories of the early interactions between gods, demigods, and mortals.

- The age of heroes (heroic age), where divine activity was more limited. The last and greatest of the heroic legends is the story of the Trojan War and after (which is regarded by some researchers as a separate, fourth period).

While the age of gods often has been of more interest to contemporary students of myth, the Greek authors of the archaic and classical eras had a clear preference for the age of heroes, establishing a chronology and record of human accomplishments after the questions of how the world came into being were explained. For example, the heroic Iliad and Odyssey dwarfed the divine-focused Theogony and Homeric Hymns in both size and popularity. Under the influence of Homer the "hero cult" leads to a restructuring in spiritual life, expressed in the separation of the realm of the gods from the realm of the dead (heroes), of the Chthonic from the Olympian. In the Works and Days, Hesiod makes use of a scheme of Four Ages of Man (or Races): Golden, Silver, Bronze, and Iron. These races or ages are separate creations of the gods, the Golden Age belonging to the reign of Cronos, the subsequent races to the creation of Zeus. The presence of evil was explained by the myth of Pandora, when all of the best of human capabilities, save hope, had been spilled out of her overturned jar. In Metamorphoses, Ovid follows Hesiod's concept of the four ages.

Phaedra with an attendant, probably her nurse, a fresco from Pompeii.

Origins of the World and the Gods

"Myths of origin" or "creation myths" represent an attempt to explain the beginnings of the universe in human language. The most widely accepted version at the time, although a philosophical account of the beginning of things, is reported by Hesiod, in his Theogony. He begins with Chaos, a yawning nothingness. Out of the void emerged Gaia (the Earth) and some other primary divine beings: Eros (Love), the Abyss (the Tartarus), and the Erebus. Without male assistance, Gaia gave birth to Uranus (the Sky) who then fertilized her. From that union were born first the Titans—six males: Coeus, Crius, Cronus, Hyperion, Iapetus, and Oceanus; and six females: Mnemosyne, Phoebe, Rhea, Theia, Themis, and Tethys. After Cronus was born, Gaia and Uranus decreed no more Titans were to be born. They were followed by the one-eyed Cyclopes and the Hecatonchires or Hundred-Handed Ones, who were both thrown into Tartarus by Uranus. This made Gaia furious. Cronus ("the wily, youngest and most terrible of Gaia's children"), was convinced by Gaia to castrate his father. He did this, and became the ruler of the Titans with his sister-wife Rhea as his consort, and the other Titans became his court.

A motif of father-against-son conflict was repeated when Cronus was confronted by his son, Zeus. Because Cronus had betrayed his father, he feared that his offspring would do the same, and so each time Rhea gave birth, he snatched up the child and ate it. Rhea hated this and tricked him by hiding Zeus and wrapping a stone in a baby's blanket, which Cronus ate. When Zeus was full grown, he fed Cronus a drugged drink which caused him to vomit, throwing up Rhea's other children, including Poseidon, Hades, Hestia, Demeter, and Hera, and the stone, which had been sitting in Cronus's stomach all this time. Zeus then challenged Cronus to war for the kingship of the gods. At last, with the help of the Cyclopes (whom Zeus freed from Tartarus), Zeus and his siblings were victorious, while Cronus and the Titans were hurled down to imprisonment in Tartarus.

Amor Vincit Omnia (Love Conquers All),
a depiction of the god of love, Eros.

Zeus was plagued by the same concern, and after a prophecy that the offspring of his first wife, Metis, would give birth to a god "greater than he", Zeus swallowed her. She was already pregnant with Athena, however, and she burst forth from his head—fully-grown and dressed for war.

The earliest Greek thought about poetry considered the theogonies to be the prototypical poetic genre—the prototypical mythos—and imputed almost magical powers to it. Orpheus, the archetypal poet, also was the archetypal singer of theogonies, which he uses to calm seas and storms in Apollonius' Argonautica, and to move the stony hearts of the underworld gods in his descent to Hades. When Hermes invents the lyre in the Homeric Hymn to Hermes, the first thing he does is sing about the birth of the gods. Hesiod's Theogony is not only the fullest surviving account of the gods, but also the fullest surviving account of the archaic poet's function, with its long preliminary invocation to the Muses. Theogony also was the subject of many lost poems, including those attributed to Orpheus, Musaeus, Epimenides, Abaris, and other legendary seers, which were used in private ritual purifications and mystery-rites. There are indications that Plato was familiar with some version of the Orphic theogony. A silence would have been expected about religious rites and beliefs, however, and that nature of the culture would not have been reported by members of the society while the beliefs were held. After they ceased to become religious beliefs, few would have known the rites and rituals. Allusions often existed, however, to aspects that were quite public.

Images existed on pottery and religious artwork that were interpreted and more likely, misinterpreted in many diverse myths and tales. A few fragments of these works survive in quotations by Neoplatonist philosophers and recently unearthed papyrus scraps. One of these scraps, the Derveni Papyrus now proves that at least in the fifth century BC a theogonic-cosmogonic poem of Orpheus was in existence.

The first philosophical cosmologists reacted against, or sometimes built upon, popular mythical conceptions that had existed in the Greek world for some time. Some of these popular conceptions can be gleaned from the poetry of Homer and Hesiod. In Homer, the Earth was viewed as a flat disk afloat on the river of Oceanus and overlooked by a hemispherical sky with sun, moon, and stars. The Sun (Helios) traversed the heavens as a charioteer and sailed around the Earth in a golden bowl at night. Sun, earth, heaven, rivers, and winds could be addressed in prayers and called to witness oaths. Natural fissures were popularly regarded as entrances to the subterranean house of Hades and his predecessors, home of the dead. Influences from other cultures always afforded new themes.

Attic black-figured amphora depicting Athena being "reborn" from the head of
Zeus, who had swallowed her mother Metis, on the right, Eileithyia,
the goddess of childbirth, assists, circa 550–525 BC.

Greek Pantheon

According to Classical-era mythology, after the overthrow of the Titans, the new pantheon of gods and goddesses was confirmed. Among the principal Greek gods were the Olympians, residing on Mount Olympus under the eye of Zeus. (The limitation of their number to twelve seems to have been a comparatively modern idea.) Besides the Olympians, the Greeks worshipped various gods of the countryside, the satyr-god Pan, Nymphs (spirits of rivers), Naiads (who dwelled in springs), Dryads (who were spirits of the trees), Nereids (who inhabited the sea), river gods, Satyrs, and others. In addition, there were the dark powers of the underworld, such as the Erinyes (or Furies), said to pursue those guilty of crimes against blood-relatives. In order to honor the Ancient Greek pantheon, poets composed the Homeric Hymns (a group of thirty-three songs). Gregory Nagy regards "the larger Homeric Hymns as simple preludes (compared with Theogony), each of which invokes one god".

The gods of Greek mythology are described as having essentially corporeal but ideal bodies. According to Walter Burkert, the defining characteristic of Greek anthropomorphism is that "the Greek gods are persons, not abstractions, ideas or concepts". Regardless of their underlying forms, the Ancient Greek gods have many fantastic abilities; most significantly, the gods are not affected by disease, and can be wounded only under highly unusual circumstances. The Greeks considered immortality as the distinctive characteristic of their gods; this immortality, as well as unfading youth, was insured by the constant use of nectar and ambrosia, by which the divine blood was renewed in their veins.

Each god descends from his or her own genealogy, pursues differing interests, has a certain area of expertise, and is governed by a unique personality; however, these descriptions arise from a multiplicity of archaic local variants, which do not always agree with one another. When these gods are called upon in poetry, prayer or cult, they are referred to by a combination of their name and epithets, that identify them by these distinctions from other manifestations of themselves (e.g., Apollo Musagetes is "Apollo, (as) leader of the Muses"). Alternatively the epithet may identify a particular and localized aspect of the god, sometimes thought to be already ancient during the classical epoch of Greece.

Zeus, disguised as a swan, seduces Leda, the Queen of Sparta.
A sixteenth-century copy of the lost original by Michelangelo.

Most gods were associated with specific aspects of life. For example, Aphrodite was the goddess of love and beauty, Ares was the god of war, Hades the ruler of the underworld, and Athena the goddess of wisdom and courage. Some gods, such as Apollo and Dionysus, revealed complex personalities and mixtures of functions, while others, such as Hestia (literally "hearth") and Helios (literally "sun"), were little more than personifications. The most impressive temples tended to be dedicated to a limited number of gods, who were the focus of large pan-Hellenic cults. It was, however, common for individual regions and villages to devote their own cults to minor gods. Many cities also honored the more well-known gods with unusual local rites and associated strange myths with them that were unknown elsewhere. During the heroic age, the cult of heroes (or demigods) supplemented that of the gods.

Age of Gods and Mortals

Bridging the age when gods lived alone and the age when divine interference in human affairs was limited was a transitional age in which gods and mortals moved together. These were the early days of the world when the groups mingled more freely than they did later. Most of these tales were later told by Ovid's Metamorphoses and they are often divided into two thematic groups: tales of love, and tales of punishment.

Dionysus with satyrs. Interior of a cup painted by the Brygos Painter, Cabinet des Médailles.

Tales of love often involve incest, or the seduction or rape of a mortal woman by a male god, resulting in heroic offspring. The stories generally suggest that relationships between gods and mortals are something to avoid; even consenting relationships rarely have happy endings. In a few cases, a female divinity mates with a mortal man, as in the Homeric Hymn to Aphrodite, where the goddess lies with Anchises to produce Aeneas.

The second type (tales of punishment) involves the appropriation or invention of some important cultural artifact, as when Prometheus steals fire from the gods, when Tantalus steals nectar and ambrosia from Zeus' table and gives it to his own subjects—revealing to them the secrets of the gods, when Prometheus or Lycaon invents sacrifice, when Demeter teaches agriculture and the Mysteries to Triptolemus, or when Marsyas invents the aulos and enters into a musical contest with Apollo. Ian Morris considers Prometheus' adventures as "a place between the history of the gods and that of man".

An anonymous papyrus fragment, dated to the third century, vividly portrays Dionysus' punishment of the king of Thrace, Lycurgus, whose recognition of the new god came too late, resulting in horrific penalties that extended into the afterlife. The story of the arrival of Dionysus to establish his cult in Thrace was also the subject of an Aeschylean trilogy. In another tragedy, Euripides' The Bacchae, the king of Thebes, Pentheus, is punished by Dionysus, because he disrespected the god and spied on his Maenads, the female worshippers of the god.

Demeter and Metanira in a detail on an Apulian red-figure hydria, circa 340 BC (Altes Museum, Berlin).

In another story, based on an old folktale-motif, and echoing a similar theme, Demeter was searching for her daughter, Persephone, having taken the form of an old woman called Doso, and received a hospitable welcome from Celeus, the King of Eleusis in Attica. As a gift to Celeus, because of his hospitality, Demeter planned to make his son Demophon a god, but she was unable to complete the ritual because his mother Metanira walked in and saw her son in the fire and screamed in fright, which angered Demeter, who lamented that foolish mortals do not understand the concept and ritual.

Heroic Age

The age in which the heroes lived is known as the heroic age. The epic and genealogical poetry created cycles of stories clustered around particular heroes or events and established the family relationships between the heroes of different stories; they thus arranged the stories in sequence. According to Ken Dowden, "There is even a saga effect: We can follow the fates of some families in successive generations".

After the rise of the hero cult, gods and heroes constitute the sacral sphere and are invoked together in oaths and prayers which are addressed to them. Burkert notes that "the roster of heroes, again in contrast to the gods, is never given fixed and final form. Great gods are no longer born, but new heroes can always be raised up from the army of the dead." Another important difference between the hero cult and the cult of gods is that the hero becomes the centre of local group identity.

The monumental events of Heracles are regarded as the dawn of the age of heroes. To the Heroic Age are also ascribed three great events: the Argonautic expedition, the Theban Cycle, and the Trojan War.

Heracles and the Heracleidae

Some scholars believe that behind Heracles' complicated mythology there was probably a real man, perhaps a chieftain-vassal of the kingdom of Argos. Some scholars suggest the story of Heracles is an allegory for the sun's yearly passage through the twelve constellations of the zodiac. Others point to earlier myths from other cultures, showing the story of Heracles as a local adaptation of hero myths already well established. Traditionally, Heracles was the son of Zeus and Alcmene, granddaughter of Perseus. His fantastic solitary exploits, with their many folk-tale themes, provided much material for popular legend. According to Burkert, "He is portrayed as a sacrificer, mentioned as a founder of altars, and imagined as a voracious eater himself; it is in this role that he appears in comedy.

While his tragic end provided much material for tragedy—Heracles is regarded by Thalia Papadopoulou as "a play of great significance in examination of other Euripidean dramas". In art and literature Heracles was represented as an enormously strong man of moderate height; his characteristic weapon was the bow but frequently also the club. Vase paintings demonstrate the unparalleled popularity of Heracles, his fight with the lion being depicted many hundreds of times.

Heracles also entered Etruscan and Roman mythology and cult, and the exclamation "mehercule" became as familiar to the Romans as "Herakleis" was to the Greeks. In Italy he was worshipped as a god of merchants and traders, although others also prayed to him for his characteristic gifts of good luck or rescue from danger.

Heracles attained the highest social prestige through his appointment as official ancestor of the Dorian kings. This probably served as a legitimation for the Dorian migrations into the Peloponnese. Hyllus, the eponymous hero of one Dorian phyle, became the son of Heracles and one of the Heracleidae or Heraclids (the numerous descendants of Heracles, especially the descendants of Hyllus—other Heracleidae included Macaria, Lamos, Manto, Bianor, Tlepolemus, and Telephus). These Heraclids conquered the Peloponnesian kingdoms of Mycenae, Sparta and Argos, claiming, according to legend, a right to rule them through their ancestor. Their rise to dominance is frequently called the "Dorian invasion". The Lydian and later the Macedonian kings, as rulers of the same rank, also became Heracleidae.

Other members of this earliest generation of heroes such as Perseus, Deucalion, Theseus and Bellerophon, have many traits in common with Heracles. Like him, their exploits are solitary, fantastic and border on fairy tale, as they slay monsters such as the Chimera and Medusa. Bellerophon's adventures are commonplace types, similar to the adventures of

Heracles and Theseus. Sending a hero to his presumed death is also a recurrent theme of this early heroic tradition, used in the cases of Perseus and Bellerophon.

Heracles with his baby Telephus (Louvre Museum, Paris).

Argonauts

The only surviving Hellenistic epic, the Argonautica of Apollonius of Rhodes (epic poet, scholar, and director of the Library of Alexandria) tells the myth of the voyage of Jason and the Argonauts to retrieve the Golden Fleece from the mythical land of Colchis. In the Argonautica, Jason is impelled on his quest by king Pelias, who receives a prophecy that a man with one sandal would be his nemesis. Jason loses a sandal in a river, arrives at the court of Pelias, and the epic is set in motion. Nearly every member of the next generation of heroes, as well as Heracles, went with Jason in the ship Argo to fetch the Golden Fleece. This generation also included Theseus, who went to Crete to slay the Minotaur; Atalanta, the female heroine, and Meleager, who once had an epic cycle of his own to rival the Iliad and Odyssey. Pindar, Apollonius and the Bibliotheca endeavor to give full lists of the Argonauts.

Although Apollonius wrote his poem in the 3rd century BC, the composition of the story of the Argonauts is earlier than Odyssey, which shows familiarity with the exploits of Jason (the wandering of Odysseus may have been partly founded on it). In ancient times the expedition was regarded as a historical fact, an incident in the opening up of the Black Sea to Greek commerce and colonization. It was also extremely popular, forming a cycle to which a number of local legends became attached. The story of Medea, in particular, caught the imagination of the tragic poets.

House of Atreus and Theban Cycle

In between the Argo and the Trojan War, there was a generation known chiefly for its horrific crimes. This includes the doings of Atreus and Thyestes at Argos. Behind the myth of the house of Atreus (one of the two principal heroic dynasties with the house of Labdacus) lies the problem of the devolution of power and of the mode of accession to sovereignty. The twins Atreus and Thyestes with their descendants played the leading role in the tragedy of the devolution of power in Mycenae.

The Theban Cycle deals with events associated especially with Cadmus, the city's founder, and later with the doings of Laius and Oedipus at Thebes; a series of stories that lead to the eventual pillage of that city at the hands of the Seven Against Thebes and Epigoni. (It is not known whether the Seven Against Thebes figured in early epic.) As far as Oedipus is concerned, early epic accounts seem to have him continuing to rule at Thebes after the revelation that Iokaste was his mother, and subsequently marrying a second wife who becomes the mother of his children—markedly different from the tale known to us through tragedy (e.g. Sophocles' Oedipus Rex) and later mythological accounts.

Trojan War and Aftermath

Greek mythology culminates in the Trojan War, fought between Greece and Troy, and its aftermath. In Homer's works, such as the Iliad, the chief stories have already taken shape and substance, and individual themes were elaborated later, especially in Greek drama. The Trojan War also elicited great interest in the Roman culture because of the story of Aeneas, a Trojan hero whose journey from Troy led to the founding of the city that would one day become Rome, as recounted in Virgil's Aeneid (Book II of Virgil's Aeneid contains the best-known account of the sack of Troy). Finally there are two pseudo-chronicles written in Latin that passed under the names of Dictys Cretensis and Dares Phrygius.

The Trojan War cycle, a collection of epic poems, starts with the events leading up to the war: Eris and the golden apple of Kallisti, the Judgement of Paris, the abduction of Helen, the sacrifice of Iphigenia at Aulis. To recover Helen, the Greeks launched a great expedition under the overall command of Menelaus's brother, Agamemnon, king of Argos or Mycenae, but the Trojans refused to return Helen. The Iliad, which is set in the tenth year of the war, tells of the quarrel between Agamemnon and Achilles, who was the finest Greek warrior, and the consequent deaths in battle of Achilles' beloved comrade Patroclus and Priam's eldest son, Hector. After Hector's death the Trojans were joined by two exotic allies, Penthesilea, queen of the Amazons, and Memnon, king of the Ethiopians and son of the dawn-goddess Eos. Achilles killed both of these, but Paris then managed to kill Achilles with an arrow in the heel. Achilles' heel was the only part of his body which was not invulnerable to damage by human weaponry. Before they could take Troy, the Greeks had to steal from the citadel the wooden image of Pallas Athena (the Palladium). Finally, with Athena's help, they built the Trojan Horse. Despite the warnings of Priam's daughter Cassandra, the Trojans were persuaded by Sinon, a Greek who feigned desertion, to take the horse inside the walls of Troy as an offering to Athena; the priest Laocoon, who tried to have the horse destroyed, was killed by sea-serpents. At night the Greek fleet returned, and the Greeks from the horse opened the gates of Troy. In the total sack that followed, Priam and his remaining sons were slaughtered; the Trojan women passed into slavery in various cities of Greece. The adventurous homeward voyages of the Greek leaders (including the wanderings of Odysseus and Aeneas (the Aeneid), and the murder of Agamemnon) were told in two epics, the Returns (the lost Nostoi) and Homer's Odyssey. The Trojan cycle also includes the adventures of the children of the Trojan generation (e.g., Orestes and Telemachus).

El Juicio de Paris by Enrique Simonet, 1904. Paris is holding the golden apple on his right hand while surveying the goddesses in a calculative manner.

The Trojan War provided a variety of themes and became a main source of inspiration for Ancient Greek artists (e.g. metopes on the Parthenon depicting the sack of Troy); this artistic preference for themes deriving from the Trojan Cycle indicates its importance to the Ancient Greek civilization. The same mythological cycle also inspired a series of posterior European literary writings. For instance, Trojan Medieval European writers, unacquainted with Homer at first hand, found in the Troy legend a rich source of heroic and romantic storytelling and a convenient framework into which to fit their own courtly and chivalric ideals. Twelfth-century authors, such as Benoît de Sainte-Maure (Roman de Troie (Romance of Troy)) and Joseph of Exeter (De Bello Troiano (On the Trojan War)) describe the war while rewriting the standard version they found in Dictys and Dares. They thus follow Horace's advice and Virgil's example: they rewrite a poem of Troy instead of telling something completely new.

Some of the more famous heroes noted for their inclusion in the Trojan War were:

On the Trojan side:

- Aeneas.

- Hector.

- Paris.

On the Greek side:

- Ajax (there were two Ajaxes).

- Achilles.

- King Agamemnon.

- Menelaus.

- Odysseus.

In The Rage of Achilles by Giovanni Battista. Achilles is outraged that Agamemnon would threaten to seize his warprize, Briseis, and he draws his sword to kill Agamemnon. The sudden appearance of the goddess Athena, who, in this fresco, has grabbed Achilles by the hair, prevents the act of violence.

Greek and Roman Conceptions of Myth

Mythology was at the heart of everyday life in Ancient Greece. Greeks regarded mythology as a part of their history. They used myth to explain natural phenomena, cultural variations, traditional enmities and friendships. It was a source of pride to be able to trace the descent of one's leaders from a mythological hero or a god. Few ever doubted that there was truth behind the account of the Trojan War in the Iliad and Odyssey. According to Victor Davis Hanson, a military historian, columnist, political essayist and former classics professor, and John Heath, a classics professor, the profound knowledge of the Homeric epos was deemed by the Greeks the basis of their acculturation. Homer was the "education of Greece", and his poetry "the Book".

After the rise of philosophy, history, prose and rationalism in the late 5th century BC, the fate of myth became uncertain, and mythological genealogies gave place to a conception of history which tried to exclude the supernatural (such as the Thucydidean history). While poets and dramatists were reworking the myths, Greek historians and philosophers were beginning to criticize them.

A few radical philosophers like Xenophanes of Colophon were already beginning to label the poets' tales as blasphemous lies in the 6th century BC; Xenophanes had complained that Homer and Hesiod attributed to the gods "all that is shameful and disgraceful among men; they steal, commit adultery, and deceive one another". This line of thought found its most sweeping expression in Plato's Republic and Laws. Plato created his own allegorical myths (such as the vision of Er in the Republic), attacked the traditional tales of the gods' tricks, thefts and adulteries as immoral, and objected to their central role in literature. Plato's criticism was the first serious challenge to the Homeric mythological tradition, referring to the myths as "old wives' chatter". For his part Aristotle criticized the Pre-socratic quasi-mythical philosophical approach and underscored that "Hesiod and the theological writers were concerned only with what seemed plausible to themselves, and had no respect for us. But it is not worth taking seriously writers who show off in the mythical style; as for those who do proceed by proving their assertions, we must cross-examine them".

Nevertheless, even Plato did not manage to wean himself and his society from the influence of myth; his own characterization for Socrates is based on the traditional Homeric and tragic patterns, used by the philosopher to praise the righteous life of his teacher:

But perhaps someone might say: "Are you then not ashamed, Socrates, of having followed such a pursuit, that you are now in danger of being put to death as a result?" But I should make to him a just reply: "You do not speak well, Sir, if you think a man in whom there is even a little merit ought to consider danger of life or death, and not rather regard this only, when he does things, whether the things he does are right or wrong and the acts of a good or a bad man. For according to your argument all the demigods would be bad who died at Troy, including the son of Thetis, who so despised danger, in comparison with enduring any disgrace, that when his mother (and she was a goddess) said to him, as he was eager to slay Hector, something like this, I believe:

> "My son, if you avenge the death of your friend Patroclus and kill Hector, you yourself shall die; for straightway, after Hector, is death appointed unto you. (Hom. Il. 18.96)"

> "He, when he heard this, made light of death and danger, and feared much more to live as a coward and not to avenge his friends, and said, straightway may I die, after doing vengeance upon the wrongdoer, that I may not stay here, jeered at beside the curved ships, a burden of the earth."

Hanson and Heath estimate that Plato's rejection of the Homeric tradition was not favorably received by the grassroots Greek civilization. The old myths were kept alive in local cults; they continued to influence poetry and to form the main subject of painting and sculpture.

More sportingly, the 5th century BC tragedian Euripides often played with the old traditions, mocking them, and through the voice of his characters injecting notes of doubt.

Yet the subjects of his plays were taken, without exception, from myth. Many of these plays were written in answer to a predecessor's version of the same or similar myth. Euripides mainly impugns the myths about the gods and begins his critique with an objection similar to the one previously expressed by Xenocrates: the gods, as traditionally represented, are far too crassly anthropomorphic.

Raphael's Plato in The School of Athens fresco (probably in the likeness of Leonardo da Vinci). The philosopher expelled the study of Homer, of the tragedies and of the related mythological traditions from his utopian Republic.

Hellenistic and Roman Rationalism

During the Hellenistic period, mythology took on the prestige of elite knowledge that marks its possessors as belonging to a certain class. At the same time, the skeptical turn of the Classical age became even more pronounced. Greek mythographer Euhemerus established the tradition of seeking an actual historical basis for mythical beings and events. Although his original work (Sacred Scriptures) is lost, much is known about it from what is recorded by Diodorus and Lactantius.

Rationalizing hermeneutics of myth became even more popular under the Roman Empire, thanks to the physicalist theories of Stoic and Epicurean philosophy. Stoics presented explanations of the gods and heroes as physical phenomena, while the Euhemerists rationalized them as historical figures. At the same time, the Stoics and the Neoplatonists promoted the moral significations of the mythological tradition, often based on Greek etymologies. Through his Epicurean message, Lucretius had sought to expel superstitious fears from the minds of his fellow-citizens. Livy, too, is skeptical about the mythological tradition and claims that he does not intend to pass judgement on such legends (fabulae). The challenge for Romans with a strong and apologetic sense of religious tradition was to defend that tradition while conceding that it was often a breeding-ground for superstition. The antiquarian Varro, who regarded religion as a human institution with great importance for the preservation of good in society, devoted rigorous study to the origins of religious cults. In his Antiquitates Rerum Divinarum (which has not survived, but Augustine's City of God indicates its general approach)

Varro argues that whereas the superstitious man fears the gods, the truly religious person venerates them as parents. According to Varro, there have been three accounts of deities in the Roman society: the mythical account created by poets for theatre and entertainment, the civil account used by people for veneration as well as by the city, and the natural account created by the philosophers. The best state is, adds Varro, where the civil theology combines the poetic mythical account with the philosopher's.

Roman Academic Cotta ridicules both literal and allegorical acceptance of myth, declaring roundly that myths have no place in philosophy. Cicero is also generally disdainful of myth, but, like Varro, he is emphatic in his support for the state religion and its institutions. It is difficult to know how far down the social scale this rationalism extended. Cicero asserts that no one (not even old women and boys) is so foolish as to believe in the terrors of Hades or the existence of Scyllas, centaurs or other composite creatures, but, on the other hand, the orator elsewhere complains of the superstitious and credulous character of the people. De Natura Deorum is the most comprehensive summary of Cicero's line of thought.

Cicero saw himself as the defender of the established order, despite his personal skepticism with regard to myth and his inclination towards more philosophical conceptions of divinity.

Syncretizing Trends

In Ancient Roman times, a new Roman mythology was born through syncretization of numerous Greek and other foreign gods. This occurred because the Romans had little mythology of their own, and inheritance of the Greek mythological tradition caused the major Roman gods to adopt characteristics of their Greek equivalents. The gods Zeus and Jupiter are an example of this mythological overlap. In addition to the combination of the two mythological traditions, the association of the Romans with eastern religions led to further syncretizations. For instance, the cult of Sun was introduced in Rome after Aurelian's successful campaigns in Syria. The Asiatic divinities Mithras (that is to say, the Sun) and Ba'al were combined with Apollo and Helios into one Sol Invictus, with conglomerated rites and compound attributes. Apollo might be increasingly identified in religion with Helios or even Dionysus, but texts retelling his myths seldom reflected such developments. The traditional literary mythology was increasingly dissociated from actual religious practice. The worship of Sol as special protector of the emperors and of the empire remained the chief imperial religion until it was replaced by Christianity.

The surviving 2nd-century collection of Orphic Hymns and the Saturnalia of Macrobius Ambrosius Theodosius are influenced by the theories of rationalism and the syncretizing trends as well. The Orphic Hymns are a set of pre-classical poetic compositions, attributed to Orpheus, himself the subject of a renowned myth. In reality, these poems were probably composed by several different poets, and contain a rich set of clues about prehistoric European mythology. The stated purpose of the Saturnalia is to transmit the Hellenic culture Macrobius has derived from his reading, even though much of his treatment of gods is colored by Egyptian and North African mythology and theology (which also affect the interpretation of Virgil). In Saturnalia reappear mythographical comments influenced by the Euhemerists, the Stoics and the Neoplatonists.

Apollo (early Imperial Roman copy of a fourth-century Greek original, Louvre Museum).

Modern Interpretations

The genesis of modern understanding of Greek mythology is regarded by some scholars as a double reaction at the end of the eighteenth century against "the traditional attitude of Christian animosity", in which the Christian reinterpretation of myth as a "lie" or fable had been retained. In Germany, by about 1795, there was a growing interest in Homer and Greek mythology. In Göttingen, Johann Matthias Gesner began to revive Greek studies, while his successor, Christian Gottlob Heyne, worked with Johann Joachim Winckelmann, and laid the foundations for mythological research both in Germany and elsewhere.

Comparative and Psychoanalytic Approaches

The development of comparative philology in the 19th century, together with ethnological discoveries in the 20th century, established the science of myth. Since the Romantics, all study of myth has been comparative. Wilhelm Mannhardt, James Frazer, and Stith Thompson employed the comparative approach to collect and classify the themes of folklore and mythology. In 1871 Edward Burnett Tylor published his Primitive Culture, in which he applied the comparative method and tried to explain the origin and evolution of religion. Tylor's procedure of drawing together material culture, ritual and myth of widely separated cultures influenced both Carl Jung and Joseph Campbell. Max Müller applied the new science of comparative mythology to the study of myth, in which he detected the distorted remains of Aryan nature worship. Bronisław Malinowski emphasized the ways myth fulfills common social functions. Claude Lévi-Strauss and other structuralists have compared the formal relations and patterns in myths throughout the world.

Max Müller is regarded as one of the founders of comparative mythology. In his Comparative Mythology Müller analysed the "disturbing" similarity between the mythologies of "savage races" with those of the early Europeans.

Sigmund Freud introduced a transhistorical and biological conception of man and a view of myth as an expression of repressed ideas. Dream interpretation is the basis of Freudian myth interpretation and Freud's concept of dreamwork recognizes the importance of contextual relationships for the interpretation of any individual element in a dream. This suggestion would find an important point of rapprochement between the structuralist and psychoanalytic approaches to myth in Freud's thought. Carl Jung extended the transhistorical, psychological approach with his theory of the "collective unconscious" and the archetypes (inherited "archaic" patterns), often encoded in myth, that arise out of it. According to Jung, "myth-forming structural elements must be present in the unconscious psyche". Comparing Jung's methodology with Joseph Campbell's theory, Robert A. Segal concludes that "to interpret a myth Campbell simply identifies the archetypes in it. An interpretation of the Odyssey, for example, would show how Odysseus's life conforms to a heroic pattern. Jung, by contrast, considers the identification of archetypes merely the first step in the interpretation of a myth". Karl Kerényi, one of the founders of modern studies in Greek mythology, gave up his early views of myth, in order to apply Jung's theories of archetypes to Greek myth.

Origin Theories

Max Müller attempted to understand an Indo-European religious form by tracing it back to its Indo-European (or, in Müller's time, "Aryan") "original" manifestation. In 1891, he claimed that "the most important discovery which has been made during the nineteenth century with respect to the ancient history of mankind was this sample equation: Sanskrit Dyaus-pitar = Greek Zeus = Latin Jupiter = Old Norse Tyr". The question of Greek mythology's place in Indo-European studies has generated much scholarship since Müller's time. For example, philologist Georges Dumézil draws a comparison between the Greek Uranus and the Sanskrit Varuna, although there is no hint that he believes them to be originally connected. In other cases, close parallels in character and function suggest a common heritage, yet lack of linguistic evidence makes it difficult to prove, as in the case of the Greek Moirai and the Norns of Norse mythology.

It appears that the Mycenaean religion was the mother of the Greek religion and its pantheon already included many divinities that can be found in classical Greece. However, Greek mythology is generally seen as having heavy influence of Pre-Greek and Near Eastern cultures, and as such contains few important elements for the reconstruction of the Proto-Indo-European religion. Consequently, Greek mythology received minimal scholarly attention in the context of Indo-European comparative mythology until the mid 2000s.

Archaeology and mythography have revealed influence from Asia Minor and the Near East. Adonis seems to be the Greek counterpart—more clearly in cult than in myth—of a Near Eastern "dying god". Cybele is rooted in Anatolian culture while much of Aphrodite's iconography may spring from Semitic goddesses. There are also possible parallels between the earliest divine generations (Chaos and its children) and Tiamat in the Enuma Elish. According to Meyer Reinhold, "near Eastern theogonic concepts, involving divine succession through violence and generational conflicts for power, found their way into Greek mythology".

In addition to Indo-European and Near Eastern origins, some scholars have speculated on the debts of Greek mythology to the indigenous pre-Greek societies: Crete, Mycenae, Pylos, Thebes and Orchomenus. Historians of religion were fascinated by a number of apparently ancient configurations of myth connected with Crete (the god as bull, Zeus and Europa, Pasiphaë who yields to the bull and gives birth to the Minotaur, etc.). Martin P. Nilsson asserts, based on the representations and general function of the gods, that a lot of Minoan gods and religious conceptions were fused in the Mycenaean religion and concluded that all great classical Greek myths were tied to Mycenaean centres and anchored in prehistoric times. Nevertheless, according to Burkert, the iconography of the Cretan Palace Period has provided almost no confirmation for these theories.

Classical Greco-Roman Mythology

During the middle ages and Renaissance, when Latin remained the dominant language in Europe for international educated discourse, mythological names almost always appeared in Latinized form. With the Greek revival of the 19th century, however, Greek names began to be used more often, with both "Zeus" and "Jove" being widely used as the name of the supreme god of the classical pantheon.

Classical Myth

Classical mythology is a term often used to designate the myths belonging to the Greek and Roman traditions. The myths are believed to have been acquired first by oral tradition, entering since Homer and Hesiod the literate era; later works by those who studied or collected the myths, or sometimes all literary works relating to mythology, are known as mythography and those who wrote them as mythographers. A classical myth as it appears in later Western culture is usually a syncretism of various versions from both Greek and Latin sources.

Greek myths were narratives related to ancient Greek religion, often concerned with the actions of gods and other supernatural beings and of heroes who transcend human bounds. Major sources for Greek myths include the Homeric epics, that is, the Iliad and the Odyssey, and the tragedies of Aeschylus, Sophocles, and Euripides. Known versions are mostly preserved in sophisticated literary works shaped by the artistry of individuals and by the conventions of genre, or in vase painting and other forms of visual art. In these forms, mythological narratives often serve purposes that are not primarily religious, such as entertainment and even comedy (The Frogs), or the exploration of social issues (Antigone).

Roman myths are traditional stories pertaining to ancient Rome's legendary origins, religious institutions, and moral models, with a focus on human actors and only occasional intervention from deities but a pervasive sense of divinely ordered destiny. Roman myths have a dynamic relation to Roman historiography, as in the early books of Livy's Ab urbe condita. The most famous Roman myth may be the birth of Romulus and Remus and the founding of the city, in which fratricide can be taken as expressing the long history of political division in the Roman Republic.

During the Hellenization of Roman literature and culture, the Romans identified their own gods with those of the Greeks, adapting the stories told about them and importing other myths for which they had no counterpart. For instance, while the Greek god Ares and the Italic god Mars are both war deities, the role of each in his society and its religious practices differed often strikingly; but in literature and Roman art, the Romans reinterpreted stories about Ares under the name of Mars. The literary collection of Greco-Roman myths with the greatest influence on later Western culture was the Metamorphoses of the Augustan poet Ovid.

Syncretized versions form the classical tradition of mythography, and by the time of the influential Renaissance mythographer Natalis Comes, few if any distinctions were made between Greek and Roman myths. The myths as they appear in popular culture of the 20th and 21st centuries often have only a tangential relation to the stories as told in ancient Greek and Latin literature.

Ages of Man

The Ages of Man are the stages of human existence on the Earth according to Greek mythology and its subsequent Roman interpretation.

Both Hesiod and Ovid offered accounts of the successive ages of humanity, which tend to progress from an original, long-gone age in which humans enjoyed a nearly divine existence to the current age of the writer, in which humans are beset by innumerable pains and evils. In the two accounts that survive from ancient Greece and Rome, this degradation of the human condition over time is indicated symbolically with metals of successively decreasing value.

Lucas Cranach the Elder, The Golden Age.

Hesiod's Five Ages

The first extant account of the successive ages of humanity comes from the Greek poet Hesiod, in his poem Works and Days (lines 109–201). His list is:

- Golden Age: The Golden Age is the only age that falls within the rule of Cronus. Created by the immortals who live on Olympus, these humans were said to live among the gods, and freely mingled with them. Peace and harmony prevailed during this age. Humans did not have to work to feed themselves, for the earth provided food in abundance. They lived to a very old age but with a youthful appearance and eventually died peacefully. Their spirits live on as "guardians". Plato in Cratylus recounts the golden race of men who came first. He clarifies that Hesiod did not mean men literally made of gold, but good and noble. He describes these men as daemons upon the earth. Since daimones is derived from daēmones, meaning knowing or wise, they are beneficent, preventing ills, and guardians of mortals.

- Silver Age: The Silver Age and every age that follows fall within the rule of Cronus's successor and son, Zeus. Men in the Silver age lived for one hundred years under the dominion of their mothers. They lived only a short time as grown adults, and spent that time in strife with one another. During this Age men refused to worship the gods and Zeus destroyed them for their impiety. After death, humans of this age became "blessed spirits" of the underworld.

Lucas Cranach the Elder, The Silver Age.

- Bronze Age – Men of the Bronze Age were hardened and tough, as war was their purpose and passion. Zeus created these humans out of the ash tree. Their armor was forged of bronze, as were their homes, and tools. The men of this Age were undone by their own violent ways and left no named spirits; instead, they dwell in the "dank house of Hades". This Age came to an end with the flood of Deucalion.

- Heroic Age: The Heroic Age is the one age that does not correspond with any metal. It is also the only age that improves upon the age it follows. It was the heroes of this Age who fought at Thebes and Troy. This race of humans died and went to Elysium.

- Iron Age: Hesiod finds himself in the Iron Age. During this age humans live an existence of toil and misery. Children dishonor their parents, brother fights with brother and the social contract between guest and host (xenia) is forgotten. During this age, might makes right, and bad men use lies to be thought good. At the height of this age, humans no longer feel shame or indignation at wrongdoing; babies will be born with gray hair and the gods will have completely forsaken humanity: "there will be no help against evil."

Ovid's Four Ages

The Roman poet Ovid tells a similar myth of Four Ages in Book 1.89–150 of the Metamorphoses. His account is similar to Hesiod's, with the exception that he omits the Heroic Age. Ovid emphasizes that justice and peace defined the Golden Age. He adds that in this age, men did not yet know the art of navigation and therefore did not explore the larger world. Further, no man had knowledge of any arts but primitive agriculture. In the Silver Age, Jupiter introduces the seasons and men consequentially learn the art of agriculture and architecture. In the Bronze Age, Ovid writes, men were prone to warfare, but not impiety. Finally, in the Iron Age, men demarcate nations with boundaries; they learn the arts of navigation and mining; they are warlike, greedy and impious. Truth, modesty and loyalty are nowhere to be found.

Virgil Solis, The Iron Age.

Aurora

Aurōra is the Latin word for dawn, and the goddess of dawn in Roman mythology and Latin poetry. Like Greek *Eos* and Rigvedic *Ushas*, *Aurōra* continues the name of an earlier Indo-European dawn goddess, *Hausos*.

In Roman mythology, Aurōra renews herself every morning and flies across the sky, announcing the arrival of the Sun. Her parentage was flexible: for Ovid, she could equally be *Pallantis*, signifying the daughter of Pallas or the daughter of Hyperion. She has two siblings, a brother (Sol, the Sun) and a sister (Luna, the Moon). Roman writers rarely imitated Hesiod and later Greek poets by naming Aurōra as the mother of the Anemoi (the Winds), who were the offspring of Astraeus, the father of the stars.

Aurōra appears most often in sexual poetry with one of her mortal lovers. A myth taken from the Greek by Roman poets tells that one of her lovers was the prince of Troy, Tithonus. Tithonus was a mortal, and would therefore age and die. Wanting to be with her lover for all eternity, Aurōra asked Jupiter to grant immortality to Tithonus. Jupiter granted her wish, but she failed to ask for eternal youth to accompany his immortality, and he became forever old. Aurōra turned him into a cicada.

Greek Mythology in Western Art and Literature

With the rediscovery of classical antiquity in the Renaissance, the poetry of Ovid became a major influence on the imagination of poets and artists, and remained a fundamental influence on the diffusion and perception of Greek mythology through subsequent centuries. From the early years of the Renaissance, artists portrayed subjects from Greek mythology alongside more conventional Christian themes. Among the best-known subjects of Italian artists are Botticelli's *Birth of Venus* and *Pallas and the Centaur*, the Ledas of Leonardo da Vinci and Michelangelo, and Raphael's *Galatea*. Through the medium of Latin and the works of Ovid, Greek myth influenced medieval and Renaissance poets such as Petrarch, Boccaccio and Dante in Italy.

Botticelli's *The Birth of Venus* — a revived *Venus Pudica* for a new view of pagan Antiquity-- is often said to epitomize for modern viewers the spirit of the Renaissance.

In northern Europe, Greek mythology never took the same hold of the visual arts, but its effect was very obvious on literature. Both Latin and Greek classical texts were translated, so that stories of mythology became available. In England, Chaucer, the Elizabethans and John Milton were among those influenced by Greek myths; nearly all the major English poets from Shakespeare to Robert Bridges turned for inspiration to Greek mythology. Jean Racine in France and Goethe in Germany revived Greek drama. Racine reworked the ancient myths — including those of Phaidra, Andromache, Oedipus and Iphigeneia — to new purpose.

Francisco Goya, *The rape of Europa (El rapto de Europa)*.

In the 18th century, the philosophical revolution of the Enlightenment spread throughout Europe. It was accompanied by a certain reaction against Greek myth; there was a tendency to insist on the scientific and philosophical achievements of Greece and Rome. The myths, however, continued to provide an important source of raw material for dramatists, including those who wrote the libretti for Handel's operas *Admeto* and *Semele*, Mozart's *Idomeneo*, and Gluck's *Iphigénie en Aulide*. By the end of the century, Romanticism initiated a surge of enthusiasm for all things Greek, including Greek mythology. In Britain, it was a great period for new translations of Greek tragedies and Homer's works, and these in turn inspired contemporary poets, such as Keats, Byron, and Shelley. The Hellenism of Queen Victoria's poet laureate, Alfred Lord Tennyson, was such that even his portraits of the quintessentially English court of King Arthur are suffused with echoes of the Homeric epics. The visual arts kept pace, stimulated by the purchase of the Parthenon marbles in 1816; many of the "Greek" paintings of Lord Leighton and Lawrence Alma-Tademawere seriously accepted as part of the transmission of the Hellenic ideal.

American authors of the 19th century, such as Thomas Bulfinch and Nathaniel Hawthorne, believed that myths should provide pleasure, and held that the study of the classical myths was essential to the understanding of English and American literature. According to Bulfinch, "The so-called divinities of Olympus have not a single worshipper among living men. They belong now not to the department of theology, but to those of literature and taste." In more recent times, classical themes have been reinterpreted by such major dramatists as Jean Anouilh, Jean Cocteau, and Jean Giraudoux in

France, Eugene O'Neill in America, and T. S. Eliot in England, and by great novelists such as the Irish James Joyce and the French André Gide. Richard Strauss, Jacques Offenbach and many others have set Greek mythological themes to music.

Centaur fighting a Lapith, detail from a metope of the Parthenon; in the British Museum, London.

Western people of all eras have been moved and baffled by the deceptive simplicity of Greek myths, and Greek mythology has had a profound effect on the development of Western civilization.

Arrival or departure of a young warrior or hero, detail of an Apulian krater.

The earliest visual representations of mythological characters and motifs occur in late Mycenaean and sub-Mycenaean art. Though identification is controversial, Centaurs, a siren, and even Zeus's lover Europa have been recognized. Mythological and epic themes are also found in Geometric art of the 8th century BCE, but not until the 7th century did such themes become popular in both ceramic and sculptured works. During the Classical and subsequent periods, they became commonplace. The birth of Athena was the subject of the east pediment of the Parthenon in Athens, and the legend of Pelops and of the labours of Heracles were the subjects of the corresponding pediment and the metopes (a space on a Doric frieze) of the Temple of Zeus at Olympia. The battles of gods with Giants and of Lapiths (a wild race in northern Greece) with Centaurs were also favourite motifs. Pompeian frescoes reveal realistic representations of Theseus and Ariadne, Perseus, the fall of Icarus, and the death of Pyramus.

The Birth of Venus, tempera on canvas by Sandro Botticelli.

The great Renaissance masters added a new dimension to Greek mythology. Among the best-known subjects of Italian artists are Sandro Botticelli's Birth of Venus, the Ledas of Leonardo da Vinci and Michelangelo, and Raphael's Galatea.

Apollo and Daphne, marble sculpture.

Through the medium of Latin and, above all, the works of Ovid, Greek myth influenced poets such as Dante and Petrarch in Italy and Geoffrey Chaucer in England and, later, the English Elizabethans and John Milton. Jean Racine in France and Johann Wolfgang von Goethe in Germany revived Greek drama, and nearly all the major English poets from William Shakespeare to Robert Bridges turned for inspiration to Greek mythology. In later centuries, Classical themes were reinterpreted by such major dramatists as Jean Anouilh, Jean Cocteau, and Jean Giraudoux in France, Eugene O'Neill in America, and T.S. Eliot in England and by great novelists such as James Joyce (Irish) and

André Gide (French). The German composers Christoph Gluck and Richard Strauss, the German-French composer Jacques Offenbach, the Russian composer Igor Stravinsky, and many others have set Greek mythological themes to music.

References

- Greek-mythology: britannica.com, Retrieved 19 August, 2020

- Romemythology: crystalinks.com, Retrieved 18 July, 2020

- Miles, Geoffrey, ed. (2006). Classical mythology in English literature: a critical anthology. Routledge. ISBN 0415147557. OCLC 912455670

- Mallory, J. P.; Adams, D. Q. (2006-08-24). The Oxford Introduction to Proto-Indo-European and the Proto-Indo-European World. OUP Oxford. p. 409. ISBN 9780199287918

- Greek-mythological-characters-and-motifs-in-art-and-literature, Greek-mythology: britannica.com, Retrieved 29 August, 2020

5
Asian Mythology

Asian mythology includes Korean mythology, Hindu mythology, Japanese mythology, Vietnamese mythology, Philippine mythology, etc. This chapter delves into origin, ritual practices, gods and literature of the different Asian mythologies to provide an easy understanding of the subject.

Korean Mythology

Geography

The Korean peninsula juts out from the mainland in Northeast Asia between China and Japan. This key location has made Korea the target of aggression by neighboring nations throughout history. To the east, Japan viewed Korea as a first and vital step to a conquest of the Asian mainland. To the west, China viewed Korea as a rightful part of its territory as the supreme power of Asia. For thousands of years, Korea managed to fend off advances and maintain cultural and political independence. It was not until 1910, when Korea became a colony of Japan, that a foreign power ruled over the Korean peninsula. For thousands of years Korea was beset on all sides, yet still managed to maintain its own unique cultural identity.

Its unique position also made it a natural conduit of culture in Asia. Much of Chinese culture was borrowed or adapted, later to be passed on to Japan. Trade was important as well, bringing news and culture as well as goods from distant lands. According to the legends, travelers came from as far away as India. Although Korea considered China to be a "big brother" nation — Korea was, for most of its history, under Chinese suzerainty — a fierce national pride preserved a unique Korean culture. King Sejong's invention of Hangul, the Korean alphabet, in the fifteenth century is an example of the independent spirit of the Korean people. Up to that point, all literature had been transmitted using Chinese characters. With the invention of Hangul, Korea now had a unique written language to match its unique spoken language — Korean, along with Japanese, is more closely related to Turkish than it is to Chinese.

The peninsula itself is very mountainous, divided by eight major mountain ranges. The larger of these ranges have historically hindered communication and interaction between the various regions of Korea. The result of this is that each province in modern-day Korea has its own distinct dialect. With regards to Korean mythology, the effect has been equally diversifying. Unlike the Greeks or Romans, who had a pantheon of gods that interacted with each other, the gods and spirits of Korea are more independent, and sometimes mutually exclusive. This is also due to the fact that what is now Korea was once five different nations.

The earliest political entities on the Korean peninsula were walled city-states that arose during the Bronze Age, not unlike the city-states of Greece. The most powerful of these states was called Chosŏn (now called Old Chosŏn to avoid confusion with the later Chosŏn kingdom). According to myth, Chosŏn was founded in 2333 BCE. near P'yŏng-yang by Tangun. Sometime around the beginning of the second century BCE, Chosŏn fell due to pressure from Yen China. A refugee named Wiman founded a new kingdom, which he named Wiman Chosŏn. Not only did he keep the Chosŏn name, he also adopted Chosŏn customs and culture, in a sense reviving the fallen kingdom. Wiman Chosŏn exerted a fair amount of power in Asia, but fell in 108 BCE to China.

Late in the next century, the first of what would later be called the Three Kingdoms emerged. According to legend, Chumong founded Koguryŏ in 37 BCE near the Yalu River. The second kingdom, Paekche, developed some time around the third century CE in the southwestern corner of the Korean peninsula. The last of the Three Kingdoms, Shilla, developed in the fourth century in the southeastern portion of the peninsula. The small nation of Gaya did exist in the south of the peninsula between Paekche and Silla, but it was conquered by Silla in the mid-sixth century. An entirely separate nation developed on the island of ghosts of Paekche and Koguryŏ were resurrected in Later Paekche and Koryŏ (from which the modern name "Korea" is derived), and Koryŏ proved victorious. The Koryŏ kingdom lasted until 1392, when a coup d'etat began the kingdom of Chosŏn. Chosŏn kings reigned for over five hundred years, until the light of their kingdom was snuffed out by the Japanese as they began their Pacific War by colonizing Korea in 1910.

Mythology in the Korean Context

Most people know what mythology is, but would have a very difficult time providing a precise definition if asked for one. Once said that a myth is "a story of great but unknown age which originally embodied a belief regarding some fact or phenomenon of experience, and in which often the forces of nature and of the soul are personified; an ancient legend of a god, a hero, the origin of a race, etc.; a wonder story of prehistoric origin; a popular fable which is, or has been, received as historical."

It denies that myth can be present ("great but unknown age," "ancient," "historical"), which is something Joseph Campbell would no doubt have disagreed with. Is age the primary condition of a myth? One would think so sometimes. It often appears that the older a story is, the more likely it is to be called a myth. The word "myth" has also come to mean "untrue story," thus raising the suspicion that perhaps veracity (or lack of it) is the measuring stick of myth.

The definition also uses the world "legend" in its definition — does that mean that all legends fall within the realm of myth? This is the true problem in defining myth: defining it in relation to the other genres, like legend, folktale, fable, fairy tale, etc. One would indeed be hard-pressed to find mutually exclusive definitions for these five genres, let alone all the others.

Now we turn to the field of Korean mythology, and we are faced with two problems. For one, scholars here have also struggled to classify and define the broad body of literature known as "tales" (seolhwa). The most common division is a three-fold one: myth (shinhwa), legend (cheonseol), and folktale (mindam). This is the division most often used, but there are others just as valid. Another three-fold division divides tales into animal tales, ordinary people tales, and anecdotes. A two-fold division would distinguish between "serious" and "fantastic" tales, while another would set myths against the group of legends and folktales. There is even a five-fold division, which arranges tales in a vertical hierarchy: supernatural tales, hero tales, ordinary people tales, humorous tales (or "idiot tales"), and plant and animal tales.

The second of the problems complicates matters even further, and this is the problem of language. The terms shinhwa, cheonseol, and mindam do not correspond exactly to myth, legend, and folktale in English. All three of the Korean terms are Sino-Korean-based on Chinese characters. To get a basic feel for the meaning of these terms.

Pronunciation	Meaning
shin	spirit, god, divine, supernatural
hwa	words, to talk
cheon	transmit, hand down
seol	to say, to speak
min	people, mankind, folk
dam	to talk, to converse

The keen observer will note that the characters hwa, seol, and dam all have a similar root (the left-hand character), which means "to speak." These three characters can be translated as either "story" or "tale." Shin refers to spirits, ghosts, monsters, and demigods as well as the gods that reside in heaven. Thus the term shinhwa would seem to refer to all supernatural tales. The term cheonseol may be interpreted as either "a story that is handed down" or as "a story of something passed down." Both apply to the Korean cheonseol. Mindam, is a tale of the common people.

Each of these genres has specific characteristics that distinguish it from the others. Before getting into these characteristics, though, it will be helpful to discuss two classification systems, both put forth by Dr. Cho Dong-Il, a professor of Korean Literature at Seoul National University. The first system is laid out in his "Classification System of Korean Tale Types.1 Here he defines the genres according to the changes in the protagonist's fortunes, a "+" representing a positive state and a "-" representing a negative state. The myth is a "+ +" type, the legend is a "+ -" type, and the folktale is a "- +" type. This is, a simplification of a very large and complex system that covers all of the Korean tale types.

Genre	Shinwa	Cheonseol	Mindam
Protagonist (P)	Deity or semi deity	Outstanding human	Ordinary or foolish human
Theme	P founds nation or performs other heroic deed with aid of heavenly benefactor/parent	P challenges existing authority or power	P overcomes adverse circumstances, often in a humorous fashion
Outcome	P is victorious	P is defeated	P is victorious
+ / - Type	+ +	+ -	- +
Self-World Conflict	supernatural self overcomes world	self is overcome by world	ordinary self overcomes world

Table immediately reveals that shinhwa and cheonseol are indeed quite different, and that mindam would appear to have more in common with shinhwa than with cheonseol. The typical motivation behind each genre is also revealed upon closer examination. Unlike other mythologies, which include creation, myths, origin myths, and various other types, the Korean shinhwa focuses almost exclusively on national-foundation myths (keonguk shinhwa). As such, the shinhwa served to legitimize the existence of a government or nation, and they were vigorously handed down to succeeding generations.

To understand the cheonseol, we must know a little about Confucianism, perhaps the most important philosophy in Asia. It will suffice to say for The purposes that Confucianism promotes a rigid vertical social hierarchy, and was adopted by the ruling classes as a means of preserving their power. The cheonseol often depicted humans who, through exceptional but earthly power, rose above their stations to challenge the existing authority. Seen from a Confucian point of view, it is natural that these heroes should fail and that legends should invariably be tragic. Cheonseol are often quite similar to what a Western audience would call an origin myth, a myth explaining how something came to be. The clue to this is to be found within the word cheonseol itself; as explained before, it can mean both "a story that is handed down" or "a story of something passed down." Thus, a cheonseol almost always leaves something behind as proof, be it a rock, a flower, or an animal.

The mindam does share more in common with the shinhwa than with the cheonseol, but it is still quite different from both. Unlike the semi-deified hero of the shinhwa, the hero of the mindam is an ordinary person, or sometimes even a bumbling idiot. He or she overcomes low station and hard times, succeeding by trickery or luck. This, goes directly against the Confucianist philosophy that everyone has their place, and here lies the difference between the mindam and both the shinhwa and cheonseol. Shinhwa and cheonseol both served the interests of the ruling aristocracy, one serving political interests and the other serving social interests. Mindam, on the other hand, were a way for the common people to escape the harsh reality that surrounded them, and served the noble purpose of making people laugh. They were truly "tales of the people."

One should be able to see by now how very different shinhwa, cheonseol, and mindam are from myths, legends, and folktales, and I hope the reader will both understand and forgive me for consistently using the Korean terms. Part of this, as we have seen, is due to Confucianism, and yet another part is due to other aspects of Korean thinking, such as Buddhism, Taoism, and folk religions (like shamanism). There are many cheonseol that would be considered myths in the Western context simply because they deal with spirits, or shin, but we must differentiate between two types of shin when discussing Korean tales. This is where those other systems of thought come in.

The shin in shinhwa are a breed apart. They are the gods who live in the heavens and more or less rule over the earth. The other shin (also called chapshin, chap meaning "various" or "miscellaneous") live on the earth and interact quite regularly with humans; these chapshin are a product of Korean folk religions. Ghosts, fairies, guardian spirits, and even what would be considered monsters in the West are all described by the term chapshin. Interestingly, ghosts and monsters in Korea do not hold the same place of horror and dread as they do in the west; there are, in fact, no truly evil chapshin. A ghost may take revenge on someone who has done them wrong, but the Western vampires, ghouls, zombies and the like — fearsome monsters evil to the core — have no counterparts in Korea. Chapshin often act as judges or guardians, punishing the evil and rewarding or protecting the good.

This harmony with the supernatural comes from the Buddhist influence with its circular worldview. Life and death are not separate states of being, they are merely part of the same process. Although this circular worldview is not so strictly adhered to in Korea as it is in Southeast Asia, the co-existence and harmony of life and death is a natural part of the worldview. We can say that the "natural" is emphasized in the "supernatural" in Korea.

There are other characters that appear in Korean tales who could easily appear in Western mythology. These are the Taoists, "the Followers of the Way," known as tosa and shinseon. Tosa ("practitioner of the Way") are humans noted for superhuman skills obtained through study of the Way. Some have, for example, the ability to run long distances in a short period of time, reminiscent of the Jewish prophet Elijah. Shinseon ("divine hermits"), on the other hand, live to extremely old age through ascetic mountain living and practicing of the Way.

The thought and philosophy of a people is revealed in their myths. In The modern, rational world, "myth" has almost become synonymous with "untruth." In ancient Greece, though, mythos was accepted as truth without question, whereas logos was a truth that could be argued and proven. This is because the Greeks recognized that the myths tell the truth about who we really are, and that is a truth that can ultimately not be argued. These days we laugh at myth, or relegate it to children's books, because we are afraid of it — afraid of what it says about us.

Webster echoes a common sentiment by denying that myth is present, but the reason that myths are still around is because they still speak to us as human beings. It is fine to know the modern history of Korea, but most people stop there and go no further into the mind of the Korean people. Hopefully a knowledge of Korean mythology will lead to a deeper understanding of Korea and her people, bringing the West a little closer to the East.

Deities in Korean Mythology

JUMONG: The god who founded the ancient kingdom of Koguryeo, from which the name Korea was ultimately derived. While Jumong's mother, the goddess Yuhwa, was hiding with King Keumwa she gave birth to an egg which contained the offspring of the sun god Haemosu. Fearful over the strange birth, King Keumwa exposed the egg to the horses of his stable, but none of them would trample it. He left it in the forest, but none of the animals would harm it. He tried to prevent Yuhwa from warming the egg, but Haemosu made a shaft of sunlight keep the egg warm, even on cloudy days.

Keumwa gave in and let Yuhwa care for the egg, from which Jumong eventually burst forth, like many other gods in Korean mythology. (See Talhae and Pakhyeokkeose, also born of eggs; Kimsuro, born of a golden egg found in a golden chest; and Kimalji, born from a golden chest alone, just to be different) Jumong could speak after just one month and grew to adulthood very quickly. He had supernatural skill as an archer and was said to be able to shoot even tiny objects like fleas from a great distance. He always outdid King Keumwa's sons, who grew to resent him, which conflict ultimately led to Jumong heading south to establish his own kingdom, with his mother's blessing (in some versions she also gives him the Five Grains to take with him).

Keumwa's troops pursued him to the Kaesa River, where there was no ferry. Not wishing to have to strike down the army of the man who had been kind to his mother, Jumong instead shot an arrow into the river and in the name of his godly heritage as the son of Haemosu and Yuhwa, commanded all the fish and turtles in the water to form a bridge for him to cross. They obeyed and after he successfully crossed, the animals gave way, letting the pursuing soldiers fall into the river.

Balladeer's Blog

Next Jumong overthrew King Songyang by obtaining a sacred drum and bugle, defeating him at an archery contest and by calling on the rain goddess Aryongjong to cause a flood that washed away Songyang's capital city (which certainly seems more effective than drums, bugles and beating the guy at archery).

The common people of the city were saved from the flood by Jumong, riding a horse-sized duck. He then used his godly power to cause a new city to form out of mist on the spot in just seven days, and this became the capital of his new kingdom called Koguryeo. His own son Yuri went on to become a great king, too. Jumong is sometimes spelled Chumong for the same reason Jeju Island is sometimes spelled Cheju Island.

HALMANG: The goddess of Jeju Island, often depicted embodying the island the way Earth goddesses are often depicted embodying the entire planet. She could also assume giantess form and roam the island at will and much of her mythic cycle deals with her activities in that mobile form. Her diahhrea after having eaten millet porridge resulted in 360 of the hills and mountains of Jeju Island. Halmang also arranged all the valleys and rivers of the island to her liking, too. Her urine caused the channel between Jeju Island and mainland Korea, or the channel between Jeju Island and nearby Udo Island, depending on the version.

When the people of Jeju Island wanted the goddess to cease walking around naked in her giantess form she told them that if they could make clothing large enough to fit her she would build them a bridge to the mainland. The people exhausted all of the material on the island but still the clothes they made were not large enough to cover Halmang, so she stopped her own efforts, leaving the bridge half-finished. (This is similar to many Philippine myths about giant gods or goddesses partially completing bridges between islands)

Another myth involves her out-doing her husband, the god Halubang, at fishing by lying in the ocean and swallowing all the fish into her vagina. (This is similar to one of the Vietnamese myths about Giat Hai outdoing Khong Lo) With that husband, the god that the large, ancient stone phalluses on Jeju Island are dedicated to, Halmang spawned Koeulla, Puella and Yangeulla, the progenitor gods of The Three Clans of Jeju Island.

HWANUNG: The god of the laws and father of the demigod Tangun, one of the important founder- heroes of northern Korean lore. Hwanung told his father, Hwanin, that he desired to live among the people who worshipped them. Hwanin designated Mount Taebaek near modern Pyeongyang for his son to establish himself. Hwanung descended there with Aryongjong, the goddess of rainfall and Yondung, the wind goddess. He gathered three thousand initial followers around him and established the Divine City, from where his rule spread.

Hwanung instituted three hundred sixty laws governing not just the affairs of humanity, like government, agriculture, morality, punishments and society but also governing natural laws on the young world. These laws pertained to lifespans, illnesses, science, etc, similar to certain concepts in Sumerian myth. When both a female bear and a female tiger prayed to Hwanung to be made human, only the bear passed Hwanung's test and became his bride, the mother of Tangun and through him many descending generations of Koreans. The mythical significance is that it was the patience of the bear, not the ferocity of the tiger, that became part of the Korean character and enabled them to survive repeated invasions by Japan and China.

KOEULLA, PUEULLA AND YANGEULLA: These three progenitor gods of the Three Clans of Jeju Island are always mentioned in unison. They are the sons of Halmang, the goddess of Jeju Island, and emerged from her womb, the ground, at a hole named Mohung near Mount Chu. This spot, called the Hollow of the Three Clans, is a landmark in modern day Jeju City. The three brothers roamed the island hunting game, eating the meat and making clothes from the skins.

One day three brides arrived for them, sent with respects from the ruler of Pyeongyang on the Korean mainland. The brides brought with them calves, colts and the Five Grains-barley, rice, soybean, millet and foxtail millet. In Korean mythology these five grains symbolize all of agriculture. Each of the three gods took a bride for himself and established settlements, with their countless offspring forming the mythical Three Clans from which all the people of Jeju Island supposedly descended. Each clan claims their progenitor was the first-born of the three gods.

HAEMOSU: The Korean sun god, usually depicted wearing a headdress of crow feathers from the gigantic crow he killed when it stole the sun and he had to retrieve it (crows have connections with the sun in Chinese myths, too and in Vietnamese mythology some versions claim that the sun goddess' palanquin is adorned with crow images instead of rooster images). For his chief weapon Haemosu wielded a solar sword that shone as brightly as the sun.

Each dawn as the sun, his home, made its way across the sky he would leave it to take its course while he flew down to the Earth on his chariot. That chariot, Oryonggeo, was drawn by five flying dragons and traveled faster than the wind. The sun god's retinue, meanwhile, accompanied him riding giant white swans that floated on multi- colored, music-producing clouds. Haemosu and his court would land at Puyeo, the ancient capital of what would eventually become the combined Three Kingdoms of Korea. There the sun god would attend to the affairs of mortals all day, returning to his solar home at sunset. Haemosu desired the goddess Yuhwa, who bore his son Jumong.

KOENEGITTO: The war god of Jeju Island, home of a shrine that bears his name. Koenegitto had a bronze gong which, when struck once, could conjure up an army of a million soldiers out of the air. When struck twice the army would disappear. Koenegitto was the son of the shrine god Sochonguk through the mortal woman Paek Chunim. When Koenegitto turned three he was so uncontrollable that Sochonguk locked him in a chest and tossed the chest into the sea.

Koenigitto escaped the chest, married the youngest daughter of the dragon god of the sea but was asked to leave the sea kingdom when his enormous appetite was emptying the dragon god's larder. He and his wife went to Chonja on the Korean mainland, where Koenegitto became a hero by driving away an invading army (led by multi- headed generals) from the north. The bronze- armored demigod then returned triumphantly to Jeju Island for revenge on his parents for tossing him into the sea. He scared them both to death, then transformed his father into a mountain ridge and his mother into a shrine.

HABAEK: The god of the Yalu River, which borders what is now North Korea and China. As such he had special significance as the watchman over the northern frontier. Habaek's daughter Yuhwa was snatched away by the sun god Haemosu and made his bride. Habaek complained to Hwanin, the Heavenly King of the gods, who ordered Haemosu to meet with his irate father-in- law. Haemosu defeated the river god in a metamorphosis duel, besting him in the forms of animals of the sea, land and air, but then benevolently acquiesced to Habaek's demand for a formal wedding ceremony. Following that ceremony the still- reluctant bride fled Haemosu, ultimately hiding with King Keumwa of Puyeo.

KIMSURO: The god sent down from the heavens to rule the Kaya region of Korea in approximately 43 C.E. Nine elders ruled the Kaya region – one from each of the main city- states, but the lack of a central authority prompted them to pray to the heavenly king of the gods Hwanin for a strong ruler to unite them. Hwanin's voice rang out from the heavens, drawing a crowd of hundreds to Kuji Mountain, where he instructed them to sing the Kujiga. After the song was sung, Hwanin lowered a golden chest from the sky, a chest containing six large golden eggs. From these eggs hatched the god Kimsuro and five of his subordinate aristocrats, all of whom grew to be nine feet tall in a matter of days. Kimsuro united the nine city-states into the kingdom of Kaya, defeated the god Talhae (future founder of Shilla) in a metamorphosis duel and refused to get married until the gods sent a wife, Hwangok, to him from India.

YUHWA: The goddess of willow trees, this daughter of the river- god Habaek was desired by the sun god Haemosu. The sun god trapped her by causing a copper palace to grow from some lines he drew on the ground. Yuhwa and her sisters, intrigued by the sudden appearance of the magnificent structure, ventured in and were lavishly entertained by Haemosu and his attendants. At a sign from the sun god the attendants made to bolt the doors so they could trap the three goddesses within. Yuhwa's sisters were swift enough to escape, but Yuhwa was captured by Haemosu and taken off to be his wife. Eventually she fled Haemosu and, while hiding with King Keumwa of Puyeo she gave birth to Haemosu's son Jumong.

TANGUN: The founder- god of the ancient Choson kingdom supposedly in 2333 B.C. Tangun was the son of Hwanung, the god of the laws who descended from the heavens to teach humanity how to live and adapt to the world when it was young. Tangun established an ancient city near Pyeongyang, which the demented Kim Jong IL of North Korea claimed to have unearthed in recent years but for some reason (HA!) refused to allow outside authorities in to confirm the claim. Tangun ruled as a combination king and high priest and is still worshipped today by many modern Koreans who follow Cheondogyo, "the religion of the heavenly way." We are told Tangun ruled for 1,500 years, then became the guardian god of Mount Taebaek.

IGONG: Also called Hallakkungi, this god tended the Flower Garden Of Life And Death. This garden contained flowers that were really the souls of each person on Earth and Igong oversaw the length and quality of each life. After ending those lives by plucking their corresponding flowers from the garden Igong also decided on the soul's merits for rebirth. This god was worshipped only on Jeju Island, the huge island off the southern coast of Korea. Jeju is also spelled Cheju because the alphabet has no true equivalent of that consonant sound from the Korean language.

Korean folklore

Korean folklore is well established, going back several thousand years. The folklore's basis derives from a variety of belief systems, including Shamanism, Confucianism, Buddhism and more recently Christianity. Mythical creatures often abound in the tales, including the Korean conception of goblins.

Types of Folklore's

There are many types of folklore in Korean culture, including Imuldam, focused on supernatural beings such as monsters, goblins and ghosts. The most common of which are the Dokkaebi, meaning goblin. However, this term differs from the European concept of 'goblin' in that they do not possess an evil or demonic characteristic. Instead, they are creatures with powers that seek to both bring delight to people and misery. These beings engage either in friendly or annoying behavior with humans. Their interactions with humans represent the belief in the supernatural and their interactions with humanity. The presence of these beings is meant to represent both difficulties and pleasures in life.

Women in Korean Folklore

In Korean folklore, there are a few legends that touch of the idea of feminism and the role of women in these tales.

Legend of Arang (Chosen Era): In the Legend of Arang, Arang is portrayed as very vulnerable. She is helpless, weak and innocent and needs to be rescued by a hero to avoid falling into the trap of her maid, who is tempting her. However, Arang's maid is seen as very beautiful but also a very evil temptress. From these two characters, it can be seen that women in the Chosen Era are seen secondary to men as they are always in need of rescue or too weak to fight for themselves. The Korean women were considered not marriageable if they were found of these traits.

Legend of Dangun: In the legend of Dangun, the bear who followed the orders of Hwanung was transformed into a beautiful woman, who eventually became the mother of Dangun. Through this tale, the reader can see that women are perceived as very patient and motherly figures.

Kumiho: Kumiho is a nine-tailed fox that appears in various Korean folktales. When this fox transforms itself into a human, it becomes a woman. One prominent trait of this fox is its trickster personality which is often used to trick men. This reflects a perception of women as being deceptive.

Hindu Mythology

Hindu mythology are narratives found in Hindu texts such as the Vedic literature, epics like Mahabharata and Ramayana, the Puranas, the regional literatures like Periya

Puranam. Hindu mythology is also found in widely translated popular texts such as the Panchatantra and Hitopadesha, as well as Southeast Asian texts.

Hinduism

Hindu mythology does not often have a consistent, monolithic structure. The same myth typically appears in various versions, and can be represented differently across socio-religious traditions. These myths have also been noted to have been modified by various philosophical schools over time and particularly in the Hindu tradition. These myths are taken to have deeper, often symbolic, meaning, and have been given a complex range of interpretations.

Texts

The Hindu Epic literature is found in genre of Hindu texts such as:

- Vedic literature.

- Puranas.

- Vedas.

Many of these legends evolve across these texts, the character names change or the story is embellished with greater details, yet the central message and moral values remain the same. According to Wendy Doniger,

Every Hindu epic is different; all Hindu epics are alike. Each Hindu epic celebrates the belief that the universe is boundlessly various, that everything occurs simultaneously, that all possibilities may exist without excluding the other. There is no single basic version of a Hindu epic; each is told and retold with a number of minor and major variations over the years. Great epics are richly ambiguous and elusive; their truths cannot be filed away into scholar's neat categories. Moreover, epics (in Hinduism) are living organisms that change constantly.

Hindu epic shares the creative principles and human values found in epic everywhere. However, the particular details vary and its diversity is immense, according to Doniger.

The Hindu legends embed the Indian thought about the nature of existence, the human condition and its aspirations through an interwoven contrast of characters, the good against the evil, the honest against the dishonest, the dharma-bound lover against the anti-dharma bully, the gentle and compassionate against the cruel and greedy. In these epics, everything is impermanent including matter, love and peace. Magic and miracles thrive, gods are defeated and fear for their existence, triggering wars or debates. Death threatens and re-threatens life, while life finds a way to creatively re-emerge thus conquering death. Eros persistently prevails over chaos.

The Hindu epics integrate in a wide range of subjects. They include stories about how and why cosmos originated (Hindu cosmology, cosmogony), how and why humans or all life forms originated (anthropogony) along with each's strengths and weaknesses, how gods originated along with each's strengths and weaknesses (theogony), the battle between good gods and bad demons (theomachy), human values and how humans can live together, resolve any disagreements (ethics, axiology), healthy goals in stages of life and the different ways in which each individual can live (householder, monk, purusartha), the meaning of all existence and means of personal liberation (soteriology) as well as legends about what causes suffering, chaos and the end of time with a restart of a new cycle (eschatology).

Dashavatara

A significant collection of Vaishnavism traditional reincarnations includes those related to the avatars of Vishnu. The ten most common of these include:

- Matsya: It narrates a great flood, similar to one found in many ancient cultures. The savior here is the Matsya (fish). The earliest accounts of Matsya mythology are found in the Vedic literature, which equate the fish saviour to the deity Prajapati. The fish-savior later merges with the identity of Brahma in post-Vedic era, and still later as an avatar of Vishnu. The legends associated with Matsya expand, evolve and vary in Hindu texts. These legends have embedded symbolism, where a small fish with Manu's protection grows to become a big fish, and the fish ultimately saves earthly existence.

- Kurma: The earliest account of Kurma is found in the Shatapatha Brahmana (Yajur veda), where he is a form of Prajapati-Brahma and helps with the samudra manthan (churning of cosmic ocean). In the Epics and the Puranas, the legend expands and evolves into many versions, with Kurma becoming an avatar of Vishnu. He appears in the form of a tortoise or turtle to support the foundation for the cosmos and the cosmic churning stick (Mount Mandara).

- Varaha: The earliest versions of the Varaha or boar legend are found in the *Taittiriya Aranyaka* and the *Shatapatha Brahmana*, both Vedic texts. They narrate that the universe was primordial waters. The earth was the size of a hand and was trapped in it. The god Prajapati (Brahma) in the form of a boar (*varaha*) plunges into the waters and brings the earth out. In post-Vedic literature, particularly the Puranas, the boar mythology is reformulated through an avatar of god Vishnu and an evil demon named Hiranyaksha who persecutes people and kidnaps goddess earth. Varaha-Vishnu fights the injustice, kills the demon and rescues earth.

Depictions of episodes from Hindu mythology.

- Narasimha: The Narasimha mythology is about the man-lion avatar of Vishnu. He destroys an evil king (Hiranyakashyapu), ends religious persecution and calamity on Earth, saves his devotee (Prahlad) from the suffering caused by torments and punishments for pursuing his religious beliefs, and thereby Vishnu restores the Dharma.

- Vamana.

- Parashurama.

- Rama.

- Krishna.

- Buddha.

- Kalki.

Japanese Mythology

Japanese mythology embraces Shinto and Buddhist traditions as well as agriculturally-based folk religion. The Shinto pantheon comprises innumerable *kami*.

Japanese myths, as generally recognized in the mainstream today, are based on the Kojiki, the Nihon Shoki, and some complementary books. The Kojiki, or "Record of

Ancient Matters", is the oldest surviving account of Japan's myths, legends and history. The Shintōshū describes the origins of Japanese deities from a Buddhist perspective, while the Hotsuma Tsutae records a substantially different version of the mythology.

One notable feature of Japanese mythology is its explanation of the origin of the Imperial Family, which has been used historically to assign godhood to the imperial line. The title of the Emperor of Japan, tennō, means "heavenly sovereign".

Note that Japanese is not transliterated consistently across all.

Creation Myth

In the Japanese creation myth, the first deities which came into existence, appearing at the time of the creation of the universe, are collectively called Kotoamatsukami.

Later, the seven generations of kami, known as Kamiyonanayo ("Seven Generations of the Age of the Gods"), emerged, following the formation of heaven and earth.

The first two generations are individual deities called hitorigami, while the five that followed came into being as male/female pairs of kami: brothers and sisters that were also married couples. In this chronicle, the Kamiyonanayo comprise 12 deities in total.

In contrast, the Nihon Shoki states that the Kamiyonanayo group was the first to appear after the creation of the universe, as opposed to the Kamiyonanayo appearing after the formation of heaven and earth. It also states that the first three generations of deities are hitorigami (individual deities) and that the later generations of deities are pairs of the opposite gender, as compared to the Kojiki's two generations of hitorigami.

Kuniumi and Kamiumi

Japan's creation narrative can be divided into the birth of the deities (Kamiumi) and the birth of the land (Kuniumi).

The seventh and last generation of Kamiyonanayo were Izanagi no Mikoto ("Exalted Male") and Izanami no Mikoto ("Exalted Female"), and they would be responsible for the creation of the Japanese archipelago and would engender other deities.

To help them to achieve this, Izanagi and Izanami were given a naginata decorated with jewels, named Ame-no-nuboko ("Heavenly Jeweled Spear"). The two deities then went to the bridge between heaven and earth, Amenoukihashi ("Floating Bridge of Heaven") and churned the sea below with the halberd. Drops of salty water formed the island, Onogoro ("self-forming"). The deities descended from the bridge of heaven and made their home on the island. Eventually, they fell in love and wished to mate. So they built a pillar named Amenomihashira around which they built a palace called Yashirodono ("the hall whose area is 8 arms' length squared"). Izanagi and Izanami circled the pillar in opposite directions, and when they met on the other side, Izanami, the female deity, spoke first in greeting. Izanagi did not think that this was proper, but they mated anyway. They had two children, Hiruko ("leech child") and Awashima ("pale island"), but the children were badly formed and are not considered gods in their original form. (Hiruko later became the Japanese god, Ebisu.)

The parents, who were dismayed at their misfortune, put the children into a boat and sent them to sea, and then petitioned the other gods for an answer about what they had done wrong. They were informed that Izanami's lack of manners was the reason for the defective births: a woman should never speak prior to a man; the male deity should have spoken first in greeting during the ceremony. So Izanagi and Izanami went around the pillar again, and this time, when they met, Izanagi spoke first. Their next union was successful.

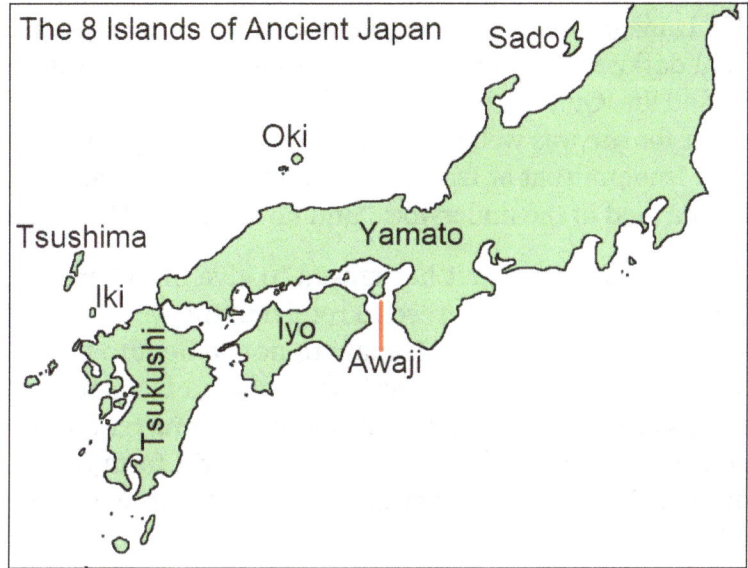

From their union were born the Ōyashima, or the eight great islands of Japan:

- Awaji.

- Iyo (later Shikoku).

- Oki.

- Tsukushi (later Kyūshū).

- Iki.

- Tsushima.

- Sado.

- Yamato (later Honshū).

Note that Hokkaidō, Chishima and Okinawa were not part of Japan in ancient times.

Izanami died giving birth to Kagutsuchi (incarnation of fire), also called Homusubi (causer of fire) due to severe burns. She was then buried on Mount Hiba, at the border of the old provinces of Izumo and Hoki, near modern-day Yasugi of Shimane Prefecture. In anger, Izanagi killed Kagutsuchi. His death also created dozens of deities.

The gods who were born from Izanagi and Izanami are symbolic aspects of nature and culture.

Izanagi in the Underworld

Izanagi lamented the death of Izanami and undertook a journey to Yomi ("the shadowy land of the dead"). Izanagi found little difference between Yomi and the land above, except for the eternal darkness. However, this suffocating darkness was enough to make him ache for light and life. Quickly, he searched for Izanami and found her. At first, Izanagi could not see her for she was well hidden in the shadows. Nevertheless, he asked her to return with him. Izanami spat at Izanagi and informed him that he was too late. She had already eaten the food of the underworld and now belonged to the land of the dead.

Izanagi was shocked at this news, but he refused to give in to her wishes to be left to the dark embrace of Yomi. Izanami agreed to return to the world but first requested to have some time to rest. She instructed Izanagi to not come into her bedroom. After a long wait, Izanami did not come out of her bedroom, and Izanagi was worried. While Izanami was sleeping, he took the comb that bound his long hair and set it alight as a torch. Under the sudden burst of light, he saw the horrid form of the once beautiful and graceful Izanami. The flesh of her ravaged body was rotting and was overrun with maggots and foul creatures.

Crying out loud, Izanagi could no longer control his fear and started to run, intending to return to the living and to abandon his death-ridden wife. Izanami woke up shrieking and indignant and chased after him. Izanami instructed the shikome, or foul women, hunt for the frightened Izanagi and to bring him back.

Izanagi, thinking quickly, hurled his headdress, which became a bunch of black grapes. The shikome fell on these but continued pursuit. Next, Izanagi threw his comb, which became a clump of bamboo shoots. Now it was Yomi's creatures that began to give chase, but Izanagi urinated against a tree and created a great river that increased his lead. Unfortunately, the shikome still pursued Izanagi, who began to hurl peaches at them. He knew that this would not delay them for long, but he was nearly free, for the boundary of Yomi was now close at hand.

Izanagi burst through the entrance and quickly pushed a boulder to the entrance of Yomi. Izanami screamed from behind this barricade and told Izanagi that, if he left her, she would destroy 1,000 living people every day. He furiously replied that he would give life to 1,500.

And so began the existence of Death, caused by the hands of the proud Izanagi, and his abandoned wife Izanami.

Sun, Moon and Storms

As could be expected, Izanagi went on to purify himself after recovering from his descent to Yomi. As he undressed and removed the adornments of his body, each item that he dropped to the ground formed a deity. Even more gods came into being when he went to the water to wash himself. The most important ones were created once he washed his face:

- Amaterasu (incarnation of the sun) from his left eye.

- Tsukuyomi (incarnation of the moon) from his right eye.

- Susanoo (incarnation of storms) from his nose.

Izanagi went on to divide the world between them with Amaterasu inheriting the heavens, Tsukuyomi taking control of the night and moon and the storm god Susanoo owning the seas. In some versions of the myth, Susanoo rules not only the seas but also all elements of a storm, including snow and hail, and, in rare cases, even sand.

Amaterasu and Susanoo

Amaterasu, the powerful sun goddess of Japan, is the most well-known deity of Japanese mythology. Her feuding with Susanoo, her uncontrollable brother, however, is equally infamous and appears in several tales. One story tells about Susanoo's wicked behavior toward Izanagi, who, tired of Susanoo's repeated complaints, banishes him to Yomi. Susanoo grudgingly acquiesces, but has first to attend some unfinished business. He goes to Takamagahara ("heaven") to bid farewell to his sister, Amaterasu. Amaterasu knows that her unpredictable brother does not have good intentions and is prepared for battle. "For what purpose do you come here?" asks Amaterasu. "To say farewell," answers Susanoo.

But she does not believe him and requests a contest for proof of his good faith. A challenge is set as to who can bring forth more noble and divine children. Amaterasu creates three women from Susanoo's sword, while Susanoo makes five men from Amaterasu's ornament chain. Amaterasu claims the title to the five attributed to Susanoo.

Both gods declare themselves to be victorious. Amaterasu's insistence in her claim drives Susanoo to violent campaigns that reach their climax when he hurls a half-flayed pony (an animal sacred to Amaterasu) into Amaterasu's weaving hall and causes the death of one of her attendants. Amaterasu, angered by the display, hides in the cave called Iwayado. As the sun goddess disappears into the cave, darkness covers the world.

Torii at Ama-no-Iwato Shrine, Takachiho, Miyazaki Prefecture.

All of the gods and goddesses strive to coax Amaterasu out of the cave, but she ignores them all. Finally, the kami of merriment, Ame-no-Uzume, hatches a plan. She places a large bronze mirror on a tree, facing Amaterasu's cave. Then, Uzume clothes herself in flowers and leaves, overturns a washtub and begins to dance upon it, drumming the tub with her feet. Finally, Uzume sheds the leaves and flowers and dances naked. All of the male gods roar with laughter, and Amaterasu becomes curious. When she peeks outside, a ray of light called "dawn" escapes and Amaterasu is dazzled by the beautiful goddess that she sees, this being her own reflection in the mirror. The god, Ameno-Tajikarawo, pulls her from the cave, which is sealed with a shimenawa. Surrounded by merriment, Amaterasu's depression disappears, and she agrees to return with her light. Uzume is then known as the kami of dawn as well as of mirth.

Susanoo and Orochi

Susanoo, exiled from heaven, comes to Izumo Province (now part of Shimane Prefecture). It is not long before he meets an old man and an old woman sobbing beside their daughter. The old couple explain that they originally had eight daughters who were devoured, one after the other, by the dragon, Yamata no Orochi ("eight-forked serpent", who is said to originate from Koshi—now Hokuriku region). The terrible dragon had eight heads and eight tails, stretched over eight hills, and is said to have eyes as red as good wine. Kushinada-hime ("rice paddy princess") was the last of the eight daughters.

Susanoo, who knew about the old couple's relation to Amaterasu, offers his assistance in return for their beautiful daughter's hand in marriage. The parents accept, and Susanoo transforms Kushinada into a comb and hides her safely in his hair. He also orders a large fence-like barrier to be built around the house. The fence has eight gates, with eight tables placed at each gate and eight casks placed on each table. Each cask is filled with eight-times-brewed rice wine.

Orochi arrives and finds his path blocked. After boasting about his prowess, he finds that he cannot get through the barrier. His keen sense of smell takes in the sake—which Orochi loves—and the eight heads are now faced with a problem. They want to drink the delicious sake, yet the fence blocks access to the sake. One head suggests that they simply smash the barrier, but that would knock over the sake. Another proposed that they combine their fiery breath and burn the fence to ash, but then the sake would evaporate. The heads begin to search for an opening. They find the hatches, and, eager for the sake, they wish to poke their heads through to drink it. Yet, the eighth head, which is the wisest, warns his brethren about the folly of such an act and volunteers to go through first to ensure that all is well. Susanoo waits for his chance. He allows the head to drink some sake in safety and to report to the others that there is no danger. All eight heads plunge through the hatches and greedily drink every drop of the sake.

As the heads finish, Susanoo launches his attack on Orochi. Drunken from drinking so much sake, the great serpent is no match for the spry Susanoo who decapitates and slays Orochi. A nearby river is said to have turned red with the blood of the defeated serpent. As Susanoo cuts the dragon into pieces, he finds an excellent sword from a tail of the dragon that his sword had been unable to cut. The sword is later presented to Amaterasu and named Ama no Murakumo no Tsurugi/"Sword of the Gathering Clouds of Heaven", which was later called Kusanagi, "Grass Cutter"). This sword was to feature prominently in many other tales.

Prince Ōkuninushi

Mostly known by his nickname Ōkuninushi, Ōnamuji was a descendant of Susanoo, and represented the power structure localized in the Izumo area. Ōkuninushi's people succeeded in unifying territory to some measure, but later relinquished control to the Yamato-based clans.

Ōkuninushi helps the White Hare

A tale of how the merciful Ōkuninushi helped the beleaguered rabbit or hare is of enduring fame, and often told as a sort of a *Mukashibanashi* or "once upon a time tale". It is found in *Kojiki* but not recorded in the "Nihongi".

Ōkuninushi (at the time he was just Ōnamuji without the august nickname) had eighty brothers who were rival suitors courting Princess Yakami/Yagami of Inaba to become her husband. They started out of their homeland of Izumo headed for the neighboring province, with Okuninushi brought along to follow and carry the luggage of his more eminent brothers. The brothers encountered a rabbit who had been flayed (by crocodile-fish, usually interpreted as sharks) and lay in agony upon a sea shore. In a wicked-hearted gesture, they advised the rabbit to bathe in the briny sea and blow himself dry in the wind. The rabbit found himself in worse agony. Ōnamuji, who came lagging behind, took pity on the creature and told the hare to wash in fresh water, then roll in the scattered fleece of cattail plants. The cured rabbit made a divined prediction that Ōnamuji would be the one to win Princess Yakami, "though thou bearest the bag,"

Princess Suseri

As the hare predicted, Princess Yakami pronounces her choice of Ōnamuji for husband before the eighty gods, and they all conspire and kill him twice over. His mother petitions Kamimusubi, one of the creator deities, and resuscitates him each time, finally sending him off to seek Susanoo who has been banished to the Netherworld (Ne-no-kuni), and to obtain his wise counsel.

Here Ōnamuji meets face to face with Susanoo's daughter Suseri-hime and they immediately marry. The crafty Susanoo tests Ōnamuji several times, but, in the end, Susanoo approves of the young boy and foretells Ōnamuji's victory over his brothers.

Although the Yamato tradition attributes the creation of the Japanese islands to Izanagi and Izanami, the Izumo tradition claims that Ōnamuji, along with a dwarf god called Sukunabiko, contribute to, or at least finish, the creation of the Japanese islands.

Ninigi's Descent to the Middle World

In the Nihongi here begins the section entitled "Age of the Gods: Part II" (kamiyo ge-kan.

The episode of the Tenson kōrin ("Descent of the Heavenly Grandson") begins with description of how the heavenly gods (Ama-tsu-kami) who dwelled in the Heavenly Plains (Takama-ga-hara) peered down upon the earth below (known by the stilted name Ashihara no Nakatsukuni ("Reedy Plains Middle World") which represents Japan specifically and not the whole world. To this land they dispatched various members of their own kind to subjugate it. Amaterasu had decreed her own grandson Ninigi to rule over the terrestrial world, but the terrestrial gods (kuni-tsu-kami) were not altogether willing to hand it over, and odd sorts of terrestrial gods were still lurking about making it too dangerous.

Some of the gods first appointed to quell the middle world were derelict in their mission, or joined leagues with the terrestrial gods. After several false starts, two gods were finally successful. They were Ame-no-ohabari (aka Itsu-no-ohabari; elsewhere this kami is said to be a sword) and Takemikazuchi. They embarked aboard the Ame-no-torifune or "Deity Heavenly-Bird-Boat" to their military campaign. These two sabre-rattling deities were able to frighten Ōkuninushi's two sons into flight, causing Ōkuninushi to abdicate and relinquish the territories to the Heavenly Grandson.

Amaterasu was now able to decree the Tenson kōrin, also referred to as amori, installing her grandson to rule over the terrestrial middle world. She endowed him the Three Sacred Treasures (Imperial Regalia of Japan):

- The necklace Yasakani no magatama (now in the Imperial Palace in Tokyo).

- The mirror Yata no kagami (now in the Grand Shrine of Ise).

- The sword Kusanagi (now in the Atsuta Shrine in Nagoya).

The mirror was to be worshipped as a representation of Amaterasu. A number of deities were made to make the descent at this time.

Ninigi and his company went down to the earth and came to Himuka (Hyūga province, today's Miyazaki prefecture), there he founded his palace.

Ninigi's Marriage

Ninigi met Konohanasakuya-hime (symbol of flowers), the daughter of Yamatsumi (master of mountains), and they fell in love. Ninigi asked Yamatsumi for his daughter's hand. The father was delighted and offered both of his daughters, Iwanaga (symbol of rocks) and Sakuya (symbol of flowers). However, Ninigi married only Sakuya and refused Iwanaga.

"Iwanaga is blessed with eternity and Sakuya with prosperity", Yamatsumi said in regret, "by refusing Iwanaga, your life will be brief from now on". Consequently, Ninigi and his descendants became mortal.

Sakuya conceived by a night and *Ninigi* doubted her. To prove legitimacy of her children, Sakuya swore by her luck and took a chance; she set fire to her room when she had given birth to her three babies. By this, Ninigi knew her chastity. The names of the children were Hoderi, Hosuseri and Howori.

Luck of the Sea and Luck of the Mountains

Ninigi's elder son Hoderi or "Fire-Shine" had the gift of the bounty of the sea, and gained his livelihood by fishing (and bore the nickname Umisachihiko or "Luck of the Sea"). The younger son Hoori or "Fire-Fade" had the gift of the bounty of the mountains, and was a hunter (and nicknamed Yamasachihiko or "Luck of the Mountains").

One day, Luck of the Mountains asked his elder brother Luck of the Sea to exchange their tools and swap places for a day. He wanted to try his bid at fishing. But he did not catch a single fish, and worse, he lost his borrowed fishhook. To make amends, he shattered the very sword he was wearing to make a hundred, then a thousand hooks to replace what he lost, but the elder brother would accept nothing but the original fishhook.

Luck of the Mountains meets Toyotama, in *Wadatsumi no Iroko no Miya*

Luck of the Mountains was sitting on a beach balefully weeping, there came to his aid Shiotsuchi-no-oji (one of the deities now enshrined at Shiogama Jinja). The tide god built him a small ship described as being *manashikatsuma*, and sent him on a journey to the fish-scaled palace of the Watatsumi (Sea God, often conceived of as a dragon-god). There he had a fateful meeting with the Sea God's daughter Princess Toyotama, and married her. After three years, he remembered his brother and his fishhook, and was longing to return home.

Watatsumi gathered his piscean minions, and soon the fishhook was found in the throat of a bream (tai) and restored to Luck of the Mountains. The Sea God also imparted two magical balls: Shihomitsutama which could cause a flood, and Shihohirutama which could cause water to recede and dry up. And he gave additional strategic advice to gain advantage from his contentious elder brother. So riding on a fathom-long crocodile-fish or shark (hitohiro-wani they returned to dry land.

The pregnant Princess Toyotama built a cormorant feather-thatched maternity house and pleaded her husband for privacy, as she would be reverting to her true shape while delivering her child. But Howori (Luck of the Mountains) was overcome with curiosity, and peeped inside to discover her transformed into a crawling 8-fathom "croc-fish" (shark, dragon), and scuttered away in fright. Ashamed and disgusted by her husband's breach of trust, she abandoned the newborn and returned to sea. The infant prince was named Ugaya meaning "cormorant house".

Ugaya married his aunt, the sea princess Tamayori and had five children, including Iwarebiko, who was later to become Emperor Jimmu. In the Nihongi, the "Age of the

Gods" section ends here, and is followed by sections under the titles of the reigns of each Emperor.

Mythical Legends of Emperors

First Emperor Jimmu

The first legendary Emperor of Japan, best known by his posthumous name of Emperor Jimmu was referred to in the records by the title of Iwarebiko. He is the son of Ugaya, descendant of Ninigi, and the sea princess Tamayori. His given name was Hiko-hohodemi.

Jimmu Tennō.

His ascension marked the "Transition from Age of the Gods to Human Age". With claimed descent from sun-goddess Amaterasu through Ninigi, Emperor Jimmu launched an expedition to capture Yamato.

After taking control of Yamato province, he established the imperial throne and acceded in the year of kanototori. His pedigree is summarized as follows:

- Izanagi is born of his own accord.

- Amaterasu is born from the left eye of Izanagi.

- Oshihomimi is born from an ornament of Amaterasu.

- Ninigi is a son of Oshihomimi and Akizushi.

- Howori is a son of Ninigi and Sakuya.

- Ugaya is a son of Howori and Toyotama.

- Iwarebiko is a son of Ugaya and Tamayori.

Jimmu's Conquest of the East

The descendants of Ninigi, including Jimmu, were rooted in Himuka Myth Road of the Hyūga province (today Takachiho, Miyazaki Prefecture).

After Jimmu's death, an elder prince named Tagishishimi (who was not first in line as successor) moved to consolidate power under him while everyone else was in mourning, and plotted to slay his two younger half-brothers. The plot was suppressed, and the younger prince who had the courage to pluck the bow and shoot Tagishishimi fatally was cede the crown to become the next emperor, Suizei.

Eight Undocumented Emperors

Of the eight emperors who succeeded Jimmu, there is very little record of their deeds, so they are described collectively under Book III of *Nihon Shoki*. Regarding Emperor Suizei, the foregoing description of how he suppressed his elder brother's insurrection. And for the other legendary rulers, not much more than their genealogy is given.

The 10th Emperor Sujin is discussed in the Nihon Shoki.

Human Sacrifice and Haniwa

Nihon shoki states that when his uncle died, all his closer retainers were buried around in perimeter around the kofun tumulus, but their wailings could be heard for days. Note: the word junshi also includes such deaths compelled upon retainers. cf. similar forced sacrificial burials were evidenced from Shang Dynasty grave sites in China. This emperor allegedly decided this practice was cruel and must cease; and, four years later, he adopted the idea forwarded by Nomi no Sukune to bury clay figurines called haniwa instead of live men.

God of Japanese Sweets

The Kojiki reports that during the reign of the 11th emperor Suinin, a man named Tajimamori was sent to Tokoyo-no-kuni ("Eternal Land") in a quest for the tokijiku-no-kaku-no-konomi He was able to gather eight vine-like trees and eight spear-like trees. But by the time he returned, the Emperor was dead. The Kojiki identifies the fruit as the tachibana, a type of small, sour citrus.

Tajimamori has later been hailed as the Kami of wagashi (Japanese confection and sweets), revered at Nakashima Shrine in Toyooka, Hyōgo, though this is little known trivia to the average Japanese.

The Nihon shoki dates Tajimamori's travel to Suinin 90, and makes him out to be the great-grandson of Amenohiboko, a Korean prince who came to Japan just two years earlier. However this is anachronistic according to Kojiki, which places Amenohiboko in a much later era.

Citrus tachibana.

Yamato Takeru

Much of the book of the 12th Emperor Keikō is taken up by the heroic deeds of his prince, Yamato Takeru.

Creatures

It is probably more typical to find lists of items and weapons that appear in the Japanese mythology. However, here is a tentative list of creatures:

Creatures in mythological tracts:

- Yamata no Orochi, the eight-headed serpent, discussed above.

- The rabbit aided by Ōkuninushi, and the wani (crocodile, modern scholars assume it to be a type of shark) that flayed it.

- Yatagarasu, a three-legged crow which guided the way to Emperor Jimmu. (In China, such a bird is said to dwell in the sun, and may be related to sunspots; cf. Moon rabbit).

- Kinshi, blindingly bright golden kite that aided Jimmu; it may be a double of the crow.

- Watatsumi, sea god, often called Ryūjin or Dragon God.

- Yato-no-kami.

Creatures in legendary tracts:

- Mizuchi.

Creatures associated with Shinto deities:

- The Oni folklore legend.

- Ōnamazu or Giant Catfish; said to dwell underground causing earthquakes, said to be quelled by the god Takemikazuchi.

- Shinigami, a Japanese god of death.

Phillipine Mythology

Philippine mythology refers to the body of myths, tales, and belief systems held by Filipinos (composed of more than a hundred ethnic peoples in the Philippines), originating from various cultures and traditions of the peoples of what eventually became the Philippines. Philippine mythology is incorporated from various sources, having similarities with Indonesian and Malay myths, as well as Hindu, Muslim, Shinto, Buddhist, and Christian traditions, such as the notion of heaven (kaluwalhatian, kalangitan, kamurawayan, etc.), hell (kasamaan, sulad, etc.), and the human soul (kaluluwa, kaulolan, makatu, ginokud, etc.). Philippine mythology attempts to explain the nature of the world through the lives and actions of deities (called anitos in the north and diwatas in the south), heroes, and mythological creatures. The majority of these myths were passed on through oral tradition, and preserved through the aid of community spiritual leaders or shamans (babaylan, katalonan, mumbaki, baglan, machanitu, walian, mangubat, bahasa, etc.) and community elders.

The Maranao people believe that Lake Lanao is a gap that resulted
in the transfer of Mantapoli into the center of the world.

The term 'Philippine mythology' has been used since the 20th century by successive generations as a general term for all mythologies within the Philippines. Each ethnic group in the Philippines has their own distinct mythologies (or religion), pantheon of deities, and belief systems. For example, the mythology of the Maranao people is completely different from the mythology of neighboring Subanon people, while the mythology of the Hiligaynon people is also completely different from the mythology of the neighboring Suludnon people. The Philippines is composed of more than a hundred distinct ethnic peoples, according to a 21st-century map published by the Komisyon ng Wikang Filipino, the *Atlas Filipinas.*

Portrait of the first man, Malakas, and woman, Maganda, who came out from a
bamboo pecked by the bird form of the deity of peace, Amihan, in Tagalog mythology.

Philippine mythologies and indigenous religions have historically been referred as Anitism, meaning "ancestral religion". Other terms used were Anitismo, a Hispano-Filipino translation, and Anitería, a derogatory version used by most members of the Spanish clergy. Today, many ethnic peoples continue to practice and conserve their unique indigenous religions, notably in ancestral domains, although foreign and foreign-inspired religions continue to influence their life-ways through conversions, inter-marriage, and land-buying. Various scholarly works have been made regarding Anitism and its many topics, although much of its stories and traditions are still undocumented by the international anthropological and folkloristic community.

There are two significant sources of Philippine mythologies, namely, oral literature and written literature.

Oral literature (also known as folk literature) are stories that have been or still are being passed down from one generation to another through oral means such as verbal communication. All sources of Philippine mythologies are originally oral literature, the same way with all known mythologies and folklore in the world ranging from Islamic, Hindu, Shinto, to Christian mythologies. As oral literature is passed on verbally, changes in stories and addition of stories through time are natural phenomenons and part of the evolving dynamism of Philippine mythology. Despite many attempts to record all oral literature of the Philippines, majority of stories pertaining to Philippine mythologies have yet to be properly documented due to a lack of scholars focusing on the subject. These oral traditions were intentionally interfered by the Spanish through the introduction of Christian mythologies in the 16th century. Some examples of such interference are the Biag ni Lam-ang and the Tale of Bernardo Carpio, where the names of certain characters were permanently changed into Spanish ones. Resurgent ripples of interest towards oral literature in the Philippines have sprang since the 21st century due to sudden interests among the masses, notably the youth, coupled by various mediums such as literary works, television, radio, and social media.

Rice terracing and its accompanied myths developed in the Philippines independently from other terracing societies in Southeast Asia.

Written literature are oral literature that have been put in physical record such as manuscripts or publications. Juan de Plasencia wrote the Relacion de las Costumbres de Los Tagalos in 1589, documenting the traditions of the Tagalog people at the time. Other accounts during the period are Miguel de Loarca's Relacion de las Yslas Filipinas and Pedro Chirino's Relacion de las Island Filipinas. Various books regarding Anitism have been published by numerous universities throughout the country, such as Mindanao State University, University of San Carlos, University of the Philippines, Ateneo Universities, Silliman University, and University of the Cordilleras, as well as respected non-university publishing houses such as Anvil Publishing. The publication of these books range from the 16th century to the 21st century. There are also printed but unpublished sources of Philippine mythologies, notably college and graduate school theses. Specific written literature should not be used as a generalizing asset of a particular story, as stories differ from town to town or village to village, despite the people of a particular area belonging to the same ethnic group. Some examples are the story of Bakunawa and the Seven Moons and the story of The Tambanokano, which have multiple versions depending on the locality, people's ethnicity, origin of story, and cultural progression.

As oral literature is always the beginning of written literature, there are still many Philippine myths that have yet to be made into written literature, as many oral literature in the Philippines have yet to be properly documented. In fact, scholars, both foreign and local, continue to document previously unheard oral literature in the Philippines even up to the 21st century. Like other religions and belief systems throughout the world, the mythologies (or indigenous religions) in the Philippines have been constantly evolving even up to modern times. Many Filipinos have reverted to their respective indigenous ethnic religions.

Shamans

Indigenous shamans (called babaylan, balian, katalonan, walian, machanitu, mumbaki, mandadawak, tao d'mangaw, bahasa, baglan, duwarta, and many other names depending on the associated ethnic group), were spiritual leaders of various ethnic peoples of the pre-colonial Philippine islands. These shamans, many of which are still extant, were almost always women or feminized men (asog or bayok). They were believed to have spirit guides, by which they could contact and interact with the spirits and deities (anito or diwata) and the spirit world. Their primary role were as mediums during pag-anito séance rituals. There were also various subtypes of shamans specializing in the arts of healing and herbalism, divination, and sorcery. Numerous types of shamans use different kinds of items in their work, such as talismans or charms known as agimat or anting-anting, curse deflectors such as buntot pagi, and sacred oil concoctions, among many other objects. All social classes, including the shamans, respect and revere their deity statues (called larauan, bulul, manang, etc.) which represent one or more specific deities within their ethnic pantheon, which includes non-ancestor deities and deified ancestors.

A Hiligaynon woman depicting a babaylan (Visayan shaman) during a festival. According to Spanish records, majority of pre-colonial shamans were women, while the other portion was composed of feminized men. Both of which were treated by the natives with high respect, equal to the datu (domain ruler).

ar with the pre-colonial noble class. In the absence of the datu (head of the domain), the shaman takes in the role of interim head of the domain. Shamans were powerful ritual specialists who had influence over the weather, and can tap various spirits in the natural and spiritual realms. Shamans were held in such high regard as they were believed to possess powers that can block the dark magic of an evil datu or spirit and heal the sick or wounded. Among other powers of the shaman were to ensure a safe pregnancy and child birth. As a spiritual medium, shamans also lead rituals with offerings to the various divinities or deities. As an expert in divine and herb lore, incantations, and concoctions of remedies, antidotes, and a variety of potions from various roots, leaves, and seeds, the shamans were also regarded as allies of certain datus in subjugating an enemy, hence, the indigenous shamans were also known for their specialization in medical and divine combat.

15th century Ifugao bulul with a pamahan (ceremonial bowl) in
the Louvre Museum, France.

Shamans were highly respected members of the community, on pUnlike Christian priests or Buddhist monks, the shamans of the many ethnicities in the Philippines always have another role in the community, aside from being spiritualists. Similar to the Shinto kannushi, among the jobs of the shaman range from being a merchant, warrior, farmer, fisherfolk, blacksmith, crafstfolk, weaver, potter, musician, and even as a barber or chef, depending on the preference of the shaman, skill of the shaman, and the need of the community. Some shamans have more than two occupations at a time, especially if a community lacks people with the needed skills to take upon the role of certain jobs. This tradition of having a second job (or more than two jobs) has been ingrained in certain cultural societies in the Philippines and is still practiced today by certain communities that have not been converted into Christianity. Specific communities that have been converted into Islam have also preserved this tradition through Muslim imams.

Historical evidence suggests that the religious realm was predominated by female shamans, with various accounts being specific about the fact that in the Philippines the majority of Animist shamans were women whose ranks were swelled by a few males who dressed as women. For example, the "Bolinao Manuscript", a document of the inquisitorial-type investigation carried out in and around the town of Bolinao during the 17th century, the Catholic missionaries identified 145 female shamans and three males who dressed as women from whom they confiscated items used during Animist rituals, a ratio of almost 50:1, highlighting the statistical imbalance between the female-to-male ratio of indigenous shamans. The "Manila Manuscript" also emphasized the auxiliary role of gender non-conforming male shamans in relation to the female shamans. These evidences, together with the fact that there were no written accounts of female sex/male gender identification amongst the women who exercised authority within the spiritual sphere, prove that spiritual potency was not dependent upon the identification with a neuter "third" sex/gender space, but rather on the identification with the feminine – whether the biological sex was female or male. Femininity was considered the vehicle to the spirit world during the pre-colonial era, and the male shaman's identification with the feminine reinforced the normative situation of female as shaman.

The Santo Niño de Cebu is the inspiration of the child rain-deity
of Visayan mythology named Santonilyo.

The negative counterparts of the shamans are collectively called as witches, however, these witches actually include a variety of different kinds of people with differing occupations and cultural connotations which depend on the ethnic group they are associated with. They are completely different from the Western notion of what a witch is. Notable examples of witches in a Philippine concept are the mannamay, witches known to the Ibanag people, mangkukulam, witches that use materials from nature and the cursee as a form of curse, and the mambabarang, witches that utilize insects as a form of curse, while notable sorcery tactics enforced by witches include *barang* (insect magic), *usik* (sharp magic), *hilo* (poison magic), *paktol* (doll magic), *laga* (boiling magic), and *sampal* (sea creature magic). As spiritual mediums and divinators, shamans are notable for countering and preventing the curses and powers of witches, notably through the usage of special items and chants. Aside from the shamans, there are also other types of people who can counter specific magics of witches, such as the mananambal, which specializes in countering *barang*. Shamans can also counter the curses of supernatural beings such as aswangs, however, as mortal humans, the physical strength of shamans are limited compared to the strength of an aswang being. This gap in physical strength is usually bridged by a dynamics of knowledge and wit.

Their influence waned when most of the ethnic groups of the Philippines were gradually converted to Islam and forcefully converted to Catholicism. Under the Spanish Empire, shamans were often maligned and falsely accused as witches and "priests of the devil" and were persecuted harshly by the Spanish clergy. The Spanish burned down everything they associated as connected to the native people's indigenous religion (including shrines such as the dambana), even forcefully ordering native children to defecate on their own god's idols, murdering those who disobey. In modern Philippine society, their roles have largely been taken over by folk healers, which are now predominantly male. In areas where the people have not been converted into Muslims or Christians, notably ancestral domains of indigenous peoples, the shamans and their cultural traits have continued to exist with their respective communities, although these shamans and their practices are being slowly diluted by Christian religions which continue to interfere with their life-ways.

Concept of Realms

Like most mythologies (or religions) in the world, the concept of realms focuses greatly on heaven, earth, and hell. These worldwide concepts are also present in the many mythologies of the Philippines, although there are stark differences between ethnic groups, with ethnic-endemic additions, subtractions, and complexities in the beliefs of ethnic realms. Additionally, unlike the general Western concept of heaven and hell, in the Philippine concept, heaven may be located in the underworld, while hell may be located in the skyworld, depending on the associated ethnic group. These differences are notably caused by both cultural diffusion (where portions of cultures are introduced through various activities such as trade) and cultural parallelism (where portions of cultures develop independently without foreign influences). These diffusions and parallelisms are also present in the many story motifs of Philippine mythologies. Some examples of the concept of realms in the many ethnic groups in the Philippines are as follows:

- Tagalog: The upperworld is called Kaluwalhatian, and is the home of specific deities who belong to the court of Bathala, the Tagalog supreme deity. The middleworld are the domains of mankind, other deities and various mythological races, while in the underworld, there are two realms, namely, Maca (realm where the spirits of good mortals go to) and Kasanaan (realm where the spirits of sinful mortals go to). Deities also dwell in the underworld, notably Sitan and his four agents. There is also Batala, a reappearing mountain realm located in the middleworld and is filled with the sacred "tigmamanukan" omen creatures.

- Palaw-an: The earthly world is composed of seven plates, one on top of the other with a center pole connecting all of them; mankind is believed to live in the middle of the fourth plate.

- Tagbanwa: The earthworld and the underworld are complete opposites as night in the earthworld is day in the underworld, and vice versa; rivers flow backward in the underworld, from sea to mountains, and rice is always eaten cold.

- Batak: The ancestral land of the Batak is called Kabatakan, which is found in the middle layer (fourth layer) of the universe; the universe has seven layers (*lukap*) consisting of a center tier (fourth layer) surrounded by ocean and inhabited by humans, animals, plants, super-human beings, and aggressive entities; Puyok, the highest sacred mountain in Kabatakan, is regarded as the original place of all malevolent *panya'en*; the Gunay Gunay, at the edge of the universe, is perceived as the place of origin of the couple divinities, Baybay (goddess and master of rice) and Ungaw (god and master of bees); the Batak believe that capitalism and the exploitation of the natural resources are signals of the destruction of the Batak culture.

- Sulodnon: The universe has three realms; the upperworld is Ibabawnon, which is divided into two realms, one for the male deities and the other for female deities; the middleworld is Pagtung-an, where the earth is located; the lowerworld is Idadalmunon, where the souls of the dead go to; initially, there was no land, only a sky and an expanse of water called Linaw; earth was established upon the excretion of an earthworm found by Bayi, a creation giantess.

Subanon people at one of Mount Malindang's waterfalls. According to tradition, the Subanon do not practice division of labor based on sex, the same way as their deities.

- Bisaya: The universe has seven layers; the first is uninhabited and nothing can be found in its vastness; the second is called Tibugnon and is made of water filled with mermaids and sea fairies who govern their separate kingdoms; the third layer is called Idalmunon which is the bowels of the earth and is inhabited by underground spirits; the fourth layer is called Lupan-on which is the earth where mankind and various supernatural beings live in; the fifth layer is called Kahanginan which is the atmosphere directly above earth and is the home of flying beings suchs as the bentohangin race and the hubot race; the sixth layer is called Ibabaw-non which is inhabited by special babaylans who intercede for man with spirits; the last layer and the highest is called Langit-non, which is the abode of Maka-ako, the creator of the Bisaya universe;

these seven layers can be classified into three categories, namely Kahilwayan, the skyworld realms ruled by Kaptan and inhabited by deities who assist him, Kamaritaan, the middleworld home of humans which is ruled by Sidapa and Makaptan and inhabited by the gods of their middleworld court, and lastly, Kasakitan, the lowerworld realms ruled by Magyan and Sumpoy; Kasakitan is said to have a unique sub-realm called Kanitu-nituhan which is ruled by the god Sisiburanen.

- Bicolano: It is believed that the sky and the waters are the first thing in existence; after the divine upheaval against the god Languit, the sun, moon, stars, and earth were formed through the bodies of his dead grandchildren; an unnamed giant is said to support the world, where his finger movements caused earthquakes; if the giant's body moves, it is said to cause the end of the world.

- Ilokano: The sky, sun, moon, stars, rivers, seas, and mountains are said to be created by the giant Anglao upon the order of an unnamed supreme deity; the underworld is guarded by the giant dog, Lobo.

- Kapampangan: The sky, earth, planets, and stars were in existence while land was created after the great divine war of the gods which was caused by the beauty of the divine daughter of Mangechay, the Kapampangan supreme deity; the gods lived in different faraway planets, and they travelled from planet to planet, with each travel taking up to hundreds of years.

- Ifugao: Initially, it is believed that there are two mythical worlds, namely Daya and Lagud. Daya is the downstream east, while Lagud is the upstream west. This notion later developed into a layered concept of the universe, where Daya became the upperworld which includes four layers, namely, Hudog, Luktag, Hubulan, and Kabunian, where Kabunian is the lowest of the upperworld, and is home to the god Liddum, the only deity who directly communicated with mankind for the deities of the upper layers of the upperworld. Each realm's upper surface layer is believed to be earthen and filled with fields and gardens, while the lower surface is made of smooth blue stone. The middleworld is the mortal world, directly below the Kabunian layer, and has the broadest circumference in the global universe, as both the upperworld and the lowerworld grow successively smaller as they approach the end of the celestial globe. The lowerworld is called Dalom, which is made of an indeterminate number of layers. The souls of those who were murdered are believed to go to its lowest level. Finally, the realm of Lagud was transformed by the layered universe concept into a far eastern sub-realm region.

- Kalinga: The universe is believed to look like a big plate (personifies the earth) with a smaller dome (personifies the sky) resting on it; the sky is not transparent, rather it is opaque and solid and its rim is three meters thick.

A double ikat weaving from Sulu, made of banana leaf stalk fiber. Among the weaving traditions of the Philippines, the most complex is of the Tausug people's.

- Kankanaey: The middleworld is believed to be carried by four huge posts which stands on the lowerworld; a giant hog causes earthquakes every time it scratches against one of the posts; the lowerworld is call Aduongan and is inhabited by cannibals.

- Ibaloi: The skyworld and the underworld were once close to each other; this changed after a great war between the two sides where a man from the underworld hit the sun god with an arrow; the sun god moved the two world apart, establishing a gap between; earth as the middleworld was afterwards established.

- Bukidnon: The Banting is a small circula space of immense brightness extant in the beginning, surrounded by a sacred rainbow; the realm called Haldan ta Paraiso (Garden of Paradise) was created by Diwta na Magbabaya from materials provided by Dadanhayan ha Sugay; the garden is where Agtayuban rests his wings; the upperworld is said to be divided into seven tiers and the underworld also has seven tiers, but only three are identifiable; the middleworld is saucer-shaped, as is the sky, but with the concavity towards the earth.

- Manobo: The world is on iron posts created by the god Makalindung who lives in the center with a python; the sky is round and ends at the limits of the sea; this limit is the sea navel, where waters ascend and descend; the underworld is below the pillars of the earth and is divided into different subsections where each Manobo nation is assigned a place; there are different sections for other tribes and even for foreign peoples.

- Mandaya: The earth is flat but pressed into mountains by a mythological woman; the earth rests on the back of a gigantic eel which causes earthquakes when agitated.

- Bagobo: Deities live in the skyworld, where various realms are present, each being ruled by a divinity lesser than the supreme deity Pamulak Manobo; the entrance to the skyworld has numerous kampilan swords who fight without any wielder; the underworld for the sinful dead is called Gimokudan, where spirits with heavy misdeeds are engulfed by flames, while those with little misdeeds are not, although their bodies are covered with sores as they lay in an acid that burns like lemon juice; a special underworld sub-realm called Banua Mebuyan, near a black river, is reserved for children who died at their mother's breast and these souls are nourished by the many-breasted goddess Mebuyan; children's souls who graduate from Banua Mebuyan go to another district to join souls that died of disease; all souls pass through Banua Mebuyan before going to Gimokudan; another special underworld district is dedicated to those slayed by swords or spears, where scars will continue to be with the soul and plants in the district are colored like blood.

- Tboli: The skyworld has seven layers, where the last layer is the dwelling of the supreme couple deities, Kadaw La Sambad and Bulon La Mogoas; earth was formed due to the body of the sterile god, S'fedat; there are different afterworlds depending on the circumstances of death; the soul of those killed via swords in battle and murder go to Kayong, where the soul is greeted with continual music; if a soul dies a natural death, it goes to Mogul, which has everything a soul desires.

- Maranao: The world has seven layers; the earth and sky are also divided into seven layers; some of the layers of the earth are the human, layer of karibangs, and the layer under the sea inhabited by nymph-like beings; each sky layer has a door guarded by a garoda; the seventh layer of the sky is heaven, where the tree of life grows and whose leaves inscribes the names of all living humans; once the leaf of a person ripens or dries and falls, the person dies; in a section of heaven, the jars containing the souls of every person alive exists; this jar area is guarded by the fearsome creature Walo.

Each ethnic group in the Philippines, which number more than a hundred, has their own indigenous concept of realms. The diversity of ethnic groups in the country contributes to the unique diversity of realms believed to be found endemically in specific ethnic domains and mythologies.

Supreme Deities of Philippine Mythology

Each ethnic group in the country has their own distinct pantheon of deities and belief systems. Some ethnic groups have a supreme deity, while others revere ancestor spirits and the spirits of the natural world. The usage of the term "diwata" is mostly found in the central and southern Philippines while the usage of "anito" is found in the northern Philippines. There is also a 'buffer zone' area where both terms are used interchangeably. The etymology of diwata may have been derived from the Sanskrit word, devata, meaning "deity", while anito's etymology may have been derived from the proto-Malayo-Polynesian word qanitu and the proto-Austronesian qanicu, both meaning "ancestral spirits". Both diwata and anito, which are gender-neutral terms, can be translated into deities, ancestral spirits, and guardians, depending on the associated ethnic group. The concept of both diwata and anito are similar to the concept of the Japanese kami. However, during the colonization era between the 16th century to the 19th century, the Spanish intentionally modified the meaning of both diwata and anito as both terms were not in line with the monotheistic concept of Christianity. This modification was supported by the Americans in the early 20th century. The meaning of diwata was transformed into "fairy or enchantress", while the meaning of anito was transformed into "ancestors and spirits", although in areas not subjugated by Spain, the original meanings of the two terms were not changed. Each of the supreme deities per ethnic people is completely distinct, even if some of their names are the same or almost the same.

Mayon volcano, within the Albay UNESCO biosphere reserve, is believed to have sprouted from the burial ground of lovers Magayon and Pangaronon. Later, the supreme god of the Bicolano people, Gugurang, chose Mayon as his abode and repository for the sacred fire of Ibalon.

The supreme deities of various ethnic groups in the Philippines must be treated as *existing* and *prevalent*, as they are still believed by many societies, the same way Christians believe in a supreme god they refer as 'God' and the same way Muslims believe in a supreme god they refer as 'Allah'. Below are some of the supreme deities (head of an ethnic people's divine pantheon of deities) in the Philippines:

- Mangechay: Supreme deity of the Kapampangan people; known as the 'net weaver' for the sky she weaved with her own fabric; the stars at night are said to be the fabric holes she envisioned in some accounts, Mengechay is female, while in others, the deity is male.

Sunset at the edge of Kanlaon Volcano. The Hiligaynon supreme goddess,
Kanlaon, resided within the huge land mass after the epic heroes,
Laon and Kan, slayed the dragon-like monster who lived there.

- Malayari: Supreme deity of the Sambal people; deity of power and strength and is believed to reside in Mount Pinatubo; albeit having almost the same name, he is ethnically different from the Kapampangan people's Apûng Malyari and the Tagalog people's Mayari.

- Bathala: Supreme deity of the Tagalog people; known as the grand conserver of the universe who lives in Kaluwalhatian; despite the similarity in name, he is different from the Bicolano people's Batala and the Bisaya people's Bathala, which was another name of their supreme god, Kaptan.

- Kabunian: Supreme deity of the Ibaloi people; despite the similarity in name, he is different from the Bontoc people's Kabunian and the Ifugao people's Kabunian.

- Kadaw La Sambad and Bulon La Mogoaw – Husband and wife, supreme deities of the Tboli people; Kadaw La Sambad is the sun god, while Bulon La Mogoaw is the moon goddess; both deities are said to reside in the "seventh heaven".

- Melu: Also called D'wata, supreme deity of the Blaan people; he possesses golden teeth and shining divine skin; he is accompanied by the sky spirit Fiuwe and, strangely, the evil spirit Tasu Weh.

- Dadanhayan ha Sugay, Diwata na Magbabaya, and Agtayabun: Trinity deities, supreme deities of the Bukidnon people; Dadanhayan ha Sugay, "lord from whom permission is asked", is depicted as an evil ten-headed being who drools continuously; Diwata na Magbabaya, "pure god who wills all things", is depicted a good human; Lastly, Agtayuban, "adviser and peace-maker", was depicted with a hawk-like head, powerful wings and a human body; the trinity of the deities symbolize the evil, the good, and the balance between the two; Diwata na Magbabaya is believed to have created the eight elements, namely *tumbaga* (bronze), *bulawan* (gold), *salapi* (coins), *bato* (rock), *gabon* (clouds), *ulan* (rain), *puthaw* (iron), and *tubig* (water), from which he created the sea, sky, moon, and stars.

- Malaon and Makapatag: Supreme deity of the Waray people; known as a single deity with two aspects; Malaon (meaning ancient one) is an understanding goddess, while Makapatag (meaning the leveller) is a stern and fearful god.

- Kaptan: Supreme deity of the Bisaya people; believed to dwell in the sky and possesses a sacred golden shell which can transform anyone into anything; also called Bathala, but is distinct from the Tagalog people's Bathala and the Bicolano people's Batala.

- Kan-Laon: Supreme deity of the Hiligaynon people; originally a resident of Mount Madia-as in Panay, she shifted her residence into the volcano, Kanlaon, in Negros island; she is also referred by the Hiligaynon as Lalahon.

- Gamhanan: Supreme deity of the Aklanon people; he was the giver of life, security, and livelihood; lives with many other gods in Mount Daeogdog, where he gives life and punished errant mortals; used to have a loyal deer-like pet and messenger called Panigotlo, which bleated as a sign of abundance to mortals or foretells floods and despairs to alert the people

- Eugpamolak Manobo: Also called Manama, Diwata, Kalayagan, and Pamulak Manobo, supreme deity of the Bagobo people; the deity is said to live in the sky and is offered white gifts by the natives; created the sun, moon and stars and gave life to a fish-like snake being called Kasili, who wraps itself around the world; controls good harvest, rain, wind, life, and death.

- Gugurang: Supreme deity of the Bicolano peoples (includes numerous ethnic groups in Bicol); he is said to live in Mayon, which he chose as the repository of the sacred fire of Ibalon; despite similarity in name and the name of his foe, he is ethnically different from the Hiligaynon people's Agurang.

- Magbabaya: Supreme deity of the Higaonon people; a ritual is performed for the deity before the utilization of land and other resources.

- Ampu: Supreme deity of the Palaw'an people (not to be confused with other ethnic peoples of Palawan province); the deity wove the world and created several kinds of humanity, hence he is also called Nagsalad.

- D'wata ng Kagubatan: Supreme deity of the Cuyunon people; she is honored in a celebrated feast, periodically held atop of Mount Caiman prior to Spanish persecution.

- Minaden: Supreme deity of the Teduray people; she created the world while her brother, Tulus, rectified some errors to better the world created by Minaden.

- Mahal na Makaako: Supreme deity of the Hanunoo Mangyan (not to be confused with other Mangyan peoples which are distinct from each other); the deity gave life to mankind by merely gazing at them.

The Sambal and Dumagat peoples believe that the foul odor of *takang demonyo* or *kalumpang* (*Sterculia foetida*) attracts two horse-like races, namely the tulung, monstrous tikbalang-like beings, and the binangunan, fire horses.

- Bagatulayan: Referred as the "Great Anito", is the supreme deity of the Itneg people; he directs the activities of the world, including his abode, the celestial realms; has a loyal servant named Emlang.

- Nanolay: Supreme deity of the Gaddang people; he is also regarded as an epic hero and a benevolent deity, never inflicting pain or punishment on the people.

- Mangindusa, Polo, Sedumunadoc, and Tabiacoud: Four supreme deities of the Tagbanwa people; the first, Mangindusa, (also called Nagabacaban) is the lord of the heavens who sits up in the sky and lets his feet dangle below, above the earth; the second, Polo, is the god of the sea and a benevolent spirit who was invoked as a healer in times of illness; the third, Sedumunadoc, is the god of the earth whose favor was sought in order to have a good harvest; and the fourth, Tabiacoud, is the god who lived in the deep bowels of the earth.

A kolago/kagwang, *Cynocephalus volans*. The Waray and Bisaya peoples believe that when such a creature cries loudly during dawn, there will be no rain for the whole day.

- Diwata Migbebaya: Also known as Diwata-sa-Langit, supreme deity of the Subanon people; scholarly works have noted that scriptures were used to be written for the deity, until such scriptures and practices were destroyed by the Spanish during colonization.

- Tahaw: Supreme deity of the Mamanwa people; various rituals are used to honor him, including a dance known as *katahawan*.

- Lumawig: Supreme deity of the Bontoc people; he is also regarded as an epic hero who taught the Bontoc their five core values for an egalitarian society; he is the son of the primordial deity, Intutungcho/Kabunian, who is different from the Kabunian in Ibaloi beliefs.

- Tungkung Langit: Supreme deity of the Suludnon people and specific Visayan peoples; known as the creator, he is also the husband of Alunsina; despite having similar names, he and Alunsina are different from the deities with the same names in other Visayan mythologies.

- Ama-Gaolay: Supreme deity of the Pangasinense people; also called Ama Kaoley, he communicated with the people through various rituals and shrines, which were destroyed by the Spanish.

- Anlabban, Bago, and Sirinan: Supreme deities of the Isnag people; Anlabban looks after the general welfare of the people and is recognized as the special protector of hunters, Bago is the spirit of the forest, and Sirinan presides over the rivers.

- Gutugutumakkan: Supreme deity of the Agta people (not to be confused with other Negrito groups, which are completely distinct from each other); has four manifestations, namely, Tigbalog, the source of life and action, Lueve, caretaker of production and growth, Amas, mover of people to pity, love, unity, and peace of heart, and Binangewan, responsible for change, sickness, and death.

- Iraya: Supreme deity of the Ivatan people; initially depicted as an androgynous deity, she oversees the people and warns them of incoming omens through cloud formations at Mount Iraya, her earth manifestation.

- Umboh Tuhan and Dayang Dayang Mangilai – supreme deities of the Sama-Bajau people; Umboh Tuhan, also known as Umboh Dilaut, is referred as the "Lord of the Sea", while Dayang Dayang Mangilai is referred as the "Lady of the Forest".

- Delan and Elag: The supreme deities of the Bugkalot/Ilongot people; Delan, the moon god, and Elag, the sun god, are believed to be a quarrelsome supreme duo, where Elag lives in Gacay; Elag has a huge *bila-o* (basket) which he uses to block Delan during their arguments, thus creating different phases of the moon; both created mankind and continue to give life and growth; Christian missionaries have tried to replace the two deities with Bible-inspired Cain and Abel figures, however, traditional Bugkalots have rejected this notion, citing Delan and Elag as their true supreme deities.

- Taganlang: Supreme deity of the Mansaka people; creator god who has a helper bird named Oribig, who obtained soil from the far corners of the universe; the soil was used by Taganlang to create the earth.

- Tagbusan, Makalindung and Dagau: Tagbusan, who rules over destinies of all other gods and mortals, is the supreme deity of the Manobo people in general; however, the Manobos around Talakogin in the Agusan valley believe that Makalindung, god of creation, is the supreme deity, while the Manobos of the Argawan and Hibung rivers believe that Dagau, the goddess of creation, is the supreme deity.

Some ethnic peoples have a multitude of deities or nature spirits but do not consider any deity or spirit as 'supreme' from the rest, despite having a deity which 'created the world'. Research on various ethnic peoples throughout the country are continually being conducted by students, government officials, and scholars to further document, acknowledge, protect, and promote the mythology, folklore, and pantheons of more than a hundred different ethnic peoples.

Cosmogony or Creation Myths

Cosmogony or creation myths usually tell how the world was created, and most of the time, also includes how mankind came into existence. Each ethnic group in the Philippines has their own creation myth, making the myths on creation in the Philippines extremely diverse. In some cases, a single ethnic group has multiple versions of their creation myth, depending on locality and sub-culture from a larger 'mother' culture. A few of the many cosmogonies known to specific ethnic groups in the Philippines are as follow:

- Ifugao: The universe has always existed and will always exist.

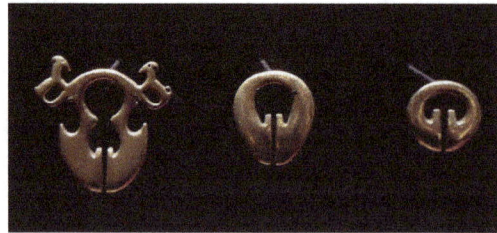

Lingling-o are jewelries that are believed to aid in fertility, and also represent
a person's social standing through the material used as medium.

- Tagalog: A sacred kite caused the sky and the sea to war; the sky threw boulders onto the sea, forming islands; the kite afterwards built a nest on an island and left the sky and sea in peace.

- Bicolano: The only thing that existed in the universe were water and sky; the grandsons of the sky god, Languit, sought to attack the sky realm to have more power; the group was led by Daga, god who controlled winds; Languit, in anger due to his grandchildren's betrayal, struck all of them with lightning, killing them instantly; Bitoon, who did not join the upheaval, looked for her brothers, but was also accidentally struck by Languit's lightning; only the sea god, Tubigan, managed to calm down Languit; the two old gods each gave the bodies of their dead grandchildren light, where Bulan's body became the moon, Aldao's (or Adlao) body became the sun, and Bitoon's body became the stars; Daga's body was not given light and, thus, became the earth.

Gongs of the Teduray people. The Tedurays base their concept of gender towards their ethnic beliefs, with a trans woman being called *mentefuwaley libun* and a trans man being called *mentefuwaley lagey*.

- Kapampangan: The sky, earth, planets, and stars were in existence before land came; during a war between the deities for the beautiful daughter of the supreme deity, Mangetchay, the earth was formed from the stones thrown by the warring deities; life on earth was created by Mangetchay in remembrance of the deity's dearest daughter who died in war.

Callao Cave is a sacred cave in the Cagayan Valley, believed to be the home of enchanted beings. In 2019, a new human species, *Homo luzonensis*, who lived between 50,000 and 67,000 years ago, was confirmed to have lived within the site.

- Ilokano: The Ilokano supreme deity ordered two primordial giants, Angalo and Aran, to become responsible for the creation of the world; the giant Anglao (or

Angalo) dug the earth and made mountains; Anglao urinated into holes in the earth and made the rivers and seas, afterwards he put up the sky, the sun, the moon, and arranged the stars.

- Ibaloi: The first thing in existence were the skyworld and the underworld; the peoples of both sides fought and one day, a man from the underworld hit the sun god with an arrow; the sun god afterwards pushed up the skyworld and pushed down the underworld, and then created the earth.

- Panay: For the many ethnic groups originating from Panay, the world was said to be formless and shapeless in the old times; the sea, sky, and earth were mixed together; from the formless mist, the deities Tungkung Langit and Alunsina appeared; the two married each other and lived in the highest realm of eternal space; one day, Tungkung Langit fought and hurt Alunsina, which forced Alunsina to be driven away; in Tungkung Langit's loneliness, he created the sea and land and took his wife's jewels to create the stars, moon, and sun; despite all of these, Alunsina chose to stay free from anybody and never returned to Tungkung Langit, thus, an early notion of divorce.

- Bisaya: One Bisaya cosmogony myth tells that a sacred bird of prey incited the sky and the sea to fight against each other so that it may find somewhere to land, thus creating the islands where the bird of prey landed on; another Bisaya cosmogony myth tells that the deities Kaptan and Magauayan (or Maguayan) fought each other for eons until, tired of the war, the great bird Manaul dropped boulders upon the fighting divinities; the rocks that dropped became islands while another Bisaya cosmogony myth tells Kaptan's son, Lihangin, who was god of the wind, and Maguayan's daughter, Lidagat, goddess of the sea, were married and produced children; three of these deities, led by Likalibutan, made an upheaval against Kaptan, angering the supreme god; Lisuga, who was looking for her brothers, was also accidentally hit by Kaptan; all the four grandchildren of Kaptan and Maguayan perished; Kaptan accused Maguayan of the coup, but was later calmed down and the two deities grieved their grandchildren; Liadlao's body became the sun, Libulan's body became the moon, Lisuga's body became the stars, and the wicked Likalibutan's body became the earth and had no light; soon, a bamboo tree grew, where the first man, Sikalak, and the first woman, Sikabay, sprang from.

- Suludnon: There was no land in the beginning; only the sky and a wide expanse of water called Linaw were present; the primordial giants, Laki and Bayi, appeared from nowhere and were responsible for the creation of many things; Bayi, the creation giantess, caught the primordial earthworm which excreted the earth; she also have birth to the wild animals that inhabit the earth.

- Bukidnon: In one Bukidnon cosmogony myth, the supreme god Magbabaya created the earth after he saw that there was only a hole, no sky and soil; he first made the eight elements, tumbaga (bronze), bulawan (gold), salapi (coins), bato (rocks), Gabon (clouds), ulan (rain), puthaw (iron), and tubig (water); from the elements, he created the sea, sky, the moon, and the stars; in another Bukidnon cosmogony myth, Magbabaya (referred as Diwata na Magbabaya) created the world with the god Dadanhayan ha Sugay; before creating mankind, the two deities created the Incantus, six guardian deities that contain good and evil qualities and can send calamities if angered.

- Manobo: Creations myths by the Manobo is diverse; one Manobo cosmogony myth from Talakogan in the Agusan valley tells that the creation of the world was due to the god, Makalindung, who set up the world on iron posts; another Manobo cosmogony myth from Argawan and Hibung rivers states that the creation goddess, Dagau, created the world; while another Manobo cosmogony myth from the upper Agusan says that the world is shaped like a giant mushroom and deities shake its core when angered by humans.

- Manuvu: In the beginning, there was nothing but a formless void; the deity Manama or Sigalungan created the deities which assisted him in creation; he took two steel bars and fashioned the bars into a frame; he then scraped off his fingernails and molded it into a mass which eventually became the earth.

- Bagobo: The world was created by Pamulak Manobo, who made the land and sea and the first humans; rain is caused when he throws water from the sky, where showers are his spit; white clouds are smoke from the fire of the deities; the sun created yellow clouds that make the colors of the rainbow.

- Blaan: The god Melu constantly rubbed his skin so that he may be pure white; he later accumulated a lot of dead skin, and in his annoyance, he used the dead skin to create the earth.

- Teduray: In the beginning, there was only sky and sea; Sualla (or Tullus-God) lived in the sky, while his sister Sinonggol lived in Bonggo, the land of the dead; Sualla visited the palace of the sun and touched one of the eight primordial wooden *khnenentaos* (statues), thus creating the first Teduray; from the rib of the man, Sualla created the first woman; when the man and woman had a child named Mentalalan, it became sick and the man sought Sualla's aid; Sualla gave a special medicine to the man, but before the man delivered the medicine to his son, a demon sent by Singgol, changed the medicine, which led to the death of Mentalalan; Sualla afterwards convened a meeting with his four brothers, Mentail, Micael, Mintlafis, and Osman Ali to buy soil from the Navi; the soil was then planted by Sualla at Colina, the center of the world; the soil grew, and Mentalalan was finally buried; from the boy's body, crops of different kinds sprouted; in anger, Sinonggol threw her comb, which turned into the first boar that aimed to destroy the crops.

Heroes in Philippine Mythology

An Ifugao woman performing sacred Hudhud chants while harvesting rice. The chanting, recognized
by UNESCO as a "Masterpiece of the Oral and Intangible Heritage of Humanity", tells a variety
of stories, including the life and journey of the Ifugao epic hero, Aliguyon.

Each ethnic group in the Philippines has its own set of stories depicting their mythical
heroes, notably through oral traditions such as epics and verbal poems. Many of these
stories have now been published in scholarly works and books by various folkloristic
and anthropological scholars and researchers throughout the country. Due to Spanish and American colonialism, some of the stories have been retrofitted with minor
changes, notably in the heroes' names. For the native people, many of these heroes are
referred as *actual* humans who lived centuries ago (others, a few hundred years ago)
and not "mythical" beings, the same way Christians and Muslims believe that their
prophets/saints were 'actual' people from the past. Among these heroes are as follow:

- Sondayo: A hero who owns a magical flying scarf called a Monsala, which can
  be ridden through lightning, in Subanen mythology; he has the power to make
  anybody fall asleep; his life and epic is much celebrated in the sacred *buklog*
  rituals.

Whang-od performing the *batok* (Kalinga tattoo). Prior to government discouragement, she used
to perform the *fi-ing* (*batok* on male headhunters) for Kalinga heroes. The last *fi-ing* was
conducted in 1972. Headhunting in the Philippines has since been illegal.

- Manggob: A young hero raised by a giant recorded in the Diawot epic of Mansa-ka mythology; he wields a golden top which had the power to bring dreams into reality; his journey focuses on his search for the golden top and his long-lost sister.

Manang, wooden idols of household deities of the Mandaya people.

- Silungan Baltapa: A noble and sinless hero from Sama-Dilaut mythology; his life is mostly about his voyages at sea, noting the tradition of maritime journeys for the Sama (Bajau) peoples; he is believed to have absolute knowledge and possesses power to speed-up time for voyages and essentially go anywhere he pleases.

- Banog: A hero named after the *banog* (Philippine eagle) by the eagle-venerating people of Bagobo Tagabawa mythology; he founded the domains of Tudaya, Binaton, Sibulan and Kapatagan.

- Tugawasi: A hero who controlled the wind from Labin Agta mythology; his heart beat is said to boom like thunder when he is fighting.

- Tud Bulul: A hero famed as the moonspeaker as he can speak with the moon and the wind from T'boli mythology; his weapons are a sword named K'filan, which can stretch to one million lakes and seas, and a shield named K'lung, made out of hardened wood.

- Agyu: A powerful hero whose journey is recorded in the Ulaging epic of Talaan-dig and Manobo mythologies of Bukidnon, while his clan's story is recorded in the Ulangihan epic of Manobo mythology of Livungan Valley; he navigates the sky through his floating ship named Sarimbar/Salimbal.

- Laon and Kan: Laon was a king of Negros from Hiligaynon mythology; he owns a head cloth named Birang, which can produce any material or food the wielder wants; Kan was a youthful hero and friend Laon; Together, they slayed a drag-on-like monster living in present-day Kanlaon volcano.

- Bantugen: His life and journeys are recorded in the Darangen chants, which has been inscribed in the UNESCO Intangible Cultural Heritage Lists, from

Maranao mythology; he owns a magic Bangka which can navigate like a sub-
marine and he can also travel the sky, walk on water, and summon ancestral
spirits.

- Indarapata and Solayman: Brothers who have slayed numerous monsters present in Maguindanao mythology and Maranao mythology; they own a sentient
  kris named Juru Pakal and a sacred plant which notifies Indarapata if Solayman
  (Solaiman in Maranao) has passed away.

- Lumalindaw: A powerful combat musician from Ga'dang mythology; he owns
  an ayoding, a musical instrument which guides him in making decisions, and a
  bolo, which produces light and music when swang.

- Tuwaang: A craftsman hero from Manobo mythology; he can speak with the
  wind, ride on lightning, and use a magical flaming skein.

- Lam-ang: A hero of Samtoy from Ilocano mythology; he is accompanied by a
  rooster which can annihilate anything through crowing, and a dog which can
  restore anything through barking.

- Urduja: A warrior princess of Tawilisi known to be unrivaled in strength from
  Pangasinense mythology; she is proficient in horse back riding, fistfight, and
  swordsmanship and leads the Kinalakian, a supreme fleet of male and female
  warriors.

- Baltog, Handyong and Bantong: Heroes recorded in the Ibalong epic from Bicolano mythology; Baltog was a *tawong-lipod* who introduced agriculture and
  defeated the Tandayag boar; Handyong, also a *tawong-lipod*, cleared the land
  of most of its monsters, inspired inventions, built *moog* (tree-house shrines for
  the deities), established a code of laws, and crafted the first boats; Bantong was
  a brave and cunning hero who defeated the beast named Rabot.

- Bernardo Carpio: A powerful figure in Montalban from Tagalog mythology;
  some sources say that he was imprisoned to hold two mountains away from
  each other, causing earthquakes every time he moves; other sources say that he
  prevented two warring mountains from clashing; there is also a version where
  he was trapped between mountains, either by enchanted beings or by the Spanish.

- Aliguyon: A powerful hero recorded in the Hudhud chants, which has been inscribed in the UNESCO Intangible Cultural Heritage Lists, from Ifugao mythology; his three-year war with Pumbakhayon ended with a peace pact due to both
  warriors' admiration for each other's capabilities.

- Labaw Dangon, Humadapnon and Dumalapdap: Demigod sibling heroes recorded in the Hinilawod/Sugidanon epic from Suludnon mythology; their romantic saga inspired various art forms in Panay.

- Ligi Wadagan and Ayo: Heroes from the Dulimaman epics of Itneg mythology; Lidi Wadagan, also called Agimlang, is known for his resoluteness in defense of his community, while Ayo, whose full name is "Ayo, si babei nga Dulimaman" and referred simply as Apo, is known for her unsurpassed fistfight combat skills and devotion to protect her family.

- Kudaman: A strong hero from Pala'wan mythology; he has the power to revive the dead by spitting them with chewed betel nut; has a purple heron named Linggisan, who he uses for transportation.

- Banna: A hero of Dulawon recorded in the Ullalim epic of Kalinga mythology; slayed numerous powerful beings and is celebrated in various Kalinga occasions such as *Bodong* peace pacts

- Urang Kaya Hadjiyula: A freedom-loving hero of Jolo recorded in the Parang Sabil (Sword of Honor) epic of Tausūg mythology; his life and journey in all facets glorifies the Tausūg's love for freedom, dignity, and honor seen in the tradition of *kamaruan*.

- Maharadia Lawana: A monkey-king recorded in the Maharadia Lawana epic of Maranao mythology who is gifted by the supreme deity with immortality; scholars have noted that the epic is the localized version of the Indian epic Ramayana.

- Suac: A cunning hunter-hero from Kapampangan mythology, who defeated various monsters and later became a ruler; has two loyal friends, namely Sunga and Sacu.

- Kawlan: A shaman hero of Sumlog from Kalagan mythology; he has the power to communicate with spirits, heal the sick, and see the souls of the dead.

- Biuag and Malana: Two rival heroes of the Ibanag, the Itawit, and the Gaddang people of Cagayan Valley; they are endowed with supernatural strength by the goddess Maginganay; one version states that the two rivals eventually became friends and did various journeys and defeated many invaders which made all their people proud of them for generations, while a more modern and Christianized version, states that during a duel, Biuag made a cowardly act and Malana flew away to the sky kingdom.

Other Human Figures in Philippine Mythology

Ipot Cave, a sacred site for the native Asi people of northwest Romblon, where the oldest surviving warp *ikat* textile, the Banton cloth, in Southeast Asia was found. The cloth exemplified myth-like patterns and was made between 1400–1500 AD, although the weaving culture in the Philippines is known to precede it by thousands of years.

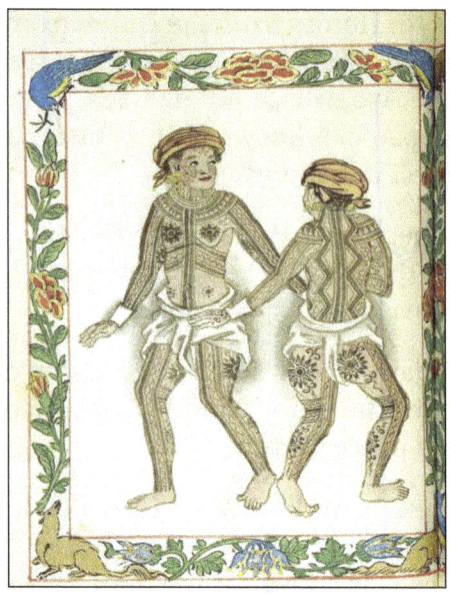

Boxer Codex depiction of "Pintados", exclusively the 16th-century
ethnic Bisaya of Cebu, Bohol, east Negros, and west Leyte.

Aside from the deities and heroes, numerous human figures, either full humans or demigods which may be mortals or immortals, in Anitism have been attributed as causers or helpers of various events in epics and poems, and their actions supplement some explanations on why things have become to what they are today. A few of these figures are:

- Daragang Magayon: A beautiful Bicolano princess of Rawis whose beauty caused the great war between Pagtuga and the people of Iriga versus her true love Panganoron and the people of Rawis; the epic war ended with a Rawis victory, but the Panganoron was killed by an arrow at the very end of the battle; in despair, Daragang Magayon went after Panganoron in the afterlife by stabbing herself with his knife; their burial ground sprouted a volcano now known as Mayon.

Detail of jar cover of one of the Maitum anthropomorphic
pottery from west Sarangani.

- Esa': The ancestor of Palawan's Batak people; he named the *Kabatakan it Tanabag* (Batak Ancestral Lands), after he followed his dog companions during a hunt for wild pigs; the landscape is said to have been created by the movement of Esa'.

- Tuglibong: A Bagobo grandmother who persuaded the sky to go up to where it is now by ranting and rebuking it repeatedly.

- Bugbung Humasanun: A binukot (well-kept maiden) of great beauty from Bohol who tasked her suitor, Datu Sumanga, to make several *mangayaw* raids from the southern frontiers such as Jolo and as far north as China; by tradition, she received each time the spoils and captives that Datu Sumanga obtained from the raids.

A couple belonging to the Sambal warrior class (Boxer Codex). The female warrior is holding a raptor, which has captured a bird, for sacred falconry.

- Ukinirot: A heavenly Bisaya hunter who shot an arrow in the sky, thus making a hole which the sky beings used as an easy entrance to the human world; the hole eventually got blocked by a huge woman who tried to enter the hole.

- Sural: The first Bikolano to have thought of a syllabary or suyat script; he carved it on a white rock-slab from Libong, which Gapon later polished.

- Timungan: A Kankanaey gardener who created a hole in the skyworld after digging up a gigantic sweet potato in his heavenly garden.

- Marikudo: The ruler of the Ati people of Panay who allowed the legendary 10 Bornean datus, including Datu Puti, to stay on the island; in gratitude, the ten datus gave Marikudo a golden *salakot* (native head gear).

- Apolinatu: An Itneg mortal who was fetched by his lover, the star goddess Gagayoma, to live with her in the upper world; the couple had a child named Takyayen, who sprang after Apolinatu pricked Gagayoma's last two fingers.

- Dinahong: The original Bikolano potter who was believed to have been an Agta (Negrito) or pygmy; helped the people learn cooking, making pots called *coron*, stoves, earthen jars, and other kitchen utensils.

- Manggat and Sayum-ay: The first man and woman in Buhid Mangyan mythology; gave the name of all trees, animals, lakes, rocks, and spirits found within the Buhid Mangyan ancestral home.

- Pandaguan: There are two Bisaya stories regarding Pandaguan, where the tales may be referring to two different persons with the same name; the first Pandaguan was the youngest son of the first man, Sikala, and first woman, Sikabay; he invented a fish trap which caught a gigantic shark; he was later lightly zapped by Kaptan after he boasted that he can defeat the deities; the second Pandaguan was a good and noble man who became a comrade of the deities, but later chose to leave his gifted immortality behind due to the reasoning that both mortals and immortals will always be afflicted with anger and sorrow no matter how short or long they live.

- Puhak: A much-hated Manobo man who defecated on the divine stairs created by the deities to connect the mortals with the upper world; due to his mockery, the stairs were permanently closed by the deities.

- Dayang Kalangitan: A legendary queen from Tondo who co-ruled initially with her husband, and later as sole ruler of her domain; fragmented Tagalog oral literature maintains that she is currently the only known legendary female monarch from a Tondo dynasty, as written records were burned by the Spanish during colonization.

- Madlawe: A Subanen prince, in the Guman epic, who saved a kingdom called Pagkatolongan; he died in battle but was revived by the maiden Pagl'lokon.

- Sawalon: Daughter of Padsilung ha Kabatlaw, enemy of Agyu; she successfully poisoned the hero Agyu of the epic Olaging and Ulahingan, however, failed as Agyu was revived later on.

- Tomitib Manaon: A dear friend of the Subenen hero Taake; he perished after a battle with Walo Sebang and was revived after Taake's wife and sister "fished back" his soul from a *tonawan* (pot of melted iron).

- Mabaning and Mabanal: Two close friends of the Maranao hero Bantugen; after finding that Bantugan has died, they rode their shields up to the skyworld and retrieved the soul of Bantugen, thus reviving him.

- Gat Pangil: A legendary ruler in Tagalog beliefs; said to have established the domains of Bai, Pangil, Pakil, and Mauban.

- Kalantiaw: A ruler from Panay who also had influence in west Negros; enacted the Code of Kalantiaw to maintain order among his people; nationally known as a historical figure until Christian scholars from a Roman Catholic university debunked his existence as "mythical" and "an urban legend" in 1968; despite this, various ethnic groups in Western Visayas, where his story originated from, continue to see him as a historical figure.

References

- KoreanMythology: tvtropes.org, Retrieved 13 June, 2020

- George M. Williams (2008). Handbook of Hindu epic. Oxford University Press. pp. 15–31. ISBN 978-0-19-533261-2

- Folktales of Southern Philippines: Rolando C. Esteban, Arthur P. Casanova, Ivie C. Esteban: 9789712724374: Amazon.com: Books. ISBN 978-9712724374

- A Brief History Of The Immortals Bonjor man. Of Non-Hindu Civilizations. Aryavart Sanatan Vahini 'Dharmraj'. p. 21. ISBN 9781329586079

- Vietnam-culture-myths: haivenu-vietnam.com, Retrieved 26 July, 2020

Permissions

We would like to thank the editorial team for lending their expertise to make the book truly unique. They have played a crucial role in the development of this book. Without their invaluable contributions this book wouldn't have been possible. They have made vital efforts to compile up to date information on the varied aspects of this subject to make this book a valuable addition to the collection of many professionals and students.

This book was conceptualized with the vision of imparting up-to-date and integrated information in this field. To ensure the same, a matchless editorial board was set up. Every individual on the board went through rigorous rounds of assessment to prove their worth. After which they invested a large part of their time researching and compiling the most relevant data for our readers.

The editorial board has been involved in producing this book since its inception. They have spent rigorous hours researching and exploring the diverse topics which have resulted in the successful publishing of this book. They have passed on their knowledge of decades through this book. To expedite this challenging task, the publisher supported the team at every step. A small team of assistant editors was also appointed to further simplify the editing procedure and attain best results for the readers.

Apart from the editorial board, the designing team has also invested a significant amount of their time in understanding the subject and creating the most relevant covers. They scrutinized every image to scout for the most suitable representation of the subject and create an appropriate cover for the book.

The publishing team has been an ardent support to the editorial, designing and production team. Their endless efforts to recruit the best for this project, has resulted in the accomplishment of this book. They are a veteran in the field of academics and their pool of knowledge is as vast as their experience in printing. Their expertise and guidance has proved useful at every step. Their uncompromising quality standards have made this book an exceptional effort. Their encouragement from time to time has been an inspiration for everyone.

The publisher and the editorial board hope that this book will prove to be a valuable piece of knowledge for students, practitioners and scholars across the globe.

Index

CPSIA information can be obtained
at www.ICGtesting.com
Printed in the USA
BVHW061831260822
645595BV00006B/775